Investing in International Real Estate

by Nicholas Wallwork

for
dummies®
A Wiley Brand

Investing in International Real Estate For Dummies®

Published by: **John Wiley & Sons, Inc.,** 111 River Street, Hoboken, NJ 07030-5774, www.wiley.com

Copyright © 2019 by John Wiley & Sons, Inc., Hoboken, New Jersey

Published simultaneously in Canada

For general information on our other products and services, please contact our Customer Care Department within the U.S. at 877-762-2974, outside the U.S. at 317-572-3993, or fax 317-572-4002. For technical support, please visit https://hub.wiley.com/community/support/dummies.

Wiley publishes in a variety of print and electronic formats and by print-on-demand. Some material included with standard print versions of this book may not be included in e-books or in print-on-demand. If this book refers to media such as a CD or DVD that is not included in the version you purchased, you may download this material at http://booksupport.wiley.com. For more information about Wiley products, visit www.wiley.com.

Library of Congress Control Number: 2019933833

ISBN 978-1-119-52752-7 (pbk); ISBN 978-1-119-52755-8 (ebk); ISBN 978-1-119-52754-1 (ebk)

Manufactured in the United States of America

C10008361_022019

Contents at a Glance

Introduction 1

Part 1: Building a Successful Real Estate Portfolio 5

CHAPTER 1: Introducing Real Estate Investment Strategies 7
CHAPTER 2: Investing at Home or Abroad: Which Is Right for You? 23
CHAPTER 3: Treating Your Real Estate Portfolio as a Business. 37
CHAPTER 4: Protecting Yourself against Market Fluctuations. 61
CHAPTER 5: Getting into the Mind-set of a Successful International
Real Estate Investor 77

Part 2: Money, Money, Money 99

CHAPTER 6: Weighing Traditional Finance Options 101
CHAPTER 7: Understanding Property Valuation 119
CHAPTER 8: Looking at More Creative Financing Options. 135

Part 3: One-Off and Shorter-Term Income Strategies 153

CHAPTER 9: Developing Properties 155
CHAPTER 10: Dealing in Property Information 179

Part 4: Ongoing and Passive Income Strategies 199

CHAPTER 11: Making Rent-to-Rent Work for You 201
CHAPTER 12: Leveraging Lease Options 223
CHAPTER 13: Delving into Houses in Multiple Occupation 243
CHAPTER 14: Renting to Students and Low-Income-Housing Tenants 265
CHAPTER 15: Providing Serviced Accommodation 285
CHAPTER 16: Providing Vacation Rentals, at Home and Abroad 309

Part 5: The Part of Tens 331

CHAPTER 17: Ten (Or So) Practical Ways to Get into the Mind-Set for Success 333
CHAPTER 18: Ten (Or So) Other Real Estate Strategies to Consider. 343

Index 353

Table of Contents

INTRODUCTION 1

    About This Book. 2

    Foolish Assumptions. 3

    Icons Used in This Book 3

    Beyond This Book 4

    Where to Go from Here 4

**PART 1: BUILDING A SUCCESSFUL
REAL ESTATE PORTFOLIO** 5

CHAPTER 1: Introducing Real Estate Investment Strategies 7

    Taking Your Real Estate Investments to the Next Level. 8

        Comparing property to other asset classes. 8

        Going beyond fixer-uppers and straightforward
        buy-to-rents 10

    Focusing on Investment Strategies That You Can
    Use Internationally 11

    Running Your Property Portfolio as a Business 12

    Getting Your Financial Ducks in a Row. 13

        Understanding financing options and valuation 13

        Getting the expert help you need 14

    Blending Real Estate Strategies to Create a More
    Robust Portfolio. 14

        Keeping an open mind about different strategies 15

        Incorporating shorter-term strategies into
        your portfolio 16

        Exploring longer-term strategies for earning a
        regular income. 17

        Avoiding spreading yourself too thin 20

    So Which Strategies Are Right for You? 20

**CHAPTER 2: Investing at Home or Abroad: Which
Is Right for You?** 23

    Deciding Whether to Invest Abroad: It's Not All
    about the Numbers. 24

        Playing on your passion 24

        Tapping into available knowledge. 25

    Considering Your Budget. 26

    Assessing Your Risk Profile 28

        Identifying where you sit on the risk spectrum. 28

        Considering country-specific risk factors. 29

        Factoring your goals into the equation 31

Figuring Out How You'll Manage Your Property 31
Drilling Down to the Right Market for You. 33
Looking at the cold, hard facts and figures 33
Developing your knowledge of that country and region 34
Focusing Your Attention on One or Two Key Markets 35

CHAPTER 3: **Treating Your Real Estate Portfolio as a Business** 37
Aiming for Passive Income as the Ultimate Goal 38
Defining passive income. 38
Looking at examples of passive income. 40
Looking at the pros and cons of passive income 40
Drafting a Dream Team 42
Getting expert advice 42
Outsourcing other aspects of your workload 44
Finding and vetting experts, at home and overseas 46
Getting the most out of your dream team 48
Investing in Systems and Technology to Grow Your Business 49
Putting the right processes in place 50
Defining effective business processes 51
Saving time through software 51
Evaluating technology solutions 53
Promoting Your Real Estate Business 53
Managing Your Cash Flow Like a Boss 55
Preparing for the rise and fall of income and expenses 55
Maintaining a safety net with a cash buffer 57
Getting the Right Insurance 57
Insuring your properties correctly 57
Making sure your chosen partners have the right insurance 58

CHAPTER 4: **Protecting Yourself against Market Fluctuations** 61
Diversifying Your Portfolio with Multiple Revenue Streams 62
Investing for the long term and the short term 62
Incorporating multiple strategies into your portfolio 63
Seeking out other ways to diversify your portfolio. 65
Finding Strategies That Work Well in a Boom Market 65
Working with the booming market. 65
Looking at suitable boom strategies. 66
Finding Strategies That Work Well in a Credit Crunch 68
Working with the challenging market. 68
Looking at suitable crunch strategies. 69
Doing the Opposite of What the Mass Market Is Doing 71

Tailoring Your Funding to Economic Fluctuations 72
    Understanding the impact on traditional finance 72
    Accessing nontraditional forms of finance 74
Considering Foreign Exchange Rate Risks 75

CHAPTER 5: **Getting into the Mind-set of a Successful International Real Estate Investor** 77
Continually Improving through Education. 78
    Tapping into a wide variety of sources. 78
    Taking time for education before you put your
    money on the line 80
Networking in the Right Places 80
    Networking offline and online. 80
    Getting the most out of networking meetings and events 81
    Maintaining and nurturing your network 82
Setting Your Goals. 82
    Figuring out what you want 83
    Committing to and working toward your goals 83
Cultivating a Positive Mental Attitude 85
    Using positive affirmations 85
    Embracing gratitude 87
Visualizing for Success 88
    Identifying the benefits of visualization .88
    Putting visualizing into practice. 89
    Getting the most out of visualization 90
Harnessing the Law of Attraction 91
    Understanding how the law of attraction works 92
    Focusing on your thoughts and feelings .93
    Putting the law of attraction into practice 94
Meditating to Manage Stress and Risk. 95
    Looking at the benefits of meditation 96
    Making meditation work for you. 97

PART 2: MONEY, MONEY, MONEY 99

CHAPTER 6: **Weighing Traditional Finance Options**. 101
Finance as a Key Element of Success and Growth 102
    Seeing the link between leverage and growth 102
    Understanding the full range of finance options 103
Considering the Main Financing Factors 104
    Looking at the property itself 105
    Deciding between fixed-rate and adjustable-rate loans 105
    Looking at the length of the loan 107
    Finding the right loan-to-value balance .108
    Weighing up repayment versus interest-only loans. 109
    Taking fees into account. 110

Assessing a Range of Traditional Finance Products..............112
    Getting a standard residential investment mortgage 112
    Seeking a commercial mortgage............................113
    Using a bridge loan 113
    Taking out a second-charge loan 115
    Getting land and development loans......................115
Finding the Right Product for You..........................117
Dipping into International Finance versus Domestic Finance 118

CHAPTER 7: **Understanding Property Valuation** 119
Defining Value and Real Estate Valuation 120
    Comparing price to value in more detail 120
    Understanding the purpose of appraisals...................121
    Looking at factors that influence value 121
    Knowing who values real estate 122
Seeing Why Valuation Is Fundamental to Property Success........123
    Understanding enough to maximize your investments 124
    Knowing the difference between yield and
    return on investment 124
    Considering how valuation methods may affect
    your financing 125
    Recognizing that appraisers are risk averse 126
    Making your own valuation case..........................127
Looking at the Three Main Valuation Methods..................128
    Market comparison approach.............................129
    Income or investment approach..........................130
    Cost approach 132
Knowing Which Method Is Best for You and How
Much an Investment Is Worth...............................132
    Evaluating on a case-by-case basis.......................132
    Doing your own appraisal research 133
Special Considerations for Valuing Property Abroad.............134

CHAPTER 8: **Looking at More Creative Financing Options**......135
You Down with OPM? Investing with Other People's Money 136
    Introducing the concept of OPM...........................136
    Looking at OPM as a route to real estate success and wealth ...137
Joining Up with a Joint Venture 138
    Knowing what's involved in a joint venture.................138
    Looking at examples of joint ventures.....................139
    Understanding why people would invest in you..............139
    Finding the right joint venture partner.....................140
    Creating a compelling business proposal for
    potential joint venture partners 142
    Dotting the I's and crossing the T's with a joint
    venture agreement.....................................145

Securing Private Lending 146
    Finding and approaching private lenders 147
    Putting it all in writing. 148
Crowdfunding Your Way to Real Estate Success. 149
Getting Control of a Property Instead of Owning It 149
Applying Creative Financing Strategies Overseas. 150

**PART 3: ONE-OFF AND SHORTER-TERM
INCOME STRATEGIES** 153

CHAPTER 9: **Developing Properties** 155
Knowing What Property Development Means 156
Deciding Which Development Strategy Is Best for You 157
    Understanding why you need to think about
    the end before you start. 157
    Looking at the main exit options. 158
    Weighing which option is right for you. 158
    Keeping your target audience in mind. 159
    Giving yourself multiple exit options 160
Sourcing Development Opportunities 161
    Assessing the property itself 161
    Deciding on the right location 162
    Finding the best properties (before anyone else). 162
Financing Your Development Projects 165
    Understanding how development financing works 165
    Knowing whether you need a development loan. 166
    Looking at other ways to fund your development projects 167
    Working out how much it's going to cost. 167
    Figuring out what improvements are needed. 168
Managing the Development 169
    Knowing where you need professional help. 169
    Creating a detailed budget. 171
    Creating a realistic schedule 174
    Communicating to keep the project on track 175
    Preparing the property for sale or rent 175
Five International Locations Where This Strategy Would Work 176

CHAPTER 10: **Dealing in Property Information** 179
Dealing in Investment Property Leads: The
Five-Minute Lowdown. 180
    How does it work?. 180
    How can you progress from an investment property
    sourcer to a retained buyer's agent? 181
    Is this strategy right for you?. 182
Generating and Selling Property Leads 183
    Finding your niche. 184

Creating value for your clients by facilitating
off-market deals 185
Understanding the financial model 186
Sourcing valuable properties. 186
Marketing the property to bring buyers and
sellers together 190
Acting as a Retained Buyer's Agent. 192
Knowing what it means to be a retained buyer's agent. 192
Understanding the financial model and agreeing
terms with buyers 193
Attracting buyers to your service 194
Sourcing properties effectively for your buyers 196
Five International Locations Where This Strategy Would Work 196

PART 4: ONGOING AND PASSIVE
INCOME STRATEGIES 199

CHAPTER 11: Making Rent-to-Rent Work for You. 201
Defining Rent-to-Rent: The One-Minute Rundown. 202
Addressing Rent-to-Rent's Image Problem .203
Applying Rent-to-Rent across a Range of Properties
and Strategies 205
What types of property are suitable for rent-to-rent? 205
What approaches can you take to sublet the property? 205
Which approach is right for you? 206
Exploring change of use in more detail .208
Margin in the Middle: Understanding the Rent-to-Rent
Financial Model 209
Looking at the startup costs. 209
Getting started on a shoestring budget. 210
Covering ongoing costs and earning an income
from the property 211
Sourcing the Ideal Rent-to-Rent Property (and Landlord). 213
Evaluating potential properties. 213
Finding a landlord who's open to rent-to-rent 216
Positioning yourself as a professional rent-to-rent operator 217
Sorting Out Your Rental Agreement. 218
Agreeing the length of the lease and other terms
with your landlord. 218
Having a tenancy agreement in place with each
of your tenants. 219
Finding Tenants and Managing the Property 220
Finding good tenants 220
Managing the property after your tenants are in place. 221
Identifying Five International Markets Where This
Strategy Would Work 222

CHAPTER 12: **Leveraging Lease Options**. 223

Understanding Lease Options and How They Work 224
Breaking down a lease option into its component parts. 224
Looking at the pros of lease options 225
Weighing the cons. 226
Deciding whether lease options are right for you 227
Understanding the Financial Model for Lease Options. 228
Earning rental income from the property 229
Earning capital growth on the property. .229
Selling the option instead of buying the property 230
Understanding the "consideration" payment 230
Considering ongoing costs. 231
Knowing What's in It for the Property Owner 232
Sourcing Lease-Option Opportunities 233
Deciding what type of property you want and
how you'll operate it 233
Looking for motivated sellers who would be open
to a lease option 234
Getting the owner onboard with a lease option. 235
Negotiating the Deal and Contract. 236
Your monthly rent. 236
The length of the agreement. 237
The purchase price 238
The consideration 238
Other safeguards. 239
Identifying Five International Locations Where This
Strategy Would Work 240

CHAPTER 13: **Delving into Houses in Multiple Occupation** 243

Introducing HMOs. 244
Breaking Down the HMO Financial Model. .245
Sourcing HMO Properties 246
Converting your existing home into an HMO 247
Buying a property to turn into an HMO. .248
Deciding Who You Want to Rent To 249
Finding the Best Location for Your HMO. 249
Staying on the Right Side of the Law 250
Complying with HMO management regulations 250
Sorting out planning requirements 251
Dealing with mandatory HMO licensing. 252
Looking at the key health and safety considerations
for HMOs 253
Managing Your HMO. 255
Sorting tenancy agreements 256
Finding and vetting tenants 258
Managing your tenants and the property 260

Scaling Up Your HMO Portfolio 262
Identifying Five International Locations Where This
Strategy Would Work 263

CHAPTER 14: **Renting to Students and
Low-Income-Housing Tenants** 265

Knowing What's Involved in Renting to Students
and Low-Income-Housing Tenants 266
 Understanding why you may want to rent to
 multiple tenants in one property 266
 Identifying your tenants' needs 266
Looking at the Pros and Cons of Renting to These
Tenant Groups 268
 Addressing the negative connotations and
 downsides 268
 Looking at the positives 269
Sourcing the Right Kinds of Property for Students
and Low-Income-Housing Tenants 270
 Finding the right location for students 270
 Identifying the right location for low-income-housing
 tenants 271
 Looking at the property itself 271
Marketing Your Property and Finding Tenants 272
 Making sure the rent is competitive 273
 Enticing students to your property 273
 Attracting low-income-housing tenants .274
 Vetting tenants 275
Drafting the Tenancy Agreement 275
 Choosing the right agreement 276
 Adding in additional clauses for these tenant groups 277
 Sorting out the security deposit 277
Physically Preparing Your Property for Use .278
 Kitting out the property for your target audience 278
 Preparing for plenty of wear and tear on the property 279
 Making sure the property is safe for your tenants 280
Managing Your Property Effectively 281
 Checking in on the property more regularly 282
 Managing tenants' behavior 282
Looking at Five International Locations Where
This Strategy Would Work 283

CHAPTER 15: **Providing Serviced Accommodation** 285

Defining Serviced Accommodation 286
 What type of accommodation does it cover? 286
 What about the "serviced" part? 287
 Who stays in serviced accommodation? .289

Looking at the Pros and Cons of Serviced Accommodation 289
Taking a glimpse at the positives 289
Assessing the downsides 292
Deciding What Level of Service to Offer. 294
Covering the basics 294
Wowing guests with personal touches. 295
Tailoring your offering to your target audience 296
Sourcing Serviced Accommodation Properties. 296
Looking at the quality and size of the property 297
Choosing the right location for your guests 297
Preparing Your Property for Serviced Accommodation Use. 299
Planning for the practicalities of welcoming guests. 299
Getting the decor and overall look of the property right 299
Equipping the property with everything your guests need. 300
Navigating Planning and Regulatory Restrictions. 301
Getting the Right Business Processes and Systems in Place 302
Managing reservations. 303
Optimizing your pricing 304
Marketing your property 304
Managing Your Serviced Accommodation Business
on an Ongoing Basis. 306
Identifying Five International Locations Where This
Strategy Would Work 307

CHAPTER 16: **Providing Vacation Rentals, at Home
and Abroad** 309
Knowing the Difference Between Vacation Rentals
and Serviced Accommodation. 310
Choosing the Right Location for You 312
Deciding which country is best 312
Drilling down to the right location 313
Doing your due diligence on the vacation market
in your target area. 313
Planning for Costs, Cash Flow, and Variations in Occupancy 314
Thinking of cash flow and costs from an
annual perspective 315
Understanding seasonality and void periods 316
Overcoming seasonality challenges 317
Sourcing the Ideal Property for Vacation Rentals. 318
Preparing Your Property for Use. 320
Providing the "wow factor" through service 320
Including all the practical things your guests need 320
Making sure your property is bursting with personality 321
Making the property as season-proof as possible 322
Paying attention to the exterior 322
Making sure the property is safe and complies
with local laws 323

Marketing Your Vacation Rental 324
    Advertising your property on the right online platforms 324
    Having your own website. 325
    Investing in professional pictures and
    awesome descriptions 325
    Cultivating great reviews 327
Managing Your Vacation Rental 327
    Working with a managing agent 327
    Pricing dynamically throughout the year. .328
Identifying Five International Locations Where
This Strategy Would Work 329

PART 5: THE PART OF TENS 331

CHAPTER 17: **Ten (Or So) Practical Ways to Get
into the Mind-Set for Success** 333
Tapping Into Education Resources 333
Using Productivity Apps and Tools 334
Learning to Be in the Here and Now 335
Cementing Your Goals Using a Vision Board or Goal List 337
Trying Out a Visualization Exercise, Real Estate Style 338
Incorporating Positive Affirmations into Your Day. 339
Recognizing and Giving Thanks for Your Successes. 340
Downloading Helpful Apps 341

CHAPTER 18: **Ten (Or So) Other Real Estate
Strategies to Consider** 343
Delving into Buy-to-Rent (Single-Tenant) Properties 344
Flipping Houses 344
Running a Bed-and-Breakfast, Guesthouse, or Hotel 345
Owning or Running a Care Home 346
Becoming a Real Estate Agent, Rental Agent,
or Property Manager. 347
Investing in Real Estate Investment Trusts 348
Offering Emergency Housing Accommodation. 349
Getting into Commercial Property 350
Trading in Freeholds 351

INDEX 353

Introduction

Welcome to *Investing in International Real Estate For Dummies,* and thank you for choosing me to guide you through the process of building a successful real estate portfolio. I'm so excited to be sharing this journey with you!

If I were a betting man, I'd wager that you're drawn to real estate because you want the chance to create financial security — and, over time, real wealth. You love the idea of working for yourself, of being in charge of your own destiny, of being liberated from the boring, 9-to-5 routine. You want to feel excited about what you do every day.

Those were certainly the things that attracted me to real estate more than 15 years ago. Back then, I had a good, grown-up job at an investment bank in the City of London. I was earning fantastic money for a young, single guy. I was doing all the things I thought I was supposed to do with my life, the way I had been taught and the way that society suggested. But I was miserable. I was desperate to escape it all and work for myself. Real estate seemed a tangible, achievable way to do that. I wasn't wrong.

I started small, renting out a room in my own house to start with. Then I rented out another room after that. Then I converted the garage to make another room, until I'd maximized that first house. Then I took on another rental property, and another after that. Pretty soon, I was expanding into other real estate strategies — and that was when things started to get *really* exciting. Within ten years, I'd built up a diverse, robust real estate portfolio worth more than £20 million (or more than $25 million), and I was running my own group of successful real estate businesses transacting many millions worth of property each and every year.

There's nothing particularly special about me. I don't have a larger-than-average brain (at least, I don't think I do!). I didn't come from a background of notable wealth or privilege. And I had no real estate experience (beyond being a homeowner) when I started out. But I was very determined, and I was willing to invest the assets I had in abundance — namely, my passion, drive, time, and energy — in immersing myself in the world of real estate. If you have the same drive and willingness to commit to your continual education, you, too, can build a successful real estate portfolio. This book shows you how to start or get to the next level.

About This Book

Many investors start out by buying a property and renting it out to a tenant or household (the standard single-tenant model). That's all well and good — and if that's your main interest in real estate, I recommend you also read Eric Tyson and Robert Griswold's excellent book, *Real Estate Investing For Dummies* (Wiley).

This book, however, is designed to go beyond simply renting out a property on a single-tenant basis, toward building a portfolio that encompasses different real estate strategies (such as renting out a property on a room-by-room basis or providing serviced accommodation). Why? Because I believe there are better ways to maximize your real estate income than the standard single-tenant model.

To put it another way, this book is designed to inspire you to grow as a real estate investor, beyond the standard route into real estate investing, and build real wealth for you and your loved ones. With that in mind, this book is built around the following core concepts:

>> By building a robust real estate portfolio — one that incorporates different strategies and multiple revenue streams — you're much better placed to ride out market fluctuations and invest for both the short and long term.

>> Passive income is the key to building real wealth and security — not to mention the freedom to live life your way. So, wherever possible, you want your investments to be as passive (hands-off) as possible. In the early days, this may not be entirely possible, but as your expertise and your portfolio grow, you'll be able to take a step back and devote more time to growing further, instead of focusing on the nitty-gritty day-to-day stuff.

>> Most real estate books tend to focus on one geographic location or another (typically, the United States or the United Kingdom), when, in fact, many real estate strategies can be successfully deployed anywhere in the world. If investing overseas doesn't appeal to you, that's fine — a number of the strategies in this book will almost certainly work just as well in your home country.

>> Continually investing in your own education and maintaining the right mind-set is critical for success as a real estate investor. In fact, one of the unique features of this book is that it devotes two whole chapters (Chapters 5 and 17) to key mind-set techniques. I believe your mind is what differentiates you from any other human being, and if you can learn to harness your mind (through education and mind-set techniques), you can do absolutely anything you want. Just dream big!

One final thing to note about this book: Within this book, you may note that some web addresses break across two lines of text. If you're reading this book in print and want to visit one of these web pages, simply key in the web address exactly as it's noted in the text, pretending as though the line break doesn't exist. If you're reading this as an e-book, you've got it easy — just click the web address to be taken directly to the web page.

Foolish Assumptions

During the writing process, most authors have a specific type of reader or audience in mind. I'm no different. So, while I was writing this book, I made some simple assumptions about you as a reader:

>> You're looking to progress beyond the standard renting-out-a-property model and build a real estate portfolio that's diverse and robust.

>> You don't necessarily know which strategy or strategies are best suited to you as an investor.

>> You may not have a lot of money to invest in growing your real estate portfolio, and you're looking for creative ways to expand and progress, without breaking the bank.

>> You aren't sure which geographic location is best for you (whether you should invest in properties at home or overseas).

If that all sounds about right (and I hope it does!), this book is for you.

Icons Used in This Book

To help you navigate this book, I use the following helpful, eye-catching icons. Here's what each of the icons is used for:

REMEMBER

I use the Remember icon to highlight critical information that you should keep in mind on your real estate journey.

TIP

The Tip icon draws your eye to handy hints and insider tips that will save you time or effort, or generally make your life as a real estate investor a little bit easier.

WARNING

As with any form of investing, mistakes can be costly. I use the Warning icon to highlight advice on what to avoid or common mistakes that many investors make (so you don't have to make them!).

TECHNICAL STUFF

Sometimes I get into the weeds a bit and give you information that's a little more technical than you absolutely need. When I do, I mark it with the Technical Stuff icon. If you're in a rush, feel free to pass by anything marked with this icon.

Beyond This Book

In addition to the book you have in your hand, you can access some helpful extra content online. Check out the Cheat Sheet for further tips on becoming a real estate pro. Just go to www.dummies.com and enter **Investing in International Real Estate For Dummies Cheat Sheet** in the search box.

I've also developed online courses that go into more detail and provide extra content to help you improve your real estate education further. You can find these courses at www.propertyforum.com/real-estate-courses.

Where to Go from Here

So, where do you want to start?

One of the great things about *For Dummies* books is that they're designed to be read in any way that works for you. So, if you want to read the entire book from cover to cover, go for it (in fact, I encourage you to do just that for maximum inspiration).

But if what really excites you is vacation rentals, you can turn straight to Chapter 16 and dive right in. Looking for creative ways to fund your investors? Chapter 8 is for you. Or if renting to students is your preferred niche, head to Chapter 14. In other words, you can pick and choose the chapters that appeal to you as a growing real estate investor, so scan through the table of contents and find what catches your eye.

And if you aren't sure where to begin, simply turn the page and see what comes next!

1
Building a Successful Real Estate Portfolio

Dip into the vast range of real estate strategies available to investors.

Weigh up whether you want to invest at home or overseas.

Run your real estate portfolio as a successful business.

Ride market fluctuations by diversifying your portfolio.

Learn critical mind-set-related skills for success as a real estate investor.

Chapter **1**

Introducing Real Estate Investment Strategies

Real estate is an asset that pretty much anyone can understand. Unlike the more complex worlds of stocks, bonds, retirement savings, and the like, real estate is a rare type of investment because it's something you have an inherent basic understanding of. It's what you live in and vacation in, day in and day out. You already know what makes a home attractive, inviting, and desirable. You already have a good understanding of your local real estate market, because you've already bought or rented in that market. In other words, you get it.

Real estate is the natural choice for many investors. They're initially attracted by

» Relatively fewer market fluctuations compared to, say, twitchy and volatile stock exchanges

» Healthy cash flow with regular income coming your way

» The ability to achieve capital growth (by selling a property and pocketing the profit) on top of a steady income

» The potential to be fairly hands off and earn "passive" income

However, just because you understand real estate, doesn't mean you'll be a successful real estate investor. You won't achieve financial security and real wealth by renting out one property; to be successful and secure, you need to build a diverse portfolio of real estate investments, and develop an understanding of the full range of real estate strategies on offer. In this chapter, I explain what that means in practice.

Taking Your Real Estate Investments to the Next Level

Many books out there show you how to rent a property and become a landlord, including the very thorough *Real Estate Investing For Dummies,* by Eric Tyson and Robert S. Griswold (Wiley). That's not my goal in this book.

This book is designed to help you go beyond the basics so that you can progress as an investor and grow your real estate portfolio — wherever you are in the world, and wherever you want to invest.

The idea for this book grew out of my own experience as an investor. Early in my real estate career, it quickly became apparent that there were tons of different strategies out there, beyond the obvious routes, for making money from property. And unlike the conventional path of buying a property and renting it out, some of the new strategies I was discovering required very little capital to get started.

I just didn't know, back then, which strategies were right for me. I could have used a one-stop guide to the various strategies out there, something to help me decide how to take my portfolio to the next level. That's where this book comes in.

Comparing property to other asset classes

I believe real estate is a much better, much more achievable route to wealth than, say, stocks or bonds. That's because property is

>> **Tangible:** You can literally touch bricks and mortar, which, for many people, makes it easier to understand.

>> **Highly controllable:** You have total control over your strategy, the properties you buy, the location you buy in, and the types of tenant you decide to target. With other asset classes, you may not get the same level of control (for example, in the case of a fund investment, someone else will be making the investment decisions for you).

>> **More accessible in terms of knowledge:** Most people have a pretty good basic understanding of property.

>> **More accessible in terms of money:** You need serious capital if you want to make serious money with stocks. But with property, you can deploy a variety of strategies with little upfront capital, and leverage is available (in the form of mortgages and loans) to help you gear up.

>> **Less vulnerable to short-term market risk:** Because you're in control, you can shift your strategy and make different investment decisions in line with what's happening in the market. If you take a longer-term view (which is sensible in property investment), then the market fluctuations are more likely to iron themselves out over time with the inherent underlying asset still holding significant value even in "bad times."

Personally, I don't get as involved in stocks or other securities like currency. There are too many factors beyond my control for my liking, I don't feel like I have enough of an understanding of macro- and microeconomic factors to do it well, and, frankly, it's just too technical. And I say that as someone who used to work in the City of London on a trading floor alongside hundreds of traders! That doesn't mean you can't make great investments through stock trading, but it takes a lot more dedication and precise knowledge, as well as more risk, in my opinion.

What was really interesting to me, working alongside traders, was that very few of them invested in stocks outside of their "day job." Despite their detailed working knowledge of the markets, my colleagues preferred to invest their own money in other assets, specifically property. That was very telling.

But even though property is, for me, head and shoulders above other types of investments, the comparison is useful because it reminds us that property is, above all, an *asset*. Real estate investments should be selected with all the care and attention that a stock investor uses when assessing which companies to invest in — and should be managed extremely carefully, like a diligent trader keeping a watchful eye on the markets.

REMEMBER

An asset is only an asset if it makes you money. If it's not making you money, it's a drain on your finances, time, and energy — in other words, it's a liability. Just like any other asset class, if you neglect your investment, take your eye off the ball, and become complacent, a property can become a liability pretty quickly.

In practice, that means if you mismanage a property or neglect it to a point where people no longer want to live in it, you'll have a liability on your hands. That's why, for the strategies in this book, I give lots of tips to help you manage your investments proactively so that they continue to be assets and make money.

Going beyond fixer-uppers and straightforward buy-to-rents

So, what's wrong with fixing up and flipping a property or owning one rental property as a retirement nest egg? Absolutely nothing at all. Done well, flipping is a decent way to make some short-term profit, and renting out a property as a standard single rental (rented to one tenant or one family) will bring in a regular monthly income with little effort required.

REMEMBER

But if you want to become a serious real estate investor, perhaps to the point where you can afford to give up your day job and concentrate on your real estate business, owning one rental property or flipping a house once in a while isn't going to cut it. You're going to have to dream bigger. One of our family mottos is "Always dream big." Why don't you make it one of yours?

Introducing multi-tenant strategies

You can grow your portfolio by having 12 properties across town that you rent out to 12 families or individuals. That's certainly one way to grow. But is it the smartest way? Maybe not. If you instead rented out your property on a room-by-room basis to young professionals or students, you'd earn significantly more rental income than you would on a standard single rental. Multiply that by multiple properties and you're really cooking.

For example, say you have a three-bedroom house that you rent to a nice young couple. You're earning $1,000 per month from your rental, and it requires little effort from you to keep the income coming in.

Now, imagine that same house is turned into a four-bedroom house for young professionals to share (four bedrooms because you've turned the dining room into an extra rental bedroom to maximize income). And each tenant is paying you $500 a month for his room. Now you have $2,000 per month coming in.

Sure, it's a little more work to find and manage four tenants than it is to deal with one nice young couple, but, in return for that little bit of extra effort, you've doubled your rental income. And that's without making expensive upgrades to the property.

Exploring other high-earning strategies

REMEMBER

Multi-tenant strategies are a great way to turbo-boost your income, which allows you to grow your portfolio more quickly. But there are also plenty of other strategies on the table to maximize your income.

For example, you could invest in apartments that are rented as serviced accommodation by the night (like an Airbnb). You'll earn significantly more in rental income than renting out the same apartments on standard 12-month contracts (albeit it with higher costs and a higher risk of *void periods,* where the property sits empty).

Some of the strategies in this book will be more appealing to you than others. Some will play to your strengths. And some will work better in your chosen location than others. The critical thing is to be aware of the wide range of options available to you as a real estate investor, so that you give yourself the best chance of building a successful real estate portfolio and achieving your goals. This book gives you that grounding, so that you can build a portfolio that's right for you and your needs.

Focusing on Investment Strategies That You Can Use Internationally

The vast majority of real estate books that I've come across are entirely focused on one country's real estate market, typically the United States or the United Kingdom. They go into great detail on filing your tax return and understanding local property management regulations to the point that the guidance is unusable outside that market and the book is out of date within a year as the tax rules and property regulations evolve.

This approach has always puzzled me. As someone who runs my real estate portfolio as a serious business, I'm not going to be poring over tax guidelines and filing my own tax returns. That's not the best use of my time as a business owner. Instead, I work with an awesome accountant and tax advisor who can help me manage my tax position and my finances in the most efficient way.

What's more, most real estate strategies can be used successfully in a huge range of countries around the world, and in fact, lots of investors are actively drawn to the idea of investing overseas. Whether it's the thought of more affordable house prices, exciting returns delivered by emerging markets, or just a passion for a particular country or region, real estate markets around the world have been attracting overseas buyers for years.

REMEMBER

This book is intended to be a more inclusive guide to real estate strategies, one that'll help you build a strong real estate portfolio at home or overseas, wherever you are in the world.

Chapter 2 helps you decide whether you should invest in your home country or internationally. As part of this decision-making process, you may

» Start with a real estate strategy from this book that appeals to you and then investigate the best market for you to deploy that strategy (not forgetting the fact that the best market may well be your domestic one)

» Start from a passion or personal interest in a specific country (again, your passion may lie close to home), and then spend time getting to know that market to find the most suitable strategy or strategies for that area

TIP

If, after careful consideration, you do decide to invest in property overseas, expert local help will be vital. You'll need to build a network of trustworthy, reliable experts who can help you manage your portfolio and individual properties. This will include a local accountant, attorney, real estate agents, and people to manage and maintain your properties. Read more about this in Chapter 3.

Running Your Property Portfolio as a Business

The fact that you've picked up this book and you haven't yet put it back on the shelf tells me that your ambitions go beyond holding one or two investment properties as a little retirement nest egg. You're looking to build a serious real estate portfolio — potentially including international investments — and generate real wealth and financial independence.

That means you need to think of yourself as a professional real estate investor and run your portfolio as a proper business. It's not a side project. It's not something you dabble in. It's a professionally run operation, and you're the entrepreneur at the helm.

REMEMBER

Some of the key aspects of running your portfolio as a business include

» **Focusing on passive income, wherever possible:** If you're doing this to escape the rat race and be free to live life your way, the last thing you want is to be working 14 hours a day managing your properties. So, as your portfolio grows, you may want to think about automating and delegating tasks when you can, just as the CEO of a company does. Read more about passive income in Chapter 3.

>> **Having the right people (I call it your "dream team" of experts), business processes, and tools in place:** This enables you to make sure your business runs like a well-oiled machine. Again, you can read more about this in Chapter 3.

>> **Future-proofing and protecting your business against market changes:** You can do this by building a varied, robust portfolio of investments. There's more on this coming up later in the chapter and in Chapter 4.

>> **Cultivating the right habits for success:** I'm a big believer in the power of mind-set and self-help. If you create the right mind-set for success, through positive habits like networking, educating yourself, thinking positive thoughts, setting goals, meditating, and so on, you've got a strong foundation that'll serve you well on your entrepreneurial journey. Turn to Chapter 5 for some powerful mind-set-boosting techniques.

You'll also need to manage your finances (both everyday cash flow and ways to finance your investments) as strictly as any business.

Getting Your Financial Ducks in a Row

My real estate portfolio didn't really take off until I began to fully grasp and take advantage of the full range of financing options and products that are available to investors.

Understanding financing options and valuation

In Chapter 6, I explore traditional financing options, like mortgages, commercial loans, and bridge loans. These are typically the first considerations for most investors, but there are other, much more creative routes to financing your investments.

For example, if you have little upfront capital for a deposit on a mortgage, or you're investing in a nonstandard project that main-street lenders won't touch, you need to be able to think outside the box and find other means of financing your projects if you don't want to miss out on great opportunities. What's more, being fully aware of the wide range of financing options can enable you to move faster and secure financing quicker than other buyers — which is handy in a fast-moving market or when you're up against other investor buyers.

Chapter 8 looks at less traditional, yet still entirely achievable, financing options, including joint ventures, private lending, and crowdfunding. All these options are about investing with other people's money (OPM). Technically, even a regular mortgage is just another form of OPM, but with these more creative options, you're generally approaching partners and private lenders directly, rather than going to the bank. This creative route is about building win–win partnerships with fellow investors that will hopefully lead to many other successful projects in the future.

TIP

Whatever financing route you choose, it's really important to get a good handle on property valuation or real estate appraisals. Knowing which valuation method a particular lender is using can make all the difference when you're searching for the most appropriate financing. Head to Chapter 7 for more on valuation.

Getting the expert help you need

Whenever you're considering your finance options, I strongly recommend you work with an expert, independent broker. Having a great broker on my side has saved me time, money, and many, many headaches over the years — a good broker will not only help you evaluate financing options and narrow down the field of lenders, but also help you pull together and file the necessary paperwork. A good broker is worth his weight in gold.

So, too, is an accountant and/or tax advisor who specializes in real estate investments and who understands your goals. She'll be able to help you stay on top of your cash flow, manage costs, and ensure that your real estate portfolio is as financially efficient as possible — a lean, mean, profit-producing machine, if you will.

Blending Real Estate Strategies to Create a More Robust Portfolio

Real estate is generally seen as a safe bet, investment-wise ("safe as houses" as the saying goes), but property markets are subject to change and fluctuations, just as any market is. Sure, the fluctuations in the real estate market may be less pronounced and unpredictable than, say, stock exchanges, but they can still hit an investor hard.

That's why, over the course of your real estate career, you'll ideally look to build a varied real estate portfolio that isn't reliant on one strategy alone. Why? Because a varied portfolio is more robust and better able to withstand market blips or changes.

If a local bubble bursts, for example, and you're not able to sell a property that you've refurbished, your immediate cash flow will suffer enormously. But if you have some income-generating rental properties as part of your portfolio, you'll be able to keep the lights on (quite literally) until the market for sales recovers. You can find more on protecting your real estate portfolio against market fluctuations in Chapter 4.

Broadly speaking, real estate investment strategies can be broken down into two categories. Ultimately, both categories may form part of your portfolio:

>> **Shorter-term strategies that are designed to deliver periodic capital growth (see Part 3 of this book):** Property development, assuming the property is sold for a profit after the development is finished, is an ideal example of this.

>> **Longer-term strategies that center on owning or controlling a property for the long haul so that you can earn a regular income from it (see Part 4):** Residential rental properties are the prime example of this.

In this section, I give a brief overview of the specific real estate strategies included in this book, from developing properties to running vacation rentals. I've personally selected the strategies that I think are best for maximizing returns and creating a varied, healthy portfolio.

Keeping an open mind about different strategies

Before we get to the strategies themselves, let me start with a pro tip: Even if a strategy isn't right for you at this point in your investment career, don't discard it from your memory altogether.

I've found that successful real estate investing is often a case of pairing the right strategy with certain scenarios or potential clients (or buyers or investors) as they come your way. So, just knowing that a strategy exists can be valuable to you — you never know when an opportunity to use that knowledge will arise.

Here's a great example of what I mean: Say you've been sourcing development opportunities to turn into luxury family homes. As part of your search, you come across some properties that perhaps aren't right for your needs, but the sellers are motivated so you file them and their properties away in your brain under "could be useful for the future."

Two weeks later, you're chatting with a fellow investor at one of your regular networking events (see Chapter 5 for the importance of networking), and she mentions that she's looking to invest in a certain type of property — and, thanks to your recent research, you have just the right sort of properties in mind. You can potentially act as a buyer's agent (subject to licensing rules that may apply in your country — see Chapter 10), and help pair this buyer with the right property, for a fee.

If you hadn't been aware of the buyer's agent strategy, in this case, you may have missed out on an opportunity to deepen your relationship with your fellow investor (which can, in turn, lead to other projects in the future) and earn a commission in the process.

So, be sure to keep an open mind about the various strategies as you read this book. Just because something isn't suitable for your portfolio right now, doesn't mean it won't work for you in future.

Incorporating shorter-term strategies into your portfolio

A large part of becoming a successful, profitable real estate entrepreneur is the ability to *add value* to a property. Property development (Chapter 9) is a great way to add value.

Developing for success

Property development can mean many things, but it commonly refers to physically improving a property by renovating it so that it's worth more, or adding value to a plot of land by building a property or properties on it.

However, property development can also cover changing the use of a property, such as turning an office block into luxury apartments, or simply changing the way a regular house is used (for example, making structural changes or changing the layout so that you can rent the property to more tenants).

Turning commercial property into residential property has proven a particularly lucrative strategy for me in recent years, although it does require a certain level of experience and expertise to successfully manage larger developments like this. If you're new to development, small projects make a better starting point.

REMEMBER

If property development appeals to you, it's vital you start by thinking about your end goal or exit strategy. Are you going to sell the property to a family or keep it and rent it out to young professionals? Is it going to be rented as a vacation home? Everything about the development process — from what kind of property you buy, to how you finance it, to how you physically develop it — will depend on your end strategy.

Another key ingredient for success as a developer is being able to source the right kind of properties — in fact, I've found that sourcing properties directly, properties that aren't yet on the market, has been a particularly valuable technique and this is something you may like to try. (Find out how in Chapter 9.) You also need to be a master at project management and communication if your development projects are to be completed on time, on budget, and without any major hiccups. I've had my fair share of hiccups and delays so I speak from many experiences of "learning the hard way."

Low-capital, shorter-term strategies

TIP

But what if you don't have the capital to develop property, but you still want to build a career in real estate? If that sounds like you, then head to Chapter 10, where you'll learn about sourcing property leads and acting as a retained buyer's agent.

Whether you're a property sourcer or buyer's agent, you're effectively trading in information or leads by bringing together people who have a property to sell and investors who are looking to buy that exact type of property. In a way, it's a bit like being a niche real estate agent who specializes in a particular type of property for investor buyers only. And like a real estate agent, you earn commission for each sale you facilitate.

Meanwhile, you're learning the market from the inside and constantly developing your own network of buyers and sellers — all of which will pay dividends if you one day want to take on your own investment projects.

Exploring longer-term strategies for earning a regular income

The thing that really drew me to property (apart from all those addictive property shows on TV) was the ability to earn a regular income from renting out property, so that I could quit the rat race and work for myself. Indeed, the ability to earn a steady income is what draws most of us investors into the real estate game.

Investing for rental income is a smart move because it gives you a certain amount of security and freedom to live life your way. Each of the strategies in Part 4 is designed to help you achieve that financial security and freedom by delivering steady returns, now and for many years to come. In this section, I give a whistle-stop tour of these income-producing strategies.

Low-capital rental strategies for cash-strapped investors

The obvious barrier to entry for real estate investors is capital, or rather, lack of it. If you haven't got the money to buy a property, how on earth can you earn money by renting it out?

But, actually, ownership isn't as important as you may think. What matters is *control* of a property. If you're managing a property that someone else owns, there's still money to be made.

Rent-to-rent (Chapter 11) is a prime example of how controlling or managing a property that you don't own can deliver a healthy monthly income. With this strategy, you rent a property from a landlord and (with the landlord's permission) sublet the property to your own tenants, typically on a room-by-room basis for maximum returns.

You earn profit by managing the property more intensively, and your landlord is happy because he no longer has to manage the property himself. Creating win–win scenarios like this is one of the things I love most about real estate.

Alternatively, you may consider negotiating a lease option (see Chapter 12). This is very similar to rent-to-rent in that you sublet the property to your own tenants, but, as part of the deal with the landlord, you also negotiate the option to buy the property in the future. That gives you income in your pocket now, and the potential for capital growth in the future. However, finding an open-minded landlord and negotiating the terms of the lease option can be complex. Turn to Chapter 12 for more on making lease options work for you.

Rent-to-rent and lease options can have a bit of an unsavory reputation; rent-to-rent because it implies slum landlords squeezing far too many people into a crappy property, and lease option because it implies taking advantage of distressed sellers who are unable to sell through other means. It's important you establish yourself as an ethical, professional operator and conduct your business accordingly. Chapters 11 and 12 show you how.

Adding value by changing how the property is used

Rather like developing properties, the income–producing rental strategies in Part 4 are all about *adding value* to a property so that you can optimize your rental income. Two awesome ways to add value to a rental property are

REMEMBER

>> **Changing the use so that instead of renting to one tenant or household as in the standard single-tenant model, you rent to multiple tenants in the same property, on a room-by-room basis:** Why should you consider renting to multiple tenants in one property? Two reasons spring immediately to mind:

- You'll earn more.

- There's enormous demand for this type of accommodation these days, and from different types of tenants, too.

You could, for example, be renting to young professionals in expensive, desirable cities who couldn't dream of having a place of their own at this stage in their lives. Or you could be renting to students, who generally embrace the house-sharing model as a way to get the most out of college life. Or you could be renting to low-income-housing tenants and satisfying a local need for comfortable housing on a tight budget.

With multi-tenant strategies like these, there's definitely more work for you (or your team) in terms of proactively managing tenants (after all, there are more of them). And you need to be on your game when it comes to keeping up with regulations, such as health and safety, and planning/zoning restrictions. But the reward is significantly higher monthly returns.

In Chapter 13, I look at renting to professionals in a *house in multiple occupation* arrangement. A house in multiple occupation is effectively a house shared by multiple tenants, but it's a very specific legal term in the United Kingdom (where this strategy is huge, and growing) and is covered by strict landlord rules. Even if you're not in the United Kingdom and subject to these strict house in multiple occupation rules, you'll still find plenty of helpful advice on renting to professionals in this chapter.

In Chapter 14, I look at renting to students and low-income-housing tenants, including practical, effective solutions to overcome the negative connotations that typically surround these tenant groups.

>> **Changing the use so that instead of renting on a standard 12-month lease, you rent the property on a nightly or weekly basis as serviced accommodation or a vacation rental:** Both of these options involve renting on a short-term basis, typically by the night or week, which will earn you much more in rental income than a standard 12-month rental agreement. I look at serviced accommodation in Chapter 15 and vacation rentals in Chapter 16.

There's a lot of work involved in setting up and running these two types of hospitality businesses. More guests means more wear and tear on the property, for example. What's more, whether you're running a large apart-hotel, a small Airbnb apartment, or a luxury beachside villa, you absolutely need to be committed to delivering an outstanding service to each and every guest.

In Chapters 15 and 16, I give lots of practical tips for providing a thoughtful, top-notch service, whatever type of hospitality accommodation you're running.

Avoiding spreading yourself too thin

As you can tell, there are many different real estate strategies out there and I'm openly advocating a varied real estate portfolio that doesn't rely on one single strategy.

The potential downside of this is that investors can take a scattershot approach to their portfolios, dipping their toes into multiple strategies at once without really mastering any of them, thereby never really maximizing their potential for returns — and, at worst, losing money because of lack of research or poor decisions. To be clear, that's absolutely not what this book is about.

It takes time and effort to really learn and master any real estate strategy, and it's important to focus that learning on one strategy at a time, instead of trying to take on three different strategies at once. Take your time to learn one strategy, establish yourself in that field, and make a success of your investments in that strategy before you even *think* about exploring another strategy.

So Which Strategies Are Right for You?

Done well, all the strategies I mention up to this point have the potential to make you money. But some strategies deliver higher returns than others, some are more work than others, some will be better suited to your individual skills than others, and some will be better suited to current market conditions than others. In other words, not all investment strategies are created equal. So, how can you tell which strategies are right for you and where you should you focus your initial efforts?

A good starting point is to think about your passions, interests, and goals (both from an investment sense and your personal goals). I talk more about these factors in the next chapter, but before you head there, take a moment now to ask yourself this: Why are you drawn to property? What is it about real estate that excites you?

For example, is it the creative aspect of visualizing something and bringing that vision to life? If so, property development sounds like your bag. Is it that your kid is going off to college and you've been introduced to the potentially very lucrative world of student housing? With your direct knowledge, you're well placed to rent to students. Or is it just that you want to be more entrepreneurial and quit your 9-to-5 job? If that's the case, high-income (and high-effort) strategies like serviced accommodation or vacation rentals may be for you.

It doesn't really matter what your initial reasons are. What matters is that you're driven by an underlying passion or goal, and that will inform your choices as you read this book and get better acquainted with the various strategies.

Another question to ask yourself is: What sort of tenants, buyers, or clients do you honestly want to do business with? Renting to students or low-income-housing tenants can be a good earner, but dealing with those tenant groups may not appeal to you. And that's fine. I prefer to rent to professionals myself, so that's where I focus the majority of my rental properties.

Budget constraints are another important factor to consider at this early stage. If you're short on capital but you have plenty of time and energy, then a rent-to-rent or lease-option strategy may be a good starting point for you.

The beauty of real estate is that there are so many options, you're bound to find at least one that works for your interests, goals, and passions — and your budget.

» Factoring in your finances

» Weighing risks

» Considering how you'll manage your property

» Identifying the best market for you

» Narrowing your focus

Chapter **2**

Investing at Home or Abroad: Which Is Right for You?

O ne of the decisions you'll face when first developing your real estate portfolio is which market, or markets, to invest in. Many people take their first step into property investing in their local market — an area they know well and feel comfortable in. But that's not always the case. Sometimes, budget, curiosity, or personal aspirations lead people to invest farther afield.

REMEMBER

Depending on the market and strategy you choose, investing abroad can deliver attractive returns on your investment, particularly in property markets that are less established or expensive than back home.

We all love those property shows about buying a place in the sun. You know the ones I mean: A couple jets off to where the sun shines brighter and the beer is always colder, to view beautiful properties that seem as cheap as chips. Those TV shows provide a wonderful bit of escapism, but when you go beyond buying a holiday home or retiring to the south of France, investing in international markets is hard, serious work and something that needs careful thought. This chapter is designed to help you decide whether it's the right step for you.

Deciding Whether to Invest Abroad: It's Not All about the Numbers

When choosing whether to invest abroad, I always ask budding investors to consider two simple questions:

>> Do you have a passion or affinity for a particular country?

>> If so, how much do you know about that market?

These questions often surprise people, because they're not about money, specific investment strategies, real estate expertise, or experience. Other important factors, such as your budget, will obviously impact your decision, and I cover them later in this chapter. But I'm addressing these two basic questions first because they get right to the heart of why some people succeed in overseas real estate investments where others fail spectacularly.

In the following sections, I cover these two facets — passion and accessibility — in more detail.

Playing on your passion

This chapter isn't about whether to buy a vacation home for your family, or a retirement spot in the sun. The considerations for purchasing a vacation or retirement home are quite different from the ones outlined here. (Of course, if you occasionally want to use an investment property for your family vacation, that's great!)

Instead, I'm talking about whether you want to build a robust real estate portfolio, using the strategies outlined in Parts 3 and 4 of this book, in an overseas market — or whether you'd actually be better off investing closer to home.

Building a robust real estate portfolio, whether at home or abroad, means treating your investment(s) as a business (see Chapter 3 for more on treating your portfolio as a business). This is why it's so important to find your passion.

Passion is what fuels successful businesses. Passion brings out the best in people and gives them the drive to succeed. After all, every business venture hits the odd bump in the road, and it's passion that keeps your enthusiasm alive when you get that call about a burst water pipe in Berlin at 6 a.m.

That's why I ask budding investors whether they have an affinity with a particular country. Have you always jaunted to Jamaica, for example? Are you fanatical about all things French? Do you dream of Denmark?

One of my passions is the Netherlands. My wife is Dutch, my kids are half-Dutch, we have family there, and I love the country. I'm definitely eager to develop a portfolio in that country. Perhaps by the time this book is published, I will have taken that step. And when I do, I know that my passion for the country will help make that learning curve easier and more enjoyable.

Bottom line is, when you like what you're doing, you do it better. So, although crunching the numbers and doing the research are important (and I get to those later in the chapter), don't be afraid to let your personal passion inform your decision making. And if your passion lies closer to home, go for that instead!

Tapping into available knowledge

Just because a country appeals to you or looks great on paper (in terms of growth prospects, return on investment, and so on) doesn't mean it's accessible for you personally as an investor. If you have no prior experience or knowledge of that country and no contacts there, you may struggle to set up and manage your investment.

After you've identified where your passion lies, you need to realistically assess how accessible that country is for you as a first-time investor in that market.

If your own knowledge and experience of a particular country is limited, don't be shy about hitting up your friends, family, and acquaintances for advice. Make a list of your contacts who have some experience of your chosen market, whether it's your colleague's brother who has a holiday home or the local barista who grew up there. Most people are happy to help by answering questions and recommending useful contacts.

Ultimately, it's not all about the numbers. Some countries, no matter how attractive they look financially, just won't stack up for you personally. Be realistic about what's achievable for you at this point in your property journey.

UNCOVERING YOUR REAL PASSION

Anita Roddick, founder of The Body Shop once said, "To succeed, you have to believe in something with such a passion that it becomes a reality." That was exactly the attitude I adopted when I first started my property business. I lived and breathed my business, literally willing it into life. Without that passion and belief, I don't think I'd have been able to create the real estate portfolio and multiple businesses that I now own.

Property was definitely my passion from the get-go, but maybe it's not yours. Maybe your passion is building a portfolio of investments that allows you to quit your job and spend more time with your family. Maybe *that's* what really lights a fire in your belly. Or maybe your passion is building financial security for you and your loved ones. Maybe your passion is simply becoming your own boss, and property provides the best way for you to achieve that goal.

It genuinely doesn't matter whether property is your prime passion, or whether your passion lies in becoming more entrepreneurial, securing a comfortable retirement, or whatever. The important thing is that you feel that overwhelming drive and passion to achieve your goals. If you're thinking of investing in Tuscany (or Tulsa, for that matter) because Bob from IT told you it was a good idea, then alarm bells should be ringing. After all, it's not Bob from IT who'll be dealing with the research, the bureaucracy, the phone calls, and so on.

Passion and drive are critical parts of real estate investing, because they link to goal-setting, positivity (including maintaining a positive attitude when things don't go according to plan) and attracting success. In other words, getting into the mind-set of a successful real estate investor is an important part of the journey.

You can read more about mind-set and discover practical techniques to get into the right frame of mind for success in Chapter 5.

Considering Your Budget

Passion aside, unless you've got plenty of funds to play with, your budget will absolutely impact your decision on whether to invest at home or abroad.

Simple budget constraints have driven many real estate investors into exciting foreign markets. For example, the London real estate market is so buoyant that beginner investors are often priced out altogether. So, if you're renting an apartment in South London and looking to get into property investing, chances are, you'll have to look farther afield. You'll certainly get a lot more for your money in Bulgaria than you will in Balham!

When you're deciding which country to invest in, budget is an important factor. You may well have a passion for Monaco, but if your budget is more slot machine than high roller, the world's most expensive property market will be way out of your reach.

TIP

It's fun to see what you can get for your money around the world. On sites like www.rightmove.co.uk and www.primelocation.com, you can get a feel for average property prices all over the world.

REMEMBER

Your budget may not be your own cash. Taking out a mortgage or other form of finance means you need less upfront capital to purchase a property. However, if you plan to buy your investment property with a mortgage, availability of financing in a given country is another factor to consider.

Some of the more mainstream investment countries like Portugal, France, and Spain will do mortgages for overseas buyers, which makes those countries more accessible to investors with limited capital. In less developed markets, however, obtaining a mortgage may not be an option.

In addition to getting a mortgage in your chosen investment country, other financing options include the following:

>> **Taking out a mortgage in your home country:** Some specialist providers offer mortgages for overseas properties, although these mortgages tend to be more expensive and difficult to obtain.

>> **Releasing equity from your home or another property you own:** This approach is a great low-barrier way to purchase affordable property overseas, because it means you can pay cash and avoid any overseas financing. On the downside, it ties your investment to your home and can put your home at risk.

>> **Taking out a personal loan:** For investors on a budget who have no equity to release and limited access to mortgage funds, a personal loan can provide a relatively quick and easy way to raise funds.

>> **Buying with friends and family:** Pooling your resources with like-minded friends and family can be a great way to boost your budget. However, you should always have a legal agreement in place that sets out who owns what proportion of the property and be clear from the outset who will be responsible for managing the property.

The low property prices in many overseas markets means you can be a bit more creative with financing options. I know one couple, friends of friends, who purchased a ridiculously cheap property in Eastern Europe by borrowing on their credit card!

Taking on additional mortgage debt or a personal loan isn't for everyone, and whether it's right for you will depend on your tolerance for risk (which I discuss in the next section). A risk-averse investor may only be comfortable with a small mortgage of, say, 30 percent of the value of the property — or even no mortgage at all — while someone who's more comfortable with risk may be willing to stretch to an 80 percent or 90 percent mortgage.

Never borrow more than you can afford to repay, no matter how mouthwatering the investment opportunity. And always talk to an independent financial advisor before making any decision. They'll be able to help you decide what you can afford and which financing option, if any, is right for you.

In Part 2, I provide lots more information on financing options, including some more creative ideas for accessing finance.

Assessing Your Risk Profile

Every investment is different, and the success of each investment depends on a wide range of factors or risks. In an overseas market, there are even more factors to consider. So, before you dive into the cool, sparkling waters of overseas property, you need to understand your personal risk profile. Why? Because your attitude to risk in general should inform any investment decision, especially whether investing overseas is the right move for you.

Your *risk profile* can best be defined as how much risk you're willing to accept, or how much risk you're comfortable with, as you work toward your real estate goals.

Of course, you should be concerned about any risk that may affect your ability to make money on a property, but some people have a greater tolerance for risk than others. Understanding your attitude to risk is an important step in deciding whether to invest overseas or closer to home.

Identifying where you sit on the risk spectrum

Consider someone purchasing an apartment in the Algarve, Portugal. Let's call our fictional investor Dave. Dave doesn't know the Algarve well, and this is his first overseas investment. So, in addition to getting up to speed on running a property as a vacation rental (see Chapter 16 for more on this strategy), Dave also has many other specific barriers to overcome:

- » The language barrier
- » Lack of local contacts
- » No knowledge of local laws
- » Currency risk (Portugal being in the eurozone)
- » Limited ability to manage the property himself (because he lives 2,000 miles away)

All these factors make the investment a higher risk than, say, a buy-to-rent apartment in Dave's hometown. Understanding Dave's risk profile essentially means understanding how concerned he is about these factors.

REMEMBER

No investment is absolutely risk free, so there's always an element of risk to contend with. The key is to work out what you're comfortable with and not push yourself beyond that point.

If Dave were very risk averse, this investment may be too high a risk. If Dave were a very adventurous investor, he may see the Algarve's stable real estate market, which is a favorite among foreign investors, as too "safe," not delivering high enough returns. Dave sits somewhere in the middle: He's comfortable with the risks associated with investing in Portugal, but he wouldn't be comfortable venturing into markets that are relatively untested for overseas investors.

In this way, risk tolerance is a spectrum, not a black-or-white issue. Are you the sort of person who likes jumping out of planes, bungee jumping, and climbing mountains? Then, in general, you have a greater tolerance for risk than I do (I'm a guy who enjoys fishing, playing guitar, and taking my family on vacation in our vintage camper van). But having started my own business in my twenties, I have a greater tolerance for risk than, say, someone who has worked for the same company, in the same job, for 30 years.

Even if your general attitude to risk is pretty gutsy, and you do enjoy jumping out of planes in your spare time, that doesn't mean you'll feel comfortable with high-risk real estate investments. The goal isn't to push yourself into one form of investing over another — it's to figure out what you're comfortable with.

Considering country-specific risk factors

You've got a passion for a particular country. You've got a base level of local knowledge, either through your own experience or existing contacts. It's within your budget. Now, how can you tell whether that country suits your risk profile?

Assessing countries for risk is kind of like assessing companies when investing in the stock market. Do you go for a newer company with huge potential for growth (and, let's be honest, utter failure), or do you go for an established blue-chip company that's expected to deliver steady returns over many years?

TIP

It's the same with international real estate. If you want a safer investment (as "safe" or reliable as any investment can get), you'll probably opt for a country that:

>> Has a stable economy (steady economic growth, minimal fluctuations in exchanges rates and interest rates, and so on)

>> Enjoys political stability

>> You understand and know well (or have the ability to access and gain knowledge more easily)

>> Has an established real estate market that's already welcoming lots of international investors

REMEMBER

With a fairly low-risk country like this, you may see smaller gains in terms of capital growth than you would in a higher-risk real estate market, but you'll also probably experience fewer crazy swings in terms of income and costs. (Turn to Chapter 3 to discover why you should be investing for income as well as capital growth.)

Like stocks and shares, as a rule of thumb, higher-risk real estate markets tend to offer higher returns. Someone with the foresight to purchase a two-bedroom apartment in East Berlin in the early 1990s, just after the fall of the Berlin Wall, would have paid as little as $9,000. Now, it would be worth easily $300,000. But investing early in untested markets like this may mean weathering years of political and financial uncertainty before you see real gains.

WARNING

Even a country with an established real estate market that attracts thousands of foreign buyers each year isn't immune to risk. If the economy isn't stable, you can still get burned. Take Greece, for example. After years of political and economic uncertainty and a crippling financial crisis, property prices in Greece have fallen more than 40 percent (at the time of writing) since 2008, while property taxes and rental taxes have increased multiple times. For the gung-ho investor, these low prices in Greece may represent an opportunity for a bargain. But if the country were to be ejected from (or opt to leave) the eurozone, prices would likely plummet further. Depending on your ultimate goal (which I talk about in the next section), this risk may not be a deal breaker for you, but for many people, it would be a huge concern.

Factoring your goals into the equation

When weighing the risks of overseas investments, you need to understand your ultimate goals, because your goals will affect your risk tolerance.

Consider the following:

>> **How long you intend to hold the investment:** If you're planning to hold the property as a long-term investment, short- and medium-term fluctuations will be less of a concern. In the context of decades, housing bubbles will pass and political landscapes will (often, but not always) smooth out. However, if you're planning to turn the property around as a short-term investment, perhaps as a development project (see Chapter 9), then political and economic fluctuations can have a huge impact on the success of your investment.

>> **Whether you're looking for capital growth (an increase in the property's value) or regular income (for example, as a rental property):** If you want to be earning income immediately and consistently, you need to invest in an established market with a ready-and-waiting target audience. You can't afford to wait for an emerging market to catch up to your vision.

>> **What strategy you intend to employ:** This ties in closely to the previous point. An ongoing income strategy like houses in multiple occupation (Chapter 13) or vacation lets (Chapter 16) likewise requires an established market.

One of my investments very much falls into the emerging market field: an apartment in Egypt. In the short and medium term, financial and political instability (compared to, say, Europe or the United States) means returns are, for now, small. But my goal for this investment was to get into the market early, buy cheap, hold the investment for ten years (maybe longer), and get a great return. In the context of this goal, short–term fluctuations and uncertainties aren't such a concern. I've also spread my risk by creating a real estate portfolio that's as diverse as possible — turn to Chapter 4 for more on diversifying your portfolio.

Figuring Out How You'll Manage Your Property

Managing a property that's farther away is more difficult than managing one down the street. (You didn't need to buy this book to figure that out.) In the early stages, when you're looking for a place to buy, it's harder to learn about the local market. Later on, after you've purchased the property, it's harder to manage relationships with tenants and other people when you can't have a face-to-face conversation and perhaps don't even speak the language.

This challenge is another reason why passion is so important in real estate investing. My business partner lives in the south of England and owns an investment property in France. Particularly in the early days, he was traveling to France regularly for meetings with local experts and tradespeople. Sometimes this involved a 16-hour day — flying over in the morning, spending the day there, and getting home late at night. Without passion, this sort of commitment gets old fast!

REMEMBER

Even if you have outstanding local contacts from the outset, be prepared to spend time in your chosen country, getting to know the local market, setting up and managing your investments, and developing those all-important relationships that will make your life easier when you're back home.

If your chosen market is a local town, it's obviously easier to build that knowledge (you know a lot about the market already) and manage your investments. If you have ten rental properties where you live, you could potentially manage them yourself, particularly in the early days if you want to save on costs. You could, for example, inspect all of them in one day and check in new tenants yourself when necessary. But if you have ten rental properties spread across the Algarve (our friend Dave has been busy!), it would be nearly impossible to manage them yourself if you didn't live there. You'd inevitably need local contacts to manage certain or all aspects for you.

TIP

This is where your "dream team" comes into play. Your dream team is made up of the people who will help you manage your investments and take care of things personally in your absence. This includes everyone from a good lawyer to a trustworthy plumber.

Whether you're investing at home or abroad, you always need reliable people you can trust, but you'll certainly rely on them more for an overseas investment. Turn to Chapter 3 for more on building your dream team.

REMEMBER

Local help comes with additional cost, so you'll need to factor this into your budget and cash flow (see Chapter 3). As an absent owner, you'll undoubtedly have higher maintenance and management costs than if you were managing the property locally yourself.

None of this should put you off investing in international property. If it suits your aims, your passion and your risk profile, it's well worth that investment of your time and money to carefully establish and run your investment.

Drilling Down to the Right Market for You

My goal in this chapter isn't to identify one catch-all international market that works for everyone. The truth is, no single choice is ideal for all investors. The best place for you as an individual to invest — whether it's in your home country or overseas — will depend on the factors I outline in this chapter.

REMEMBER

Start the decision-making process by identifying countries that you're passionate about rather than focusing solely on cold, hard facts and figures. After you've identified your passion, you can get more analytical and assess that country in terms of your budget, your risk profile, and so on.

But what if you're certain you want to invest abroad, but you don't have a passion for a particular country? Or your passion pulls you in two different directions? Or the country you love doesn't match your budget or risk profile? That's where this section can help.

Looking at the cold, hard facts and figures

If you're in a position where you need to narrow down your international options, the Internet will fast become your best friend (as if it isn't already). Online you can find a raft of information about real estate markets all over the world.

In addition to researching the real estate market in a given country, you should also carefully weigh practical considerations such as the following:

>> **If you don't speak the local language, how widely is English (or your native language) spoken?** Will you struggle to find a certified translator or deal with local tradespeople for instance?

>> **How easy is it for you to physically get to the country?** After you're established, and with your dream team in place, you shouldn't need to be on the ground often. But you never know when something unforeseen may crop up that requires your physical presence (especially in countries with a love of bureaucracy). Owning property that's an expensive 12-hour flight away may not be ideal if you're new to overseas investments.

>> **Will you be able to build a trusted dream team in that country?** In many countries, there are still elements of corruption and horror stories of investors getting ripped off, so don't scrimp on your research and due diligence. You absolutely need to be able to trust the people who will be looking after your property on your behalf.

>> **Will your preferred strategy apply in that country?** As I explain in Parts 3 and 4 of this book, multiple strategies can be successfully deployed abroad, and your preferred strategy will influence your country choice. In each of the strategy chapters, I set out some ideas for international real estate markets where that particular strategy may perform well.

You then need to drill down further from the overall country level to pinpoint your chosen town or region within that country. Again, that involves assessing specific regions in relation to the points outlined in the preceding list, as well as the following:

>> **What are the hot locations and property sectors in that country?** In Germany, for instance, student rental apartments in major cities like Berlin and Hamburg are currently performing well.

>> **What is the best geographical location for your chosen strategy or strategies?** If you want to run the property as a vacation rental, proximity to a beach or a ski or lake resort may be your preferred choice.

REMEMBER

If you want to market the property to tourists, you'll also need to consider factors like local infrastructure (such as highway access), facilities (shops, restaurants, and so on), whether English or other languages are widely spoken, and other potential barriers to attracting international visitors or out-of-towners.

Developing your knowledge of that country and region

After you've settled on a country and a specific region within that country, you need to start developing your knowledge and understanding of that market.

TIP

When you're investing in a new market, you can never spend too much time on the three Rs: *research, research, research.* As a starting point, here's what I do when I'm getting to know a new area:

>> **Read up on investing in that country.** Devour any information you can get your hands on regarding your chosen country, including property blogs and websites, economic forecast data, and political news.

>> **Research local agents before you set foot in the country.** Are there multiple agents to choose from or, if it's a less-developed market, is there just one local agent? Do they have a professional website? Are they certified by that country's accreditation body? (Read more about finding and vetting local experts in Chapter 3.) If it's a less developed market, are you going to have to

do the legwork and source your own opportunities by talking to local property owners?

>> **Spend time in the place.** Internet research is great, but there's no substitute for spending time there, getting to know the lay of the land, immersing yourself in the local properties, demographics, infrastructure, facilities and the like.

>> **Meet with local agents face to face.** No one knows the local market like the local agents, so invest time in establishing, developing, and nurturing those relationships. It will pay dividends in the long run.

>> **Get to know the local property ownership laws, planning regulations, tax issues, and other rules that are relevant to your particular strategy.** In some countries, the bureaucracy is both legendary and mind-boggling. Even the locals struggle! So source a reliable local lawyer, financial advisor, and other relevant experts (an architect, for example) as early as you can. Turn to Chapter 3 for information on the sorts of experts you'll need on your dream team.

WARNING

Don't take one agent's opinion on face value. There are lots of great agents out there — and there are lots of cowboys out there, too, looking to make a fast buck off naïve buyers. You always need to do your own due diligence and build a thorough picture of the facts by talking to multiple experts.

As you can tell, you need to go through several layers of thought processes and research. The lists in this section are by no means exhaustive — the specifics will depend on your chosen country and investment strategy (or strategies).

REMEMBER

Ultimately, whether a country, region, and investment opportunity is right for you will depend on you as an individual: what's accessible for you, what appeals to your interests, what suits your risk tolerance, and so on.

Focusing Your Attention on One or Two Key Markets

So you've decided that investing overseas is the right step for you. Awesome! However, as with any investment, it's important not to get carried away and spread yourself too thin.

No matter how mouthwatering the investment potential of multiple countries, spreading your investments across many diverse international markets can end up costing you a lot in terms of time, money, and stress.

If you do want to invest in international property, you're better off really developing your knowledge of one international market — and ideally focusing on a specific region of that country, at least at first. By focusing your efforts in one specific region, you can develop a strong foothold in that area, getting to know the market and local experts in great detail. You also benefit from economies of scale.

In other words, when you're ready to add other investments in that region, you already have your dream team of advisors and experts in place. Your second investment in that area will be a heck of a lot easier to establish than your first investment was. The third investment should be even easier than the second, and so on.

Then, having mastered that market, with your investments well established and your dream team running everything like a tight ship, you may feel ready to take advantage of the opportunities available in a different international market. That's fine — great even — but keep in mind that you'll be starting from scratch in terms of getting to know a new market and establishing your local dream team.

Even as your real estate portfolio becomes more developed and your confidence grows, I still recommend limiting yourself to no more than three different international markets. Investing in more than three countries at the same time is best left to advanced real estate investors who have deep pockets full of capital and an army of advisors.

IN THIS CHAPTER

» **Building a team of experts and helpers**

» **Automating tasks with business processes and systems**

» **Getting the word out about your business**

» **Keeping track of your money**

» **Protecting your property with insurance**

Chapter **3**

Treating Your Real Estate Portfolio as a Business

For some folks, owning a rental property or flipping the occasional house is rewarding enough, both financially and in terms of satisfaction. (And if that's your primary focus, you may want to check out Eric Tyson and Robert Griswold's excellent book *Real Estate Investing For Dummies,* 3rd Edition [Wiley].)

Other investors have seriously ambitious goals, ultimately aiming to build a robust and varied real estate portfolio, perhaps including international property investments.

TIP

If your ambitions stretch beyond one or two investments, you need to start thinking like a professional real estate investor, someone who runs her portfolio like a proper business. That's not to say you have to register as a company, employ dozens of people, and rent swanky offices — you just need to think of your portfolio as a business, not a fun side project, and manage your investments accordingly.

This chapter is all about the practical side of treating your portfolio as a business. If you want to find out more about the personal development and mind-set skills necessary for real estate success, head to Chapter 5.

Aiming for Passive Income as the Ultimate Goal

When people think of making money through real estate, their first thought is often capital growth (for example, buying a property for $200,000 and selling it six months later for $270,000). That's a solid approach to making money, and capital growth projects certainly make up part of my own portfolio.

REMEMBER

However, if you're going to treat your property portfolio as a business, you need to think about income, as well as capital growth. Investing for income tends to be less risky and more reliable than capital growth — because money in the bank this month, and next month, and the month after that is safer than relying on future growth.

That's not to say you won't achieve capital growth alongside income. If you own a collection of rental and serviced accommodation properties, for instance, those properties will likely grow in value over time. In this way, capital growth is like a cherry on top of a delicious income sundae.

Generating income from real estate is so exciting because it's relatively hands-off compared to, say, working 9 to 5 for a paycheck. In that way, it can be described as *passive income.*

Defining passive income

The great Warren Buffett once said, "If you don't find a way to make money while you sleep, you will work until you die." So, if you like the idea of making money while you slumber (and, honestly, who doesn't?), then the passive income mind-set is for you.

REMEMBER

Passive income is the key to building real wealth. Think of passive income as another name for *yield* (the money you make on an investment). What makes it *passive* is that, after it's up and running, the investment requires minimal input from you for the income, or *yield,* to keep coming in, month after month.

In other words, you invest some of your time and money upfront, and you get money back in return on a regular basis. Your money starts working for you, not the other way around. Sounds good, right?

It's important to note that passive income isn't just about making more money (although that is, of course, a big attraction). It's not about greed. It's about rethinking the fundamental nature of work and developing the means to live life your way. For me, that means being there to drop the kids off at school and spend quality time with my family. For you, it may mean putting in a few hours in the morning and having the rest of the day off, or having a four-day weekend, or never wearing a suit again! In short, passive income gives you more freedom — to do whatever you want.

MY FIRST TASTE OF PASSIVE INCOME

I sort of fell into passive income. As a young, cash-strapped homeowner, I started renting out one of my spare bedrooms to help cover the mortgage. Then, when I started renting out the second spare bedroom, I was earning enough to cover the mortgage outright — in other words, I no longer had to worry about making the mortgage payment each month. "This is all right," I thought to myself. "What's next?" So, I converted the garage to make a third rental bedroom, and the £500-a-month profit I made from *that* room was my first taste of passive income.

My interest in passive income grew from there. At the time, I was working for an investment bank in London, working all hours. (Anyone who works in that world will know what I'm talking about — working late almost becomes a competition, and no one wants to be the first one to log off at night.)

I was desperate to escape the rat race. A profit of £500 per month profit may not seem like much, but that little bit of passive income pointed the way to a brighter future — one where I didn't have to work all hours to earn a living. A future where I could focus my efforts on doing what I loved, in both a business and personal sense, while still building wealth. A future where life was more . . . fulfilling.

You can guess what happened next. I quit my job, kissing goodbye to my six-figure salary in the process, to focus on creating more passive income through property. I had to live frugally at first (even back then, £500 a month didn't go far), and it wasn't easy. But having the time and freedom to focus on my passion for property more than made up for it.

Passive income isn't a get-rich-quick scheme. It takes time to build up a good level of passive income. So, if you're looking to quit your job and devote yourself to real estate full time, it may be a while before you're comfortable giving up the security of your existing income.

Looking at examples of passive income

Anything that generates money and isn't directly tied to your effort or output (in the way of a regular job) is considered passive income. So, investing in the stock market can be considered passive income. So, too, can real estate.

What's great about real estate is that there are so many exciting sub-strategies for generating a regular income. In fact, the sheer range of real estate strategies is what prompted me to write this book in the first place.

The strategies outlined in Parts 3 and 4 of this book can pretty much all be considered passive income strategies, including the following:

>> Property development (see Chapter 9)

>> Rent-to-rent (see Chapter 11)

>> Houses in multiple occupation (see Chapter 13)

>> Student and vacation rentals (see Chapters 15 and 16, respectively)

If you think passive income ventures like these require a lot of upfront capital, think again. Rent-to-rent, for instance, requires nothing more than the first month's rent and deposit to get started — and sometimes less than that! In this way, property can offer a fairly low-capital route to passive income.

This is why I believe real estate is probably the most achievable path to passive income for the average person on the street. It can create serious wealth, too, if done right.

Looking at the pros and cons of passive income

I can only really talk about my experience, but here are the pros and cons of passive income, as I see them. On the plus side passive income gives you:

>> **More time and freedom:** Assuming you build up to a level of passive income where you no longer have to work 9 to 5, you have much more choice in how you live your life and more time for the things you love.

>> **Better work–life balance:** You can be there to take the kids to school and pick them up at the end of the day, and manage your real estate investments when it works for you.

>> **The ability to indulge your passion — and your talents:** Concentrating on passive income has allowed me to invest in projects that genuinely interest and excite me. I can spend my time on the parts of the business I find most interesting or are the best use of my time. The rest I can outsource to people who are better qualified (see "Drafting a Dream Team," coming up next).

REMEMBER

Passive income gives you the means to reach your full potential. What could be more satisfying than that?

On the downside, with passive income:

>> **You have to take a longer-term view.** Passive income isn't about getting rich overnight. It's about rethinking the way you work and earn money for the long haul.

>> **There's a cost to being more hands-off.** As your portfolio grows, you'll probably have to outsource some of your workload to other people and/or invest in technology to take care of certain tasks for you. This means sacrificing some of your income to cover these costs. For me, the additional cost is well worth it because it frees me up to focus on new opportunities and profit-enhancing activities.

>> **You can't get away with putting in zero effort.** "Low" or "minimal" effort, sure. But not zero effort. You need to invest some time in your investments, both in terms of establishing your new projects and checking in on them regularly.

WARNING

When you've got a property up and running nicely, and you're generating a regular income from it, don't make the same mistake as a lot of investors and ignore the property. If things go wrong because you've stepped off the gas, you'll have to devote lots of time and energy to getting things back on track.

I've fallen into this trap myself, when one of my former rental agents wasn't managing a property well enough. I let things slide for a while, hoping he'd get his act together. But, of course, I had to step in eventually, and I had to devote much more time than if I'd intervened earlier. To keep your investments on track, you're far better off spending a little time often than spending a lot of time only occasionally.

Drafting a Dream Team

You may have heard of the famous Pareto principle, also known as the 80/20 rule. It states that 80 percent of results (be it leads, sales, income, or whatever) come from 20 percent of your effort. So if 80 percent of your effort isn't directly generating income, why spend your time on those tasks?

TIP

For your real estate income to be as passive as possible, aim to focus on that results-delivering 20 percent of your effort and eliminate, outsource, or automate the remaining 80 percent.

REMEMBER

Trying to do everything yourself is not very passive. And sometimes you may not even be the best person for the job. There are times when paying someone more qualified and experienced to do a job for you just makes better business sense. As management guru Peter Drucker said, "Do what you do best and outsource the rest."

For example, I'd be a lousy accountant, I don't particularly relish the day-to-day side of property management, and my plumbing skills are nonexistent, so I outsource those jobs to people who are experts in their fields. They'll always do a better job than I can, and it frees me up for activities that create greater value for me, such as taking a more strategic view of my portfolio and identifying new investment opportunities.

In this section, I introduce the concept of outsourcing various aspects of your workload to experts and accessing other kinds of business support — in other words, building your very own "dream team."

Getting expert advice

The exact expert advice you'll need will depend on your chosen real estate strategy (or strategies), geographic location, and scale of your portfolio. But in this section, I try to list as many of the expert advisors as possible that the average real estate investor may need.

TIP

Wherever possible, try to get your experts in place before you make your first investment. This means you can get the advice you need (whether it's guidance on tax implications or an idea of renovation costs) before you commit to a project.

That said, I appreciate that some investors will prefer to scale up and gradually add to their dream team as their portfolio grows. For example, you'll probably want to engage a mortgage broker for your first investment, but you may not want to pay for a property manager until your portfolio is a little bigger. In that case, you can start off managing tenants yourself and, over time, outsource this task to a property manager. Find a balance and scale that works best for you.

The real estate–focused experts that you'll need to call upon may include the following:

>> **Mortgage broker:** A mortgage broker can help you find the right financing when you're ready to buy a new property.

>> **Tax advisor:** Real estate investments can have tax implications, and a good tax advisor will be able to explain the impact for you.

>> **Independent financial advisor:** This person can offer unbiased financial guidance, looking at the big picture of your finances, not just your real estate investments.

>> **Real estate lawyer:** You need someone who specializes in real estate to handle all the legal aspects of buying and selling properties.

>> **Real estate agent:** A real estate agent can help you find the right property opportunities when you're looking to buy, as well as help you sell the property when you're ready to unload it.

>> **Property manager:** If you're renting the property, a property manager can take care of finding tenants and managing the property on your behalf (collecting rent, handling repairs, and so on).

>> **Insurance agent:** Find an agent who specializes in real estate insurance to make sure you're properly covered.

>> **Architect:** If you're looking to renovate your properties, an architect will help with floor plans and elevation design drawings.

>> **Planning consultant:** A planning consultant can advise you on local planning laws and building codes and explain where you need permission or permits for building work or alterations.

>> **General building contractors and tradespeople (plumbers, electricians, and so on):** These experts will help you build, convert, develop, and maintain your properties. At this point in my real estate journey, I have a wide range of contractors and tradespeople to call upon, depending on the size and scale of the project at hand. Your own team will scale up as your portfolio grows.

>> **Translator:** You'll need a translator for overseas investments where you aren't fluent in the local language.

How can you access these experts and other support services? Turn to "Finding and vetting experts," later in this chapter.

Outsourcing other aspects of your workload

As an international real estate investor, you'll have to contend with a wide range of general business tasks associated with the day-to-day running of your investments.

TIP

As your portfolio grows, make a list of all the tasks you do to establish your investments and keep them ticking along, from logging income and expenses to running credit checks on tenants. Assess whether any of these tasks can be eliminated altogether or automated through technology (see "Investing in Systems and Technology to Grow Your Business" later in the chapter). Then, with whatever's left, go through and see if any of those tasks can be outsourced.

Here are some of the tasks that I outsource:

>> Marketing and social media

>> General administration

>> Web design and management

>> Sales and customer service

>> General accounting and bookkeeping

REMEMBER

You don't have to outsource everything in one go. You can start with one or two tasks — I'd begin with the most time-consuming and cost-effective areas first — and scale up to outsourcing more as your income grows. This strategy will give you more time to put back into your portfolio and generating more income.

Aim to outsource those areas that you're not very good at (tasks that someone else can do quicker and better than you can) or ones that you simply don't enjoy doing. Lots of traditional business advice I've read says you should work hard to improve the areas you're not good at, but that seems crazy to me. Why not spend your time on the things you *are* good at, and let other people take care of the rest?

TIP

I highly recommend getting a *virtual assistant* — a freelancer who works from home and normally carries out admin and secretarial tasks. A virtual assistant isn't just there to answer phone calls. A skilled virtual assistant— can help with researching properties and new business opportunities, saving you many hours of legwork.

You can even consider outsourcing areas of your personal life, such as laundry and cleaning. Think about it: What's the better use of your time — scrubbing the bathroom for an hour, or spending an hour on your real estate portfolio (or, for that matter, playing ball with the kids)? Over the years, I've had my virtual assistants book theater tickets, send flowers (sorry, Mum, I did that once!), and even research holidays.

TIP

In the early days, finding *multi-skilled freelancers* — people who can help you with multiple aspects of your business — offers great value for your money. For example, one of my first freelancers helped me both with managing rentals and general admin tasks. So, she'd advertise properties on online portals, conduct occasional viewings for me, keep on top of my paperwork, and help to manage my time. As you grow, you'll be able to give people more dedicated roles.

IS OUTSOURCING WORTH THE COST?

People generally accept that they need to cough up for expert advisors, like a lawyer or plumber — you know, the kinds of things that may get you into hot water (legal and literal) if you tried to do it yourself. But there's often a reluctance to pay for more general support that you feel you can just do yourself, like a virtual assistant, a bookkeeper, or even a property manager to manage tenants.

Yes, outsourcing tasks to other people does cost more, but it's a natural progression to make as you begin to treat your real estate portfolio like a business.

For example, I still use external management companies to look after some of my farther-afield properties — conducting viewings, vetting prospective tenants, managing tenants, and so on. It costs more than if I just did those jobs myself, but it massively frees me up to focus on growing my portfolio and doing more of the things I enjoy. Ultimately, it creates greater value for me — and increased income in the long run.

In startup, ambitious entrepreneurs don't try to do everything in the business — from engineering to marketing — themselves. They know that the smartest way to grow the business is to employ people who are more skilled than they are in those areas, leaving them to concentrate on the leadership, strategy, and growth side of things.

Instead of focusing on cost, try to focus on *value*. In other words, is the cost worth it?

How can you figure out whether outsourcing a particular task is worth the cost? Your time is valuable, so what you need to ask yourself is: "Would it cost me more to do it myself?" To answer this question, you need to calculate your effective hourly rate. You can do this by taking your net income for the last 6 or 12 months and dividing that figure by the number of working hours. Then look at the hourly rate someone would charge to do the task in question. If it costs less to outsource it than to do it yourself, go

(continued)

(continued)

ahead and outsource it. If it costs more to outsource it, keep doing the task yourself until your hourly rate increases or you can find a more cost-effective option.

Say, for example, your effective hourly rate is $25 per hour. You can then outsource tasks that would cost less than $25 per hour, because it would cost you more to do them yourself. So, if a freelance bookkeeper would charge $20 an hour to keep track of your finances, then go for it!

Eye-opening, isn't it?

Remember: Having outsourced tasks and freed up some of your time, you can't just sit around eating cereal and watching Netflix all day. For outsourcing to create maximum value for you, you need to wisely spend the time you've gained on income-generating tasks.

Eventually, you may reach a point where it makes more financial sense to bring tasks back "in house" and hire full-time employees to work for you. That's where I'm at in my real estate journey, and I now have multiple property-related businesses with full-time, in-house staff for a number of jobs. If your business is large and profitable enough to warrant it, and it would cost less to employ people than it would to pay freelancers, this approach makes perfect sense.

Finding and vetting experts, at home and overseas

Whether you're investing in your local town or overseas, the same general approach to finding and vetting your "dream teamers" applies. Thanks to the Internet and online platforms like Upwork, it's never been easier to tap into additional resources and support whenever and wherever you need it.

TIP

Here are my tried-and-tested methods for finding the right support:

>> **Network, network, network.** Join your local general business networking group and seek out any property-specific networking groups in your area. (You can find more on networking in Chapter 5.)

>> **Don't forget online networking opportunities.** With sites like Property Forum (www.propertyforum.com), which is part of my group of businesses, you can network with property experts and tap into their knowledge.

» **Ask your contacts for recommendations.** Many of my support team members have come to me via recommendations from people I know and trust.

» **Search via the accrediting organization, where appropriate.** For certified professionals, like lawyers and real estate agents, the certifying body will often provide a listing of professionals in your area. If you're based in a different country from the expert in question, it's a good idea to search for professionals who have direct experience working with international clients.

» **For more general business tasks, online platforms like Upwork (**www. upwork.com**) and Fiverr (**www.fiverr.com**) can connect you with skilled freelancers from all over the world.** If you prefer to work with someone local to you, seek out a local virtual assistant or business support agency. (Again, your local networking group will be a great resource for this.) Many business support agencies can handle anything from admin and research to marketing and web support.

When you find your potential dream teamers, research them thoroughly before meeting with them and certainly before you enter into any sort of agreement. You wouldn't employ a contractor to renovate your house without getting references, would you? It's exactly the same with your dream team.

Vetting your experts and freelancers can be as simple as answering the following questions:

» **Are they doing the job full time and getting paid for it, or is it a side project or hobby for them?** Your next-door neighbor's brother may be handy with a wrench, but that's no substitute for a qualified, full-time plumber!

» **Do they have a professional website?** The website should clearly outline their skills, experience, and expertise, and show testimonials from previous clients.

» **Where appropriate, are they licensed or certified?** They must also be fully insured for the work you're hiring them to do.

» **What experience do they have with your specific type of property investment?** A commercial real estate lawyer might not be the best expert for you if you're purchasing a vacation rental.

» **What do previous and existing clients have to say about them?** Always ask to speak to two or three of their clients for a reference. For a building contractor, ask to visit properties the contractor has worked on recently.

>> **Are there online reviews of their services?** Reviews aren't just for hotels and restaurants anymore. These days, just about any business can be reviewed online. Check out Yelp (`www.yelp.com`), Trustpilot (`www.trustpilot.com`) and other review platforms to see what people have to say about the business.

>> **Do they respond to your emails and calls quickly?** Are they easy to get a hold of? If you have to work hard to get their attention, that's not a great sign.

You can do a lot of this research and vetting online and over the phone, but, if possible, it's always a good idea to meet with members of your dream team, particularly the real estate agents. Even if you're investing overseas, you should definitely go and meet potential agents face to face; in-person meetings like this are crucial for establishing trust and building those all-important relationships.

TIP

Especially if you're investing overseas and don't know the local area that well, the real estate agent will be probably be the first person on your dream team. You can then leverage the real estate agent's contacts to start building your dream team in that region. Your agent's recommendations for builders, lawyers, and so on will be invaluable in the early days. Tapping into your agent's network is a great way to get started when you're new to an area.

WARNING

Of course you should be wary of relying solely on your agent's recommendations. "Backhanders" aren't uncommon, so you want to make sure you're getting a genuine recommendation, not helping your agent scratch someone else's back. It's your back the agent should be scratching! Always do your due diligence on any company that your agent recommends.

Getting the most out of your dream team

TIP

When you find the right people for your dream team, you want to keep them. So, you need to maintain and nurture those working relationships and ensure things run as smoothly as possible. This means:

>> **Keep in touch regularly.** This oils the wheels of communication and helps to build rapport.

>> **Be absolutely clear about your expectations.** Agree upfront what work you want done and to what standard.

>> **Review your arrangement regularly (at least every six months, more regularly in the early days).** If anything isn't working for you, address it head on and try to find a solution.

>> **Treat your team members' time as carefully as your own.** That means not wasting people's time or calling them at 10 p.m. to ask something that can easily wait until the next day.

>> **Talk about your future plans for growth.** This helps to build trust and rapport, but it also serves a more practical purpose. If your dream teamers have an idea of your future aspirations, they'll be more invested in the success of your portfolio and can keep you informed on potential opportunities they've heard about on the grapevine.

>> **Promote your contacts around your network.** Providing there's no conflict of interest, why not recommend your dream teamers to others in your network? *Remember:* Referrals work both ways. So, if you're happily recommending your tax advisor to your contacts, they'll be more likely to do the same for you among their own networks.

>> **Always say thank you for a job well done.** Showing your appreciation provides a welcome boost to motivation and morale.

Investing in Systems and Technology to Grow Your Business

As your business grows, you'll get an increase in customers, tenants, business contacts, and incoming enquiries that need servicing. You're no longer a part-time landlord or property developer or investor; your business is growing and you've got ambitious plans to grow further.

Your dream team will no doubt scale up to accommodate this growth and increased workload. But you should also look for opportunities to simplify and automate tasks. You can do this by creating business processes and systems for regular tasks, and/or investing in technology to take care of tasks for you.

REMEMBER

Again, there's always a cost associated with good technology. If you want quality solutions, you have to pay for them. Likewise, creating business processes and procedures takes valuable time. But instead of focusing on how much time and money all this will cost you, try to think about *value*. Is the technology or process worth it? Will it ultimately save you time and money? Will it help your team do a better job?

Putting the right processes in place

Software is only part of the picture. As your business grows and your workload increases (or the workload of your employees or freelancers increases), you need to put the right processes in place to ensure that you and the people who work for you are working consistently, effectively, and efficiently.

REMEMBER

Every business needs processes and systems in place for completing core business tasks. It's the same with your property investments. With easy-to-follow processes in place, you don't have to micromanage your people to make sure things get done the way you want.

Business processes function as a sort of training manual for your people. When procedures are set out on paper, you're no longer training everyone personally in how to complete tasks. The people you trained have the framework they need to be able to train other people. In this way, processes and guidelines are critical for scaling up your business.

As an example, here are a few of the processes I have in place for some of my rental properties:

>> **Property advertisements:** These guidelines set out exactly what information should be included about the property, in what format. The guidelines also cover images: how many photos are needed, what rooms need to be photographed, image quality, image size, and so on. This way, my team can advertise properties online consistently and effectively, without my having to tell them what to do.

>> **Tenant onboarding process:** My team has helped create and now follows a structured process for setting up new tenants. This includes a welcome letter that thanks them for choosing our property, details the information we need to complete the credit check, sets out our bank account details for paying the deposit and monthly rent, and includes information on the UK's tenancy deposit protection rules. A simple template letter like this ensures that new tenants are all onboarded quickly and consistently — and nothing gets overlooked.

>> **Credit check and reference procedures:** These step-by-step procedures set out exactly what the team needs to do to check a tenant's credit history and gather appropriate references.

>> **Rental contract templates:** We have a range of boilerplate contracts to use for different properties and rental arrangements (student rentals, houses in multiple occupation, single rentals, and so on).

Defining effective business processes

TIP

The right processes for you will depend on your chosen real estate strategy. But here are my general tips for defining effective processes:

>> **For tasks that are repeated frequently and involve multiple steps, create a simple flowchart.** This chart will help ensure this task is done correctly and consistently and that nothing gets skipped.

>> **Set out the required steps in plain English.** A total novice should be able to read the instructions and understand what you mean.

>> **Detail is good, but don't go overboard.** If your guidelines for rental advertisements stretch to ten pages, you're going into too much detail. People are more likely to read and digest guidelines that are short and snappy. *Remember:* Flowcharts are great for communicating multiple steps in a small space.

>> **Create template letters, emails, and forms for communicating with clients at key stages (for example, at the start and end of a tenancy, to inform tenants of an inspection, and so on).**

>> **Ensure that the processes and templates are accessible to everyone who needs them.** A simple shared folder, such as a Dropbox, Google Drive, or iCloud folder, will suffice.

>> **Always save separate backups elsewhere.** When multiple people have access to documents in a shared drive, accidents can happen. Make sure your hard work is backed up somewhere safe.

In time, as your dream team becomes more established, your team members will be experienced enough to devise their own processes and procedures. Embrace and encourage this level of initiative, but make sure you understand each process they're setting out and that it works for your business.

Saving time through software

There's a range of technology solutions out there designed to help you run your real estate portfolio more effectively, from general business and accounting software to technology solutions that are specifically designed for real estate businesses.

REMEMBER

As your business grows, you need to start acting like a real business. That means thinking about efficiency, automation, customer service, and so on.

Not all of these will apply in your own business, but here are some of the technology solutions that my team and I use to work more efficiently and provide outstanding service:

>> **Electronic signature system:** This speeds up the contract process significantly and allows us to process contract admin in a much shorter amount of time. We use Signable (www.signable.co.uk) for this, but two other popular options are Adobe Sign (https://acrobat.adobe.com/us/en/sign.html) and DocuSign (www.docusign.com).

>> **Customer relationship management (CRM) software:** We use Infusionsoft (www.infusionsoft.com) to manage our customer and contact list effectively. Other popular options include Salesforce (www.salesforce.com) and Zoho (www.zoho.com). We keep a record for each contact (tenants, agents, and so on) and note what's discussed in each conversation. This helps to improve our sales processes and customer service. Small details like remembering our agent's new baby's first name or where they went on holiday can really help build rapport, which in turn increases sales and service levels. Depending on the CRM software you choose, you may be able to use it for sending mail shots and other marketing communications. Infusionsoft also does this very well for small to medium businesses and automates a lot of your marketing effort, meaning your sales team are dealing with hotter incoming leads rather than wasting valuable time making tons of outgoing calls.

>> **Social media marketing software:** We use Hootsuite (www.hootsuite.com) to manage our social media accounts and automate and schedule our posts in advance. We can set up a whole month of posts in a single day, making this element of our marketing highly efficient. TweetDeck (www.tweetdeck.com) and Sprout Social (www.sproutsocial.com) are popular alternatives.

>> **Content management system (CMS):** If you have a website, make sure it's built on a CMS platform that's easy to use and update in house with minimum fuss and web expertise. If not, you can end up paying your web designer to make updates and post new content for you, which, if you plan to publish regular articles, for instance, can end up costing a small fortune. Depending on the size and complexity of the website, we like WordPress (www.wordpress.com) as a CMS. Another popular option is Squarespace (www.squarespace.com).

>> **Bookkeeping software:** We use Xero (www.xero.com) to quickly create invoices (from preset templates), run profit-and-loss management reports, automate recurring payments and invoices, and chase late payers. It saves so much time on the administrative side of things! Opt for a system that allows you and your bookkeeper or accountant to both access and manage records. Two other popular options are FreshBooks (www.freshbooks.com) and QuickBooks (www.quickbooks.com).

REMEMBER

Technology can save you time and allow you to focus on tasks that create greater value for you. These solutions don't even have to be expensive.

Some specific real estate software platforms can help you manage your properties more effectively. For example, Rent Manager (www.rentmanager.com) is a great tool for landlords and includes functions for collecting rent, managing leases, and sending correspondences/notices. It also includes a strong financial element and can handle accounts receivable, accounts payable, and financial reporting. What's more, Rent Manager, also offers built-in marketing features to help you post advertisements and track the success of your advertising. It's a great all-round solution. Rent Manager is just one example. Do some research to find the specific real estate tools are right for you. Your individual business and strategy may mean your requirements could be different from mine.

Evaluating technology solutions

TIP

Carefully evaluate any software solutions before you splash out any cash:

>> To narrow your options, compare the different software solutions in terms of features, technical support, hardware requirements, and, of course, cost.

>> Research the software provider's reputation and customer reviews online.

>> Talk to people in your circle who are already using the software to find out how easy it is to operate and any common problems. This is where your networking groups come in really handy.

>> Consider the software's ability to scale up alongside your needs. For example, if a rental management software program is suitable for, say, up to 20 units and you're already at 10 units with firm plans to expand, you'll soon outgrow the program.

>> Trial a free demo version (most software providers offer a limited free trial with no questions asked) before you buy any software. You want to make sure it serves your needs fully and is easy to use before you commit.

Promoting Your Real Estate Business

If you just want to buy one or two investment properties and that's all, you'll probably be wondering why on earth you need to bother with promoting your business. If your plans are to stay small, you won't need to think much beyond advertising your properties to buyers and tenants — something you could do yourself for free if you wanted to.

REMEMBER

However, this chapter is all about going beyond real estate investing as a nice little sideline, and thinking about your portfolio as an actual business. Like any business, you need to really invest in marketing and advertising if you want to grow.

Understanding what you need to promote is the first task. This will depend on your chosen real estate strategy or strategies but is likely to include the following:

>> Units (either rooms or entire properties) that you have available to rent

>> Properties for sale (for example, if you've developed or refurbished a property)

>> Your real estate brand (moving beyond bringing in leads to sell or rent your properties toward establishing a reputation for quality properties, so that people actively want to do business with you)

>> Growing your individual profile and brand as an expert in your chosen field, further helping to attract quality leads, contacts, and opportunities

TIP

Marketing and advertising is a specialist field so I strongly recommend that you invest in professional support. For marketing your properties, a sales or rental agent will be able to manage the process for you. For marketing your brand and expertise, a freelance marketing manager will get right to the heart of your overall brand goals and establish effective marketing steps to help you achieve those ambitions.

If you want to handle your own promotion activities, options for marketing and advertising include the following:

>> Advertising properties through online sales and rental portals, like craigslist (www.craigslist.org), Zillow (www.zillow.com), and Hotpads (www.hotpads.com) to name just a few. In the UK, SpareRoom (www.spareroom.co.uk) is a popular choice.

>> Advertising properties via Google advertisements and banner ads on relevant property websites like Property Forum (www.propertyforum.com) and social media groups

>> Advertising properties and establishing your brand via your own website

>> Growing your brand reputation and establishing your expertise via your own social media activity

>> Expanding brand awareness by attending local networking groups

>> Demonstrating your expertise among your existing network, including family and friends (don't be shy about discussing your property ventures and aspirations among your social circle)

TIP

Regularly posting on property-related groups and pages on LinkedIn (www.linkedin.com) and Facebook (www.facebook.com) is an effective and inexpensive way to demonstrate your knowledge, establish your reputation, and get your name out there, particularly in the early days.

Managing Your Cash Flow Like a Boss

Accounting is obviously a complex, specialist subject, so my intention here isn't to give you all the accounting info you need in just one small section of a chapter. (I assume you'll be working with an accountant or bookkeeper to maintain correct accounting records and practices.) Instead, my intention in this section is to draw your attention to the importance of managing your cash flow correctly.

Say, for example, you're a property developer and you currently have five development projects in your portfolio. If you run out of cash in the bank and you have mortgage payments to make and owe money to your contractors, you'll get into trouble pretty darn quickly.

TIP

Managing your cash flow can be as simple as having a spreadsheet that lists all your income and expenses, month by month, including contractor payments, utility bills, and fixed overheads such as insurance and staff costs.

As your business grows, and your income and expenses become larger and more complex, you'll likely progress beyond a simple spreadsheet. Accounting software will help you manage your cash flow more effectively (see "Saving time through software," earlier in this chapter, for recommendations).

Preparing for the rise and fall of income and expenses

Keep in mind that your expenses will fluctuate from month to month and year to year. For example, if you have a development project, you may have a lot of materials to buy one month as a one-off cost and the next month have almost no materials to buy. Managing your cash flow correctly means allowing for these fluctuations with a sufficient cash buffer.

The same is true of income fluctuations. So, for my rental properties, I have my property manager advise on occupancy rates and any upcoming void periods (where a property or room is sitting empty) so I can plan for these income fluctuations.

REMEMBER

Get your cash flow sheet as accurate as possible. That means accounting for fluctuations. Don't assume that your income and expenses will remain constant.

TIP

Setting up long-term leases and negotiating flat fees with your dream team will all help to minimize wild swings in income and expenses.

Macro-economic factors — things that are beyond your control — can cause your income and expenses to fluctuate. If interest rates rise and your properties are financed through mortgages or other forms of lending, the cost of borrowing that money will rise. Labor costs also go up and down depending on wider market factors. In the UK right now, labor availability is fairly low so I'm paying more for labor than I was, say, two years ago. On the upside, positive market shifts like a booming rental market has seen my rental income rise.

If your investments are located overseas, you'll also need to stay abreast of fluctuations in currency exchange rates and local interest rates.

TIP

It's not all about monthly costs. You also need to set aside funds for those annual expenses that can be easily overlooked, such as annual property taxes and any income tax that may be due on your earnings.

HOW INVOLVED SHOULD YOU BE AS THE BUSINESS GROWS?

If you're treating you're portfolio like a business, you need to know every element of your income and expenses in great detail. So, even when you're working with an accountant, you still need a strong handle on the figures and a clear idea of where you're at from month to month.

In addition to working with an accountant or bookkeeper, it's also a good idea to get advice from a specialist tax advisor. A tax advisor will be able to save you money by advising on upcoming tax bills and any tax that can be reclaimed through smart tax planning. Many accounting firms have these specialist advisors in house, so choose a multifaceted firm in the early days so you can more easily tap into that expertise when you need it down the road.

Maintaining a safety net with a cash buffer

Especially with fluctuating income and expenses, it's really important to keep a buffer of cash in the bank. I've read so many horror stories of multimillionaires and even very established companies going under because they ran out of cash.

REMEMBER

For any business, cash is king, and maintaining your cash flow is vital for success. This means you'll always, always need a suitable buffer of cash in the bank. This buffer needs to increase as your business grows. So, given the size of my real estate portfolio, my monthly mortgage commitments are well into five figures! At the time of writing, I also have two large development projects on the go, each with 30-odd contractors working on site. If my buffer doesn't cover these commitments, I'll be in for some sleepless nights.

That said, there's a balance to be struck between having a sensible buffer in the bank and not making the most of your money. For example, if you're financing a development project through borrowing, and you leave a big chunk of that money sitting in the bank, you're effectively paying interest on money that's just sitting there, doing nothing.

TIP

So, how much of a buffer should you have? What's right for you will depend on your income and expenses, as well as your risk tolerance. My personal rule of thumb is to always have a buffer of three to six months — so, if my income drops or dries up for some reason, I have enough cash in the bank to cover my outgoings for three to six months. That would give me a reasonable amount of time to make changes, turn things around, and get that income climbing again. If your costs are fairly low (say, for a portfolio of rental properties), then a buffer of two to three months may be more suitable for you. As time goes on and you become less focused on growth, you'll also be aiming to increase your buffer substantially.

Getting the Right Insurance

You never know what's around the corner and, just as with any important area of your life (from your home to your health), protecting your real estate investments through proper insurance is vitally important.

Insuring your properties correctly

The exact coverage you need will depend on your chosen real estate strategy, so be sure to consult a certified insurance broker with specialist property expertise. Some of the risks you may face won't be obvious (some of my projects have even had to be insured against terrorism), so your insurance broker will be an important part of your dream team. Listen to what your broker has to say and don't take any chances.

REMEMBER

With the right insurance coverage, you'll be protected against things like fire, flood, storms, and burglary. But insurance isn't just about protecting you against actual, material losses; it's also about protecting you against legal claims and lawsuits.

Appropriate coverage for your real estate portfolio may include the following:

>> Suitable buildings and contents insurance for buy-to-rent properties (your insurer will need to know that the property is being rented to tenants)

>> Property development coverage for refurbishments and developments, covering the value of the property and materials on site

>> Liability insurance (for example, where there are tradespeople working — building sites are dangerous places!)

WARNING

In our increasingly litigious society, that last point, liability insurance, may one day save your bacon. Good liability insurance will cover you for personal injuries and losses suffered by people on the property (where the injury or loss is the result of dangerous or defective conditions). Liability insurance will also cover the legal costs associated with defending any claim and damages. Legal costs in particular can spiral pretty quickly, so don't scrimp on this cover. Your broker will be able to advise you on what level of coverage is appropriate for you so you can sleep easy at night!

Making sure your chosen partners have the right insurance

In addition to insuring your investments carefully, you also need to check that the tradespeople and partners you work with (architects, lawyers, and so on) have the right level of insurance for your properties. They need to be suitably insured for the size and scale of the project at hand.

For example, a building contractor or architect with indemnity insurance worth $1 million won't cut the mustard for a big development project comprising 40 apartments worth many millions. If the contractor goes bust after you've shelled out for a lot of materials, or there's a critical flaw in the design of the building, it may cost you an awful lot to fix the issue.

TIP

The value of your partners' insurance needs to cover the value of the work, plus remedial work to correct any errors. Make sure you see a copy of their insurance and consult your own insurance broker on whether their level of coverage is sufficient.

WARNING

Your bank or lender may stipulate that your partners have a certain level of coverage, so be sure to factor that into your considerations.

I'm not saying any of this to scare you or put you off. Obviously there are risks involved in any property project — or any business venture for that matter. But with the right insurance in place (both for you and your chosen partners), you can move forward with confidence.

Chapter **4**

Protecting Yourself against Market Fluctuations

In any asset class — whether it's real estate, shares, bonds, or whatever — the market itself plays a big role in how well you're able to make money. That's not to say building a real estate portfolio is about gambling on the market or relying on the market going up to make a buck (never a great approach for a serious real estate investor). But, sure enough, the wider economic landscape is something you should factor into your decision making.

What I love about real estate as an asset class (compared to, say, stocks) is that real estate gives you the opportunity to make money by *adding value* (for example, by refurbishing a property, changing its use, or providing quality rental accommodation). This gives you an element of control — an opportunity to make money whatever the wider economic situation — that's difficult to find with other asset classes.

REMEMBER

Particularly if you're going down the passive-income route (see Chapter 3) and investing for long-term income, real estate can offer you some degree of protection against market fluctuations.

As I explain in this chapter, you can also protect your investments by diversifying your real estate portfolio — in other words, not putting all your eggs into one revenue basket. Read on to learn more about building multiple revenue streams and discover which strategies work well in a booming market and which are suited to a more challenging market.

Diversifying Your Portfolio with Multiple Revenue Streams

I have a confession to make: I actually spend very little time thinking about property markets and the economy. Of course, I research market factors such as pricing and supply and demand, especially the long-term demand for the products I'm offering. But for the most part, I can blissfully ignore short-term shifts in market opinion and expert predictions. Why? Two reasons: (1) I'm mostly investing for long-term income, as opposed to short-term capital gains, and (2) I've spread my risk by building multiple strategies, even multiple businesses, into my overall portfolio.

REMEMBER

The strategies set out in Parts 3 and 4 of this book are all designed to make money in pretty much any market. But there will be times when certain investments will perform better (or worse) than others. For example, in a credit crunch, property prices will probably fall and lack of affordable finance will mean many developers stop developing and first-time buyers drop out of the market faster than you can say "property ladder." But at times like this, the rental market may strengthen because these would-be buyers turn to renting instead.

TIP

In this way, it makes sense to diversify your real estate portfolio through different strategies, so that you're not reliant on one revenue stream. Building multiple revenue streams is also an important facet of the passive income mind-set. Circle back to Chapter 3 to learn more about building passive income streams.

Investing for the long term and the short term

Some of the strategies in this book are more short term. Developing a property, for instance — whether that involves completely refurbishing a house, turning a house into separate apartments, or even building new properties on an old parking lot — is short term compared to owning a rental property for 20 years. Generating real estate leads is another short-term example, in the sense that each project (or lead) is (if you're good at the job) successfully traded to a suitable client quickly. Turn to Part 3 to read more about these strategies.

Developing real estate, in particular, can provide a great way to boost your capital in a relatively short space of time. And it's a strategy that works particularly well in a buoyant market (see "Finding Strategies That Work Well in a Boom Market" later in the chapter). But what happens if financing dries up and real estate sales take a nosedive? You need *income* to fall back on.

REMEMBER

Smart real estate investors strike a balance between capitalizing on shorter-term opportunities and investing for long-term income. With longer-term investments that generate a regular income, you can often ride out economic storms and market shifts. In this way, taking a longer-term, income-focused view helps to reduce your risk.

The strategies outlined in Part 4, including houses in multiple occupation (Chapter 13) and vacation rental properties (Chapter 16), can be comfortably deployed over many years. In fact, with some of my income-generating projects, I'm thinking in terms of *decades* rather than years.

So, if the bricks-and-mortar value of a house in multiple occupation property that I own dips, even if it takes years for the market to recover, I don't really feel the effects of that market shift, because the investment is still bringing in a very healthy monthly income.

In the UK at least, the rental market is booming, and it's unlikely that will change anytime soon. With high property prices (particularly in London and the South East) and stagnant wages, many tenants, especially young professionals, have little choice but to rent — maybe even into their forties. But let's imagine for a moment that this did suddenly change and that property suddenly became more affordable, wages soared, and owning your own home was no longer a pipe dream. In that rose-tinted scenario, the rental market (at least in terms of renting to young professionals) would slump and my rental income would take a hit.

So, it's good that I don't rely on renting to professional tenants as my *only* income stream and that my portfolio includes multiple different strategies.

Incorporating multiple strategies into your portfolio

In addition to thinking both long term and short term, diversifying your portfolio also means not being reliant on one single strategy to earn money.

So, if we continue the example of young professionals dropping out of the rental market, I would still have renting to students and low-income tenants (two groups who will always need access to affordable rental properties) to fall back on.

Then there are the other strategies that I deploy, including *serviced accommodation* (fully-furnished property that's rented on a short-term basis, with hotel-like service features, see Chapter 15 for more details), new developments (Chapter 9), and sourcing properties for other developers and investors (Chapter 10).

REMEMBER

By incorporating more than one strategy into your portfolio, you're better prepared to withstand any market fluctuations or full-blown crises. If one part of your portfolio takes a hit, the other strategies tend to compensate.

WARNING

However, diversifying your portfolio through multiple strategies doesn't mean spreading yourself too thin. You need to strike a balance between protecting your portfolio against fluctuations and developing in-depth knowledge and expertise in your chosen strategies.

So, how can you strike that balance and not spread yourself too thin? Partly it's about working with your strengths and not trying to shoehorn in strategies that don't suit your goals and skills. In other words, it's about finding the strategies that you have a natural affinity for. When a property strategy links beautifully to your individual skills and attributes, then it's a whole lot easier to come to terms with and master that strategy. For example, maybe you're a real people person, in which case, sales-based strategies, such as sourcing property leads, would work well for you. Or maybe, as a details person, the nitty-gritty of property management is your bag.

Start small and develop your expertise in one field before you begin to incorporate another strategy. That means spending a good six to nine months (maybe more) really learning your first strategy and getting your initial project(s) up and running smoothly before you try embarking on a new strategy.

TIP

Ultimately, you should look to build two or three different strategies into your overall real estate portfolio. But don't dive into all of them at the same time! Really nail one before you think about taking things further.

Keep your long-term goals (see Chapter 5 for more on goal setting) and your individual strengths in mind as you develop your initial expertise. If you can keep one eye on the future in this way, you'll start to notice new opportunities as your skills grow. Exciting avenues will reveal themselves as you get more experienced, and, because you've always got your goals and skills visualized in your mind, you'll be better placed to assess and act on those opportunities.

Seeking out other ways to diversify your portfolio

Diversifying your income stream isn't necessarily only about different types of real estate investments, like buy-to-rents and property development. There are other ways to spread your risk and make money through real estate.

TIP

Stay alert to other ways to diversify your income streams, including the following:

>> Invest in more than one geographic region or country — again, with the caveat of not spreading yourself too thin.

>> Find other passive-income business opportunities. For example, I own www.propertyforum.com the world's largest international real estate chat forum, educational hub, and news platform for all things real estate.

>> Tweak strategies to suit your skill set. For example, if the nitty-gritty of rentals and property management plays to your strengths, you can diversify even more by offering this as a service to other busy landlords, earning a steady monthly fee in the process.

Turn to Chapter 18 to find other exciting ways to make money through property.

Finding Strategies That Work Well in a Boom Market

Picture a buoyant property market and what that means for real estate investors. Prices are strong, and rising month after month (maybe even, as we saw in the last property bubble, rising steeply month after month). There is an ample supply of buyers. Demand is high, and properties sell fast. This is what's known as a *seller's market.*

REMEMBER

These conditions are clearly ideal for strategies that are based on sales and capital growth. That's not to say these are the only strategies that will work well in a strong market (they're not), but strategies where the end goal is to sell a property (or sell property information) are particularly well suited to these market conditions.

Working with the booming market

When the market is especially strong, you gain added uplift from that market and even very short-term strategies can bring capital growth. Before the financial crisis of 2007–2008, plenty of investors were making money by buying properties and quickly reselling them (what's known as *flipping houses*) for a profit. Many of these investors did minimal or no work on the property at all, but the rising market still delivered nice returns.

REMEMBER

With a sales-based strategy, I always advocate *adding value* rather than relying on a rising market for profit. Adding value may mean changing the property's use (for example, from an office block to an apartment block), refurbishing the property, or anything else that helps to increase the property's value. The important thing is not to gamble solely on the market.

In my opinion, the housing bubbles of the future won't be as dramatic as the last one — we're more likely to see slow, steady increases and prices rising at a more sensible rate. My hope is that this will deter inexperienced investors from clamoring to flip properties quickly without adding value.

WARNING

Even so, there are still lots of reasons to be cautious with a sales-based strategy, particularly if you're financially reliant on selling the property quickly. If you get your timing wrong and the market is changing, or for some reason the sale takes longer than you think, you're stuck with the property in the meantime. If you've funded the property through finance, you're stuck paying the mortgage and bills.

In this way, the risks are higher than if you're investing for income. That's why the lion's share of my portfolio is about investing for steady, long-term income.

TIP

For any investment where the goal is to sell the property, I always like to have a plan B in mind. For example, if the market shifts, I feel more comfortable knowing I can easily rent the property instead of struggling to sell it. This may mean I focus less on luxury family houses (which would have a fairly niche target rental market) and more on smaller, more affordable houses and apartments (which would rent well).

Looking at suitable boom strategies

Here are some of the sales-based strategies that are well suited to a strong real estate market:

>> **Developing properties:** *Property development* is a broad term and can mean anything from a simple refurbishment or remodel, to building a whole block of apartments. As a strategy, it can work in both booming and challenging markets. But combined with the characteristics of a booming, seller's market, property development is a particularly attractive option. If you want to delve more into developing property, turn to Chapter 9.

>> **Dealing in property information:** Generating and selling property leads and sourcing properties for buyers is a great strategy to deploy in a strong real estate market. There are lots of people buying property, and wanting to buy property. Plus, there's the added bonus that, when prices are strong, so is your commission! This strategy is particularly worth considering if you're interested in being more hands-on and learning about the property market firsthand. If you're eager to turn property leads into profit, turn to Chapter 10.

WHY RELYING ON RISING PROPERTY PRICES IS A BAD STRATEGY

The couple of years prior to the most recent 2008 financial crisis were heady times for real estate investors and developers. New housing stock was being built all the time, and buying off-plan from developers (sometimes even a year or two before the project was due to be completed) was commonplace. Things had gotten crazy. The idea of adding value to a property had gone out the window. Instead, many investors were banking on rising real estate prices to deliver them rich rewards.

Ron (not his real name) was one such investor. I was regularly hearing stories of investors buying 10 or even 20 units off-plan in one transaction, which seemed nuts to me. Ron bought 27 units off-plan in one go, with the intention of selling them on immediately after construction was finished. (By the time construction was finished, he figured the rising real estate prices would deliver a tidy profit.) That's 27 one- and two-bedroom apartments, all in the same apartment block, through the same developer, and construction was barely underway. This was early 2007.

When the banking crisis spread, it wasn't long before construction companies, developers, and many other businesses for that matter, started feeling the pinch. The developer on Ron's investment went bust, and the project collapsed. Ron was left high and dry.

Even if that particular developer hadn't gone bust and the project had been finished, who would've been able to buy those properties? First-time buyers were unable to get mortgages unless they had a large deposit in the bank (or parents with deep pockets), and those who were already on the property ladder were struggling to sell their existing properties. Luckier investors than Ron were left with finished properties that they couldn't sell, perhaps they were even in *negative equity* (where the value of their property was less than the mortgage loan owed on it!).

The moral of the story is twofold: (1) Invest for income as well as capital growth, and (2) Never rely on a rising market to make money for you. Instead, look for opportunities where you can make money by adding value.

>> **Flipping houses:** Again, I have to stress the importance of buying, adding value, and then selling, rather than buying and quickly reselling purely on the basis of rising house prices. If you'd like to flip (pardon the pun) through more information on the buy-and-flip strategy, check out Eric Tyson and Robert Griswold's book, *Real Estate Investing For Dummies* (Wiley).

Finding Strategies That Work Well in a Credit Crunch

A financial crisis that leads to a *credit crunch* (a sudden drop in the availability of financing) is challenging for most real estate investors, especially in the first 12 to 24 months of the crisis. There's a lot of uncertainty, verging on what can sometimes feel like pandemonium. The value of assets is dropping, perhaps sharply, meaning your properties are worth less than they were the year before, or even the month before.

WARNING

During the first 12 months of a financial crisis, it's not a great idea to go running headfirst into a new strategy that you've never deployed before. In my experience, those early months are the worst. Depending on your overall goals, your level of expertise, and your financial situation, this may be the best time to sit tight, focus on the investments you already have, and see how things shake out once the initial market panic subsides.

REMEMBER

My intention here is not to get you jumping into investment decisions at the first sign of crisis; instead, it's about positioning yourself and your portfolio in a way that means you can still make money during a credit crunch. Because, even in falling or stagnant markets, there are still many strategies that can work brilliantly.

Working with the challenging market

It stands to reason that the middle of a credit crunch is not a great time to be trying to sell a property, or property leads for that matter. Without ready access to finance, fewer people are willing or able to purchase your properties, no matter how great your product is. In a tough market, your income-focused strategies are your best friends. For the most part, this will mean rental income — after all, people who can no longer get a mortgage will be forced to rent until the banks will lend to them.

REMEMBER

If you're investing for income, you're better positioned to weather the kind of storms that negatively impact capital-growth strategies.

These may be the ideal conditions for income-based strategies, but you still have to work hard to make a success of it. You've still got to make sure that your product is right for your target audience (so, don't try to target a property as a student rental when it's 20 miles away from the university). And you still need to add value for your customers. If your customers are tenants, that means offering the kind of quality accommodation that makes them want to stay put.

WARNING

When times are tough, managing your cash flow properly is more important than ever. And that means carefully factoring in fluctuations in your income and costs — for example, by planning for *void periods* (where a property or a room is sitting vacant). Turn to Chapter 3 for more on managing your cash flow.

TIP

If you're feeling confident and you're financially able, this can be an excellent time to expand your real estate portfolio. It's a *buyer's market* after all, with low prices and highly motivated sellers, meaning you can pick up some bargain properties. Read more about this in "Doing the Opposite of What the Mass Market Is Doing," later in the chapter.

Looking at suitable crunch strategies

Let's take a look at some of the income-based strategies that work well in a challenging market:

>> **Rent-to-rent:** This strategy involves renting a property from an existing landlord and then (with permission) subletting it out on a room-by-room basis. What's great about this strategy is that, in the middle of a credit crunch, if you're struggling to access financing for your property ventures, rent-to-rent requires little startup capital, at most the first month's rent and a security deposit. Make your way over to Chapter 11 if you want to make rent-to-rent work for you.

>> **Houses in multiple occupation (HMOs):** This is a fast-growing strategy, particularly in the UK and Europe. An HMO strategy involves renting out rooms in a property to multiple individual tenants (typically three or more separate tenants to qualify as an HMO). It's a bit like rent-to-rent, except you own rather than lease the property (which is even better if you can buy the property cheap in a market slump). Because you're renting rooms to multiple separate tenants, rather than renting a property to one tenant, you can significantly increase your income — and still cover the mortgage and bills even if a room or two stands empty for a while, also making it, in my view, a low-risk strategy. Head to Chapter 13 for more on HMOs.

>> **Renting to students and low-income-housing tenants:** Students and low-income-housing tenants tend to get a bad rap, and many investors avoid

these target markets like the plague. But with the right product and careful management, this strategy can deliver steady-as-she-goes income in a down or flat market. Turn to Chapter 14 to discover how to turn this strategy to your advantage.

TIP

Variations on the rent-to-rent theme can offer some "outside the box" opportunities in a credit crunch, even if you've got little capital to grow your real estate portfolio. Say, for example, someone in your circle of contacts is struggling to pay his mortgage because he's been let go from his job. You can agree to cover his mortgage costs; lease the property from him; and get stable, long-term tenants in there to more than cover the cost of the mortgage.

SUCCESSFULLY WEATHERING THE 2007–2008 CREDIT CRUNCH

One of the things that really saved my bacon during the global financial crisis was having a number of different properties and strategies in my portfolio. I was already investing with the passive-income mind-set firmly in mind, and I'd been prioritizing beefing up my monthly rental income (across a range of different strategies) as opposed to prioritizing capital-growth investments.

And, boy, was I pleased I'd done that. Because, when the credit crunch hit, the sales side of my business fell flat; property prices plummeted, and the availability of mortgages for the average person dried up (if you didn't have a 30 percent deposit, you could kiss mortgage opportunities goodbye for the foreseeable future). Trying to develop or refurbish and sell on properties in that market was very challenging, and such projects went on the backburner.

As a full-time property investor by that point, I didn't have the security of a monthly wage to fall back on. Without my rental properties, cash would've dried up pretty quickly. It was those income-generating properties that kept the money coming in (and literally the lights on) when other parts of the income portfolio weren't doing so well.

Sure, the market value of those rental properties had dipped. In fact, in the first 16 months after the financial crisis struck, the price of the average UK house dropped 20 percent. But the short-term value of those properties didn't matter to me at that time. (Prices have since recovered to the point where the properties are now worth more than they were pre-2007.) My priority was the income those properties were generating — and that income remained stable while property prices kept falling, quarter after quarter.

Likewise, someone who's looking to sell up and downsize as she approaches retirement, who has been unable to find a buyer for her large property, may be very open to your renting the property from her and subletting rooms to tenants. It provides both of you with a steady income when others are feeling the pinch. In tough times, there are lots of examples of people who would be very open to having their mortgages paid.

Doing the Opposite of What the Mass Market Is Doing

It may sound counter-intuitive, but one year after the credit crunch hit was a great time for my portfolio. Some degree of market stability had returned, and, although the market was still depressed, it felt like a sensible time to get into new strategies and expand my existing strategies by buying up cheap properties. So, that's exactly what I did.

REMEMBER

Sometimes, there's value in going against what the majority of the market is doing. For example, when limited financing is available, the property market slumps, and the wider economic landscape is uncertain (particularly jobs), everyday buyers will shy away from purchasing property — either because they can't afford to buy or, as you'll often hear people say, "It's not the right time to buy." But if you're a smart property investor, it may be exactly the right time to buy. You can snap up some real bargains.

WARNING

In this way, observing the general market trends and wisdom can inform your strategy decisions and point you in not-so-obvious directions. That's not to say you should take note of the market and then blindly go in the opposite direction. Instead, you should look to understand *why* the market is doing what it's doing and pinpoint how that information can help you make money.

After all, your knowledge and experience as a real estate investor will give you an edge over the average market participant. Everyone likes to think he understands property as an asset class ("It's a good investment" being the oft-quoted mantra). But the average, everyday buyer in the marketplace won't have the same depth of knowledge as you, someone who's devoted a lot of your time and energy to making money through property. Use that knowledge to your advantage.

In the last credit crunch, investors who did the opposite of the general market by buying up cheap properties did very well — including me! I acquired a lot of great properties in the aftermath of the financial crisis, some of them for half what they're worth now.

REMEMBER

Crucially, though, my intention wasn't to resell these properties quickly and turn a fast profit. That would've been difficult to say the least. Instead, I was looking to the future and investing for the long-term, stable rental income these properties would generate. So, although there was some element of swimming against the market tide in my decisions, I still had to heed the general market position that it was a terrible time to sell. I guess what I'm saying is, you want to be half brave salmon swimming upstream, and half sheep that stays within the safety of the flock. That's quite an image!

Tailoring Your Funding to Economic Fluctuations

A key part of learning about property investing is learning the many different ways to fund property investing. In Part 2, I provide lots of helpful information on traditional and creative sources of funding and show you how property valuation works. In this section, I explore how those funding options may be affected by market changes.

Understanding the impact on traditional finance

First things first: In a really tough market, traditional funding options like mortgages and loans may no longer be an option for you. In the last credit crunch, 95 percent and 100 percent loan-to-value (LTV) mortgages disappeared from the market overnight, leaving buyers no choice but to find large deposits (typically 30 percent) if they wanted to secure a mortgage. If that's not an option for you, turn to the next section, where I talk about nontraditional finance.

TECHNICAL STUFF

When I say a "95 percent loan-to-value mortgage," I mean you borrow 95 percent of the value of the property from the bank. The remaining 5 percent comes from your own pocket and is your down payment on the mortgage.

Assuming a traditional mortgage is still an option, you'll have to decide whether a fixed-rate mortgage or variable mortgage (also known as an adjustable-rate mortgage) is right for you. You can learn more about the different mortgage options in Chapter 6.

Whenever you're seeking a mortgage or looking to switch mortgages, it's important to talk to both an independent financial advisor and a mortgage broker. They won't be able to advise you on what interest rates are likely to do, but they can advise you on which products will suit you. Do your own research to make sure you're being presented with a genuinely independent, full-market view of available financing products. In practice, this may mean talking to at least three licensed brokers to compare advice — that way, it should be pretty obvious when someone has a clear bias and is trying to steer you toward products that aren't right for you.

Knowing when to fix

Fixed-rate mortgages tend to cost more in terms of setup and get-out costs, and they're set at a higher interest rate. But because they offer you a fixed rate of interest on your loan, your monthly repayments stay the same, whatever happens to the interest rates. In a fluctuating market, that can be very attractive.

This is where you need to think about your goals and your chosen strategy for the property. If you're planning to hold the property for only a short period of time, unless interest rates are rising sharply, it's probably not worth fixing the rate because you'll end up paying more.

As a general rule, I don't bother fixing the rate if I'm holding the property for less than three years. But if I intend to own the property for longer than three years, then I'll certainly considering fixed-rate lending.

Factoring in interest-rate rises

For a medium- to long-term investment, fixing the rate offers protection against rising interest rates. For example, my business has some 20-year fixed-rate loans that we're paying 4.5 percent interest on. That's high compared to the Bank of England's current base rate (which, at the time of writing, is 0.75 percent). But we're taking a 20-year view on these projects, and if interest rates rise in the next 20 years above 4.5 percent, we'll be better off.

How likely is it they'll rise about 4.5 percent during the course of the loan? Well, interest rates are in constant shift. In July 2007, before the global financial crisis kicked off, the base interest rate in the UK was 5.75 percent. By August 2016, that had fallen to 0.25 percent, the lowest level in 300 years. It has since risen to 0.75 percent, and it's pretty obvious to me that UK rates are only going to go in one direction: up. The highest UK interest rate on record was reached in my lifetime: 15 percent in October 1989.

If you're unsure whether to go fixed or variable, work out what your mortgage or loan payments would be at the current rate, and play around with different scenarios from there (such as interest rates rising to 3 percent, 5 percent, and so on). For each scenario, calculate what your mortgage payments would be, and assess whether you're willing — and able — to cover such a rise.

Looking at the full picture

As you can see, many factors will inform whether a fixed or variable mortgage is right for you:

» Your planned strategy for the investment and how long you're intending to hold the investment.

» The likelihood of interest rates going up. You'll need to do some research to assess how likely this is and consider how a rise would affect your repayments.

» Your personal risk profile (see Chapter 2). I'll often fix the rate on a longer-term project, but if you have a greater appetite for risk, you may prefer not to and take your chances that interest rates (and, in turn, your repayments) will remain low.

Always make sure you can comfortably cover your monthly mortgage payments, whatever the scenario. This means it's a good idea to have a cash buffer on hand. Circle back to Chapter 3 for more on managing your cash flow and maintaining a buffer.

Accessing nontraditional forms of finance

As the saying goes, "Necessity is the mother of invention." In the last credit crunch, people had to find new ways of doing business. On the one hand, you had ultra-high-net-worth individuals struggling to find suitable investments that would deliver the kinds of returns they were looking for — and the share indexes certainly weren't cutting the mustard at that time. On the other hand, you had real estate investors like myself struggling to finance projects through traditional methods, even though I knew those projects had fantastic income-generating potential.

As a result, joint ventures between myself and cash-rich investors (wherein, I brought the property expertise and they injected the capital) provided a good way for me to continue expanding my portfolio in a down market. And I wasn't alone. Real estate joint ventures became much more common in the aftermath of the financial crisis to the point where crowdfunding has even taken off in the real estate world as an alternative method of financing.

Crowdfunding, or *peer-to-peer lending,* is a relatively new option for raising funding. It works by connecting people seeking funding with investors who are willing to contribute funds. Read more about crowdfunding in Chapter 8.

Even though a challenging market can present opportunities to buy up properties at bargain prices, if traditional finance dries up, you may struggle to find the capital to make purchases. So, what should you do if you don't have a lot of capital in the bank, but you don't want to miss out on stellar investment opportunities? Turn to Chapter 8 and discover creative ways to finance your investments, including joint ventures and private lending.

Considering Foreign Exchange Rate Risks

If you're investing overseas, then fluctuating foreign exchange (FX) rates are an unavoidable risk.

Whenever you earn money in one country and spend it in another, you're at the mercy of FX rates. For example, say a U.S. investor owns an investment property in Dublin (meaning, she earns her rental income in euros but spends that income at home in dollars). When the value of the dollar surges, her euro income translates into fewer dollars.

Many investors have been caught out this way on overseas investments and found that their income is suddenly less than they're used to. So, what can you do about this? Well, you can't control the global FX market any more than you can control the weather. But you can pack an umbrella.

When FX rate shifts don't work to your advantage, you can mitigate the problem by

>> **Leaving the money where it was earned, if you can afford to:** Say, for example, our U.S. investor had family in Ireland and was ultimately planning to retire there. She could hold her rental income in her Irish bank account ready for her future life (or, indeed, to fund another investment).

>> **Carefully watching the markets and transferring money when the rate is more favorable:** FX rates are constantly in flux. They're affected by all sorts of global and local factors, so just because the rate is terrible today doesn't mean

it will be next week. So, hold your money in the overseas country when the rate isn't great and transfer when it's improved.

>> **Timing your purchases well:** If you're looking at expanding your overseas portfolio, try to transfer the funds for those purchases at more favorable times and not at the last minute.

REMEMBER

Again, it's important to have a cash buffer that gives you some wiggle room if you're hit hard by FX swings or need to leave your earnings overseas for a while. I offer more information on managing your cash flow and creating a cash buffer in Chapter 3.

IN THIS CHAPTER

» Setting and committing to your goals

» Tapping into powerful personal development and self-help techniques

Chapter 5

Getting into the Mind-set of a Successful International Real Estate Investor

Whether you want to be a wealthy real estate investor, a successful CEO, or even a champion boxer, mind-set is a critical part of success. In this chapter, I set out the main mind-set and personal development skills and techniques that have helped me grow my real estate portfolio and businesses. I truly believe that this is one of the most important chapters in this book — if there's one chapter you revisit occasionally for inspiration, make it this one!

REMEMBER

As with any new skill, repetition is key. You can't learn to drive or speak a new language by only doing it once every six months, and the same is true of developing the right mind-set for success.

If you really want to supercharge your success, the approaches set out in this chapter should become a part of your everyday routine, like brushing your teeth or remembering to wear shoes. Turn to Chapter 17 for some practical tips and exercises that will help you incorporate these mind-set approaches into your daily life.

Continually Improving through Education

Knowledge is power, as the saying goes. But I prefer to think of knowledge as a tool — a tool for building wealth and personal freedom. A bit like a spanner or a wrench, only slightly more glamorous.

REMEMBER

In most professions, continual education is key to staying on top of your game. The people who progress well and succeed are the ones who are continually evolving. Real estate is no different, and if you want to become (and remain) a successful real estate investor, you need to invest time in your education and improvement.

TIP

Even as your real estate portfolio becomes more established, never be fooled into thinking you know it all. You'll be missing out on so many important opportunities to grow and learn. I love learning from those who know more than I do, whether that comes from networking, reading books, or wherever. Even if I only get one useful nugget from a book — a tidbit that changes my mind-set or improves the way I do something — it's well worth my time.

Tapping into a wide variety of sources

So, what exactly do I mean by continual education and continual improvement? Well, real estate is a very accessible industry with little in the way of formal qualifications needed to succeed, so you'll have to think outside the formal education box when looking at ways to continually learn and grow.

Thankfully, these days it's easier than ever to access information quickly and easily, often for free or extremely cheap. Your mission is to make like a sponge and soak up all that information. This may include

>> **Reading as many books as you can get your hands on about your chosen real estate strategy:** If you struggle to find time to read, try listening to audiobooks in the car or while you're at the gym. If you commute to work every day for 30 minutes each way that's a potential hour of audiobook training time every day, which equates to 240 hours a year! It soon adds up. . . .

>> **Becoming a general business, entrepreneurship and self-help book junkie, like me:** I love reading both the practical how-to-succeed-in-business types of books and the more mind-set/self-help kinds, and even autobiographies by business leaders and entrepreneurs. I find it particularly inspiring to read about how people became successful and their personal formula for success. You'll be surprised how many similar traits successful people have — and you can learn these traits and techniques, so keep reading!

>> **Staying alert to potential new real estate strategies that are a good fit with your portfolio, skills, and passion.**

>> **Keeping up to date on the latest technology developments, from social media platforms to productivity apps and software for managing your real estate investments:** You don't need to be a tech genius to thrive in real estate, but you don't want to miss out on opportunities to connect with people more easily and streamline your processes.

>> **Harnessing the wealth of information available for free online by joining property forums (like ours at** www.propertyforum.com**), delving through relevant thread archives on forums, signing up for relevant industry newsletters, and subscribing to blogs.**

>> **Attending education seminars held by property investment and development companies:** These seminars often free to attend because the goal of the seminar is usually to sell you a product or investment. So, although I wholeheartedly encourage you to tap into these free sources of education, never buy anything on the day. Always go away and do your homework after the seminar because there are plenty of paid courses not worth the paper they're printed on.

>> **Signing up for online real estate and business courses, such as those available through Udemy (**www.udemy.com**) and Coursera (**www.coursera.org**).**

>> **Attending big annual property shows and exhibitions:** These shows provide fantastic educational and networking opportunities and are a great way to immerse yourself in the market and to learn what others are doing.

>> **Being open to new mind-set-related, self-help techniques and approaches, like some of the ones set out later in this chapter (for example, positive affirmations, visualization, the law of attraction, and meditation).**

>> **Taking the time to build mind-set-related, self-help techniques into your daily routine:** Turn to Chapter 17 for some handy mind-set tips and exercises that will easily fit into a busy life.

WARNING

As in any industry, there are operators out there looking to make a quick buck from inexperienced real estate investors who are keen to learn. So don't automatically believe everything you're told by someone in a seminar where the end goal is to sell you something. Soak up their information; then assess that information against other sources as well. If multiple different sources are telling you that Morocco is a great place to invest, that's very different from one guy pushing Moroccan investments at a seminar.

Taking time for education before you put your money on the line

Although continual education is an important part of success, I also recommend taking time to immerse yourself in real estate and learn as much as you can *before* you embark on your first investment. Learning as you go is great, and I'm still learning every day, but mistakes in your early days can be costly.

TIP

Immerse yourself in property education for at least six months before you put your money on the line with an investment. Why not set yourself some education targets to hit before you start seriously scouting for investment opportunities? For example, you can set yourself a target of reading one inspirational book a month, attending six property shows this year, and participating in property forums once or twice a week.

Networking in the Right Places

Without a network, you'll have no customers for your products, no dream team to help you manage your portfolio successfully (see Chapter 3), and no one to learn from. Does that sound like how you want to do business? I hope not! So, if you're serious about making it as a real estate investor, you need to become seriously good at networking.

Networking offline and online

Networking groups are a fantastically useful way to establish your network and learn new things. I recommend seeking out property-specific networking groups rather than general business networking groups. However, in certain circumstances, a general networking group may work well for you (for example, if you're selling properties direct in a specific area and looking to build your own buyers list, or if you're seeking an investment partner).

TIP

Look online and on Facebook for local networking groups that are relevant to your market and strategy. This can be as simple as a regular coffee meeting among local landlords. Or it can be an official organized group with formal networking meetings and events. If you live in a more remote part of the country, you may have to travel a couple of hours to your nearest property group, but the connections you make will be well worth it.

Wherever possible, network in your chosen geographic market. For example, if you're investing in London but you live in Leeds, it would be worth traveling into London for relevant networking meetings.

Granted, this gets more difficult if you're investing overseas, but nonetheless you should still spend some time building your network in person whenever you begin to immerse yourself in a new region or country. After you've established some valuable connections, you can maintain that network online from home.

REMEMBER

These days, networking online is just as important as (if not more important than) networking offline. So, don't overlook the power of online networking opportunities, such as Facebook and LinkedIn groups and online forums. These groups have no geographical boundaries, and you can get a good overall feel for what people are investing in at that time and what investment strategies are currently working well.

Getting the most out of networking meetings and events

If you're new to networking meetings, I recommend you take a look at *Business Networking For Dummies* by Stefan Thomas (Wiley). Although it's about networking in general business circles, it contains lots of helpful tips for making a great impression and getting the most out of networking.

TIP

Here are my tips for making sure the time you spend at networking events is time well spent:

>> **Practice your introductions in advance.** In a formal networking setting, you may only have a brief amount of time to get to know someone. If you practice introducing yourself and summarizing what you do in advance, you can give a snappy, relevant introduction that's free of awkward waffle.

>> **Be sociable and speak to plenty of people, but remember you're looking to make meaningful connections.** Don't be that guy who rips through the room, talks to everyone for just 30 seconds, grabs their business cards, and then leaves! Everyone hates that guy.

>> **Bring plenty of business cards with you.** Also, bring any relevant flyers or brochures that describe your business. (Don't shove brochures under the nose of every unsuspecting person — simply keep them to hand out if it will help the conversation along.)

>> **Whenever a contact is of value, arrange a specific follow-up chat for sometime after the meeting to develop the conversation further.**

>> **When talking to people, be alert to how you can help them, not just how they can help you.** Networking is a two-way street, and it should create value for everyone (not just you). So, if you know someone or something that can help the person in front of you, share it gladly and they'll be more likely to reciprocate.

Maintaining and nurturing your network

So, you're going to regular networking meetings and making meaningful new contacts. How can you best capitalize on all this networking effort?

>> **When you meet a new contact, add her to your electronic contacts or marketing customer relationship management (CRM) system (see Chapter 3), so you can keep in touch more easily.** Paper business cards can easily get lost.

>> **Send a follow-up message the same day of the "nice to meet you, great to hear about your business/investments" variety.** Finish off by saying something like "If my network or I can help you in any way, let me know."

   In your follow-up message, also ask if she minds if you keep in touch regularly. If you have a mailing list, ask for permission to add her to the list for future newsletters. Recent EU General Data Protection Regulations (GDPR) mean that you must get consent before you add an EU citizen to your mailing list, and you must provide an obvious way for people to "opt out" or unsubscribe from future emails. Having an easy way to unsubscribe is essential under U.S. law, too.

>> **Touch base at regular intervals, whether that's by emailing to say hello, sharing useful articles or news items, sending your regular newsletter (with permission), or even meeting up for a coffee.**

>> **If you have a mailing list or CRM software, be sure to keep contact details up to date and always allow an option for people to unsubscribe from future newsletters.**

REMEMBER

If you don't keep in touch regularly, your network won't grow. To prevent your contacts from withering on the vine, invest time in keeping those connections alive.

Setting Your Goals

You must be clear about what you want out of life. If you aren't, how do you expect to achieve what you want? Therefore, being able to set and commit to your goals is an important part of becoming a successful property investor. (It's an important part of succeeding in any area of life, in fact.)

REMEMBER

Setting and recording your goals is the cornerstone that underpins all the mind-set-related techniques coming up in the rest of this chapter. Set and record clear goals for yourself and you'll be in the best possible position to capitalize on these techniques.

For example, when you're clear on your goals, you can design your own positive affirmations that link to and support those goals. Or you can begin to visualize those goals in a clear and powerful way. (See "Using positive affirmations" and "Visualizing for Success" later in the chapter.)

Figuring out what you want

To figure out what you want to achieve, start with some blue-sky thinking. If you could be anything, do anything, or have anything you wanted, what would it be? Set aside the practicalities of achieving those things for now — just focus on identifying what they are. You don't want to end up with a list of 100 goals, so keep it simple and focus on what's most important to you.

TIP

Try not to get too caught up on just material things, like objects or a specific amount of money. Instead, also mainly think about the way achieving those things will make you feel and the benefits they'll bring. So, instead of focusing on becoming filthy rich, understand *why* you want that. Is it so you can be your own boss, work when it suits you, and have the freedom and financial security to spend quality time with your loved ones?

REMEMBER

At this stage, don't put a time limit on your goal or goals. Right now, you're just looking to clarify what you want. For the purposes of this exercise, let's say that you've identified that you really want to create an independent income from real estate that's large enough and stable enough for you to quit your day job.

Committing to and working toward your goals

Having distilled your thinking down to one or maybe a few clear goals, you're ready to start getting more specific. Here's how:

>> **Commit to your goals on paper.** This can be a simple list on the refrigerator, or it can be a full-on vision board. (Turn to Chapter 17 to see how I've made vision boards and goal lists work for me.) Seeing your goals on paper (or on a screen) focuses your mind and can even be used as a prompt for visualization exercises.

>> **Break each larger goal down into smaller sub-goals.** Imagine your goal is on the other side of a river — your sub-goals are the stepping stones that will get you across the river to the other side. For example, if your goal is to earn

your main income through property, you might break this goal down as follows:

- Identify the right real estate strategy that suits your capabilities and will deliver regular income (for example, student rentals).

- Attend seminars and sign up for online courses about becoming a landlord.

- Network among local property groups and build your contacts in advance.

- Meet with a financial advisor and mortgage advisor to assess your funding options.

- Research the top student rental locations.

- Visit as many student apartment buildings as you can to get a feel for the market and the way they're built to cater for that specific market.

>> **Come up with a suitable timeframe.** Many people say not to put a time limit on your goals, and I do see the logic in that. But personally, I find it helpful to set deadlines for when I'll achieve something, particularly when it comes to the smaller sub-goals. (Some goals will have a natural timetable of their own. For example, if you're doing this to create a comfortable retirement income, then you need to have your investments up and running smoothly before you actually plan to retire.)

>> **Block out time for achieving these milestones.** Life is busy and we all have lots of demands on our time. But investing real time in working toward your goals is an investment in your future. If you put off tasks, you're only cheating yourself. You can't just set goals, sit back, and do nothing, and expect them to materialize! You have to take action.

>> **Check in against your sub-goals and timeframes at regular intervals, ideally weekly.** Visualize yourself achieving them and keep them at the forefront of your mind. Are you on track to move across that first stepping stone? Are you looking ahead and preparing for the next stepping stone after that? If not, what can you do differently to make that happen?

>> **Revisit and update your list of goals every few months.** Sometimes goals change, and that's okay. They may not be relevant anymore, or as your expertise grows, you may decide you want to challenge yourself more. You want to maintain focus, but you also don't want to be too rigid, so allow yourself the freedom to amend your goals when appropriate.

>> **Create a mix of goals, making some fun and some business related.** For example, I have the goal of meeting my guitar idol Slash one day! I also have growth goals for my property portfolio and passive income levels, which will allow me to live the life I have planned in the future to enjoy with my family.

>> **Remember to *think big!*** I always set goals that seem almost un-achievable. That way, if I hit 50 percent of a goal, it's better than hitting 100 percent of a much smaller one. Don't make it too easy for yourself. Aim high. Don't sell yourself short. You'll be amazed at what you can achieve when you follow these steps.

Cultivating a Positive Mental Attitude

Have you ever been ill — maybe with the flu, maybe with an evil hangover — and found yourself focusing on how much you were suffering? How did that make you feel? Worse, I bet. That's because negative thoughts always make us feel worse, both physically and mentally. But when we think positive thoughts, our bodies and our minds feel the benefit.

TIP

On a small scale, positive thinking can help you mentally prepare for the day ahead, or perhaps a meeting that you've been anxious about. By focusing on the positive outcome that you want from your day, you're creating the ideal conditions for achieving that outcome. On a larger scale, you can use positive thinking to focus on goals that you want to achieve in life.

REMEMBER

In this way, positivity is not just a tool for coping with the more challenging aspects of life (or a really bad hangover); it's a way to create the world we want to see around us.

Let's look at two powerful tools that I use all the time to cultivate a positive attitude: affirmations and gratitude.

Using positive affirmations

If you believe you won't amount to anything in life, or that your investments will fail, you'll get what you focus on (see "Harnessing the Law of Attraction" later in the chapter). But if you tune your mind to positive thoughts of yourself as a successful real estate investor, you're more likely to be aware of and open to opportunities that deliver that goal. Positive affirmations are a great way to define and reinforce these positive thoughts.

Affirmations are brief, simple statements that motivate and inspire you. Muhammad Ali declaring "I am the greatest" is one famous example of an affirmation in action. Other examples include

>> I am confident.

>> I am open to success.

>> I am brimming with energy.

>> I am ready to become a successful real estate investor.

>> My real estate portfolio is growing and thriving.

>> Every day, in every way, I am becoming more abundant.

"I am" is a powerful phrase in affirmations, as opposed to "I want to be"!

If you had a parent or teacher tell you that you could achieve anything you wanted, you'll immediately understand how powerful it is to hear that kind of uplifting message. Affirmations give us a practical way to reinforce positive messages on a regular basis, making them one of my favorite tools for focusing the mind and boosting positivity.

Making affirmations work for you

What I love about affirmations is that they're so flexible. You can update and tailor them every day if it helps you. In fact, I find they're more powerful when I *don't* repeat the exact same thing to myself every day, and you may find the same. You can tailor them to suit your mood — so, if you're feeling anxious, use affirmations that boost your confidence or lift your mood, and if you're feeling happy and excited about something, use affirmations that build on that energy and excitement — or you can use them to focus on a specific goal.

Affirmations can be said in the morning, throughout your day, just before you go into a meeting, or whenever works best for you. They can be said quietly to yourself or shouted at the top of your voice in the shower or in the middle of a field. Again, do what feels right to you. The important thing is not how loud, where, and when you say them, but that you make the practice a part of your daily routine.

To be successful at anything, you have to be extremely focused. Incorporating affirmations into your daily routine brings a structure and focus to your thoughts, putting you in the right frame of mind for success. I'm a strong believer that we can train our brains to make us successful, just like learning to drive or learning how to speak another language. Some of the techniques I'm introducing to you will help you do just that! Turn to Chapter 17 for practical ways to make positive affirmations a daily way of life.

Believing in the affirmation . . . and yourself

A big part of making affirmations work for you, aside from making it a daily habit, is learning to believe in yourself and, crucially, believe in your affirmations. You have to wholeheartedly believe in an affirmation for it to have any real effect. You have to believe you'll achieve the things you want.

If self-belief isn't one of your strong points, I urge you to spend some time working on that. In my early days as a property investor, self-belief was all I had. My friends and family thought I was nuts for giving up a well-paying job to pursue my real estate dreams, and I had no actual experience or formal real estate education to back me up. Without that unwavering self-belief to make it work, I don't think I'd have gotten very far.

TIP

Visualization is a really useful tool to deploy alongside affirmations if you need a little boost in the self-belief department. Turn to "Visualizing for Success" later in the chapter.

Embracing gratitude

Being thankful is another powerful way to bring more positivity to your day. Being grateful for what you have, even when times are tough, brings you calm and happiness in the present moment. Appreciating the present moment is an extremely important skill because it helps you let go of stresses and any anxieties about the day or week ahead. Plus, from a law-of-attraction perspective (see "Harnessing the Law of Attraction," later in the chapter), focusing on the things you already have, rather than on what you don't have, will only help you attract more of the same abundance and prosperity. Also, see the "Meditating to Manage Stress and Risk" section (at the end of this chapter), which also gives you meditation-related tips on how to appreciate the present moment.

That's why I make gratitude a part of my everyday routine. Each day, I take time out to notice the things that have gone well for me and my loved ones, and to feel grateful for the wonderful people around me. It's hard to think of a better way to inject a little positivity into your life.

REMEMBER

You can be thankful for small, specific things (like an upcoming lunch with a friend you haven't seen in ages) or huge things (like good health). The important thing is to tune your mind to the more positive aspects of life, whatever they may be, so that you'll then be aware of and open to more positive things around you.

Turn to Chapter 17 for specific ideas for injecting a little gratitude into your day.

Visualizing for Success

Did you ever stare out of the window in history class and picture yourself as a famous sportsperson or prizewinning poet? Do you ever sit in a rainy traffic jam and fantasize about jetting off for a three-week holiday in the sun? Do you ever daydream about telling your boss what you really think of them? If so, my friend, visualization is right up your alley.

REMEMBER

Visualization, also known as *creative visualization*, is the practice of using your imagination to visualize specific outcomes. In other words, it's using your natural ability to daydream, but in a more focused, structured way that helps you achieve your goals.

As a technique, visualization has been around for a long time, and often forms a key part of other practices, such as neuro-linguistic programming (NLP) and meditation. It's a well-known business and self-help technique (going as far back as Napoleon Hill's iconic 1937 book *Think and Grow Rich*), and it's also used widely in fields such as health, education, entertainment, and sports.

In fact, the famous golfer Jack Nicklaus once said his success was 10 percent technique, 40 percent position, and 50 percent creating a mental picture of each shot. That mental picture is visualization in action.

Identifying the benefits of visualization

By visualizing what you want, you begin to live with those goals in mind, which, from a law-of-attraction perspective (see "Harnessing the Law of Attraction," later in the chapter), creates the ideal conditions for bringing that goal to life. Practicing visualization regularly can also help you feel more focused, positive, and calm, and give you a greater feeling of purpose. It certainly does for me.

Think about it: Most people are plagued by thoughts of what *could* go wrong or what has already gone wrong in the past. That's not great for our mental health or our stress levels. Using visualization, you can occupy your mind with powerful positive images that bring your attention to the future, not the past, and everything that can go right, not wrong.

But it's not just about improving your mental well-being and achieving your personal goals. Visualization can also have very real physical benefits. Studies have shown that patients who use visualization techniques heal faster than those who don't.

Putting visualizing into practice

You can use visualization to focus on larger life goals, like becoming a successful real estate investor, or plan for specific outcomes in the day or week ahead.

To get the most out of visualization, it's best to focus on a specific goal or outcome, rather than general wishes like health, wealth, and happiness.

I regularly use visualization to picture relatively small-scale things, like an important meeting. For example, I might spend five or so minutes at the start of the day visualizing how I want the day or the meeting to go. This brings dramatic results. I find I deliver far better in a meeting that I've visualized in advance. In this way, visualization is actually a really useful planning tool, helping you prepare for any kind of situation or personal event.

I meet a lot of people who think they're excellent planners because they use diaries and calendars, they write to-do lists, and they set reminders on their phones. They think that, by doing all this, they're planning their day or week. They're not. They're only planning their *time*. They're not planning their performance or specific outcomes. Visualization is a really powerful way to plan for the outcomes you want.

Visualization can also help you change your behavior. Say, if you're a reluctant or nervous public speaker, like I am, you can use visualization to picture yourself at a networking event, speaking to a rapt audience, and *enjoying yourself* in the process. Doing that regularly helps to reprogram your mind, so that you start to think and *act* like someone who's a confident, enthusiastic public speaker.

Like affirmations, visualization is pretty flexible and fits easily into everyday life. You can do it first thing in the morning, last thing at night, and/or at various points throughout the day. It's a really useful technique to turn to when negative thoughts, doubt, or anxiety creep in. By visualizing a positive outcome, either related to that specific situation I'm in or something from my wider list of goals, I find I can return to positivity quickly, feel calmer, and perform better as a result.

THE LIFE-CHANGING POWER OF VISUALIZATION

In her book *The Universe Has Your Back,* Gabrielle Bernstein talks about how she used visualization to achieve her career goals. When she was writing her first book, she didn't have a publisher lined up. But she held visions in her head of herself as an author. She also visualized herself as a speaker and teacher, speaking on the same stages as her heroes, people like author and motivational speaker Dr. Wayne Dyer. "My certainty gave me a sense of peace," she writes.

Gabrielle signed her first book deal in 2009. A few years later, after publishing three more books, she gave a talk to a huge audience at the Javits Center in New York, standing in the exact spot where Wayne Dyer had given a speech years before (while Gabrielle sat watching from the front row). Her long-held vision had come true. She is now a *New York Times* best-selling author and international speaker.

Hal Elrod tells a similar story in his best-selling book *The Miracle Morning.* While working on the book, he would visualize himself every morning writing with ease and enjoying the process of writing a book. He would visualize himself writing freely with no fear or writer's block. And he visualized the end result: the finished book, and people reading and loving it. He delivered the outcome he wanted in his mind, and it became reality.

Getting the most out of visualization

There are some essential things to consider if you want to really make visualization work for you:

TIP

>> **You need to be very clear about your goals.** Visualization doesn't work so well for general stuff. For example, instead of just wishing to be happier, visualize yourself thriving as a property investor, working for yourself, and having the freedom to be there when the kids get home from school, giving you a happier, more relaxed family life.

>> **Refer to your list of goals or vision board before visualizing.** It'll serve as a helpful prompt.

>> **You have to *believe* in what you're visualizing.** For you to achieve what you really want, you need to be *certain* of the outcome. You need to believe it can, and will, happen. You need to believe your visualization is the absolutely true version of your future. If you don't, your unconscious mind recognizes the visualization as a lie and the whole process is undermined.

>> **To get the most out of visualization you need to practice it regularly —
ideally daily, but at least a few times a week.** You need to make time to
practice this skill, regardless of what's going on around you. If you feel too
busy or stressed, that's all the more reason to visualize and focus your mind
on positive outcomes.

>> **You need to know that nothing changes without action.** You need to stay
focused and take appropriate measures to bring you closer to your goals. So,
when you've identified what you want and put it on paper, and you spend
time each day visualizing and believing in it, you need to take steps and stay
open to opportunities that help you deliver those goals. In other words, you
can't visualize yourself as a successful real estate investor, and then sit back
on the sofa and wait for the universe to deliver your goal into your lap.

TIP

Turn to Chapter 17 for a practical and quick visualization exercise that you can
adapt to suit your own goals.

Harnessing the Law of Attraction

Like a lot of people, I read *The Secret* when it first came out in 2006, after a friend
had raved about it and told me I had to read it. This was a little after I started my
own real estate company, and the simple idea behind the book (the law of attraction) immediately made sense to me.

REMEMBER

The law of attraction is centered on the principle that "like attracts like," which
means that both good things and bad things are attracted to us by our thoughts
and feelings. In other words, we get back what we put out there.

This simple statement, "Like attracts like," neatly distilled what I had felt
instinctively — that being positive brings positive results and being negative
delivers negative results. This understanding would go on to shape my actions as
I grew my business and worked toward my personal and professional goals.

The law of attraction draws upon many other business self-help tools and techniques, like positive thinking, affirmations, visualization, setting goals, meditation, and so on. Perhaps that's the reason it's so powerful — it neatly draws so
many important strands together to keep you on the path to success.

Understanding how the law of attraction works

The law of attraction is a universal law of nature, and it runs through all aspects of life: relationships, business, money, health, everything. When you think about it, it's common sense. But that doesn't make it any less powerful.

Thinking of yourself as a magnet

The law of attraction says that your thoughts emit a powerful magnetic force that attract, just like a magnet does, the things that you think about most.

REMEMBER

Good or bad, you attract the things you think about most. So, if you focus your mind on success and prosperity, that's what you'll bring into your life. Whereas if you think about debt a lot, even if you're thinking about how much you want to get out of debt, chances are, you'll only bring more debt into your life.

Maybe you know someone or have read stories of people who attracted a lot of wealth, then lost it all, then made it all back and more in a pretty short space of time — a tale of boom, bust, and then more boom. The law of attraction explains this very simply: Such people become wealthy because they focus their thoughts on wealth (as opposed to how much money they *don't* have). Then, when they become wealthy, they worry about losing it all. Sure enough, they manifest that misfortune. Then, with their thoughts turned back to wealth, they prosper again.

REMEMBER

When harnessed properly and used systematically as a tool for achieving what you want, the law of attraction delivers incredible results.

Looking at everyday examples of the law of attraction

Here's a real-life example from my own business. Not so long ago, I had a problem with one of my developments being delayed because of planning issues. It was difficult to deal with, and it dragged on for far longer than I would've liked. Over time, it chipped away at my positivity, and this began to show in my attitude at work.

As a leader, it's vital that I model the right behavior around those who work with me and for me. However, as my negativity around this project began to show, a culture of negative comments began to form around the office, and in just a short space of time, morale started to dip. I had forgotten that like attracts like.

To turn things around, I had to remember to stay positive and demonstrate the attitude I wanted to see from others. As I changed my behavior, I noticed an almost immediate adjustment in those around me. I projected a positive attitude, which made me *feel* even happier, and, unsurprisingly, this manifested as a dramatic change in those I work with. The challenging development was successfully resolved and, in the end, it turned out to be a really profitable project for the business. More important, it was a profound learning experience for me.

TIP

If you aren't convinced, try this small experiment. The next time you go into a supermarket or coffee shop, make eye contact with the person behind the till, then smile and ask how her day is going. Watch as her face lights up, and be aware of her reflecting that friendly, positive attitude right back at you.

Focusing on your thoughts and feelings

Clearly, the key to making the law of attraction work for you is learning to harness the power of your thoughts, so that you can attract more of what you want, not what you don't want. It sounds obvious, but the first thing you need to do is think positive thoughts.

Of course, it's not possible to monitor every single thought we have. I don't know about you, but my brain is constantly pinging between thoughts, from the emails I need to send to what to eat next. The good news is you don't have to keep track of every single thought. Instead, you can simply tap into your feelings as a way of gauging your thoughts.

TIP

Your feelings are a bit like the dashboard on your car: they give you a quick overview of what you're thinking, and whether something might be wrong, without having to analyze every single thought.

In other words, when you feel good, relaxed, happy, or comfortable, that gives you an indication that you're largely focusing on positive thoughts. And when you feel tense, nervous, angry, or sad, you know that your thoughts have taken a negative turn.

TIP

It's important to take time throughout the day to gauge your emotions and modify them when necessary. If you're not feeling so great, try to shift your emotions to a more positive place. Put on a song that makes you want to sing or dance or look at pictures that make you happy. Focus on the way those positive things make you feel. I take a moment to feel grateful for what I already have and enjoy that moment. I also keep a list of positive shifters as a note on my phone, these are a list of things I'm grateful for and that make me happy. Referring to that list when I'm not feeling very positive helps me shift my mind-set to a positive one very quickly.

I live by a rule that, if something or someone in my life makes me feel negative, I simply remove it from the equation as soon as possible. This means I surround myself with the most positive people who lift me up emotionally and don't drag me down. I surround myself with successful people who go after what they want in life. And I don't listen to people who say I can't do something. *Impossible* isn't a word in my vocabulary. If I believe it can be done, then it can.

Putting the law of attraction into practice

Embracing the law of attraction isn't necessarily like nurturing other positive habits, like eating well or running every night after work. Those habits slot neatly into a routine, but the law of attraction is something that should be running in the background all the time.

To put the law of attraction into action and keep it ticking along in the background, try following these five steps:

1. Set your goal.

You must be clear about what you want. If you aren't, how do you expect to manifest it? By clarifying your goals, you're starting to attract what you want to you. You're also making yourself accountable, and that's another powerful motivator for ensuring you hit your goals.

2. Trust it's coming.

Having decided what you want, trust that it will be yours. Embrace the certainty that what you want is definitely coming your way, and relax into that certainty. Admittedly, this phase is not an easy thing to achieve instantly. It takes a lot of confidence to let go and trust that things will come your way. But continue to work at it, and you'll build confidence in the process the more you do it.

3. Live the life.

I could so easily have called this step "Talk the talk and walk the walk," but that was a bit too long! Essentially, this step means you should live the life you want right now. It means you should think, speak, and act as if you've already achieved your goal. This is a sentiment I identify with strongly. When I was starting my business, I didn't have a lot of cash to throw around, but I lived with a prosperous mind-set and acted with confidence, as though I'd already made it. I moved through each day with the attitude and confidence of a successful businessperson, and that's what I became. For me, this step is about attitude as much as anything.

4. **Focus on abundance.**

   You can't attract positive things to you if you're focusing on the things you don't have. Therefore, this step is about nurturing those feelings of abundance and gratitude every single day. This means feeling as though you live an abundant life, that the world is full of abundance, and that there are enough of all the good things (including real estate opportunities) to go around. Try feeling as though you're a successful real estate investor, feeling as though there is an abundance of great opportunities out there, and so on. When you feel good, you attract good things.

5. **Eat, sleep, repeat.**

   For the law of attraction to work, you need to live these steps daily. Therefore, consciously return to steps 2, 3 and 4 until they become second nature. Catch yourself when you start to say something negative, and turn it into something positive. Or when you're feeling negative, do something to shift your mind-set. Keep at it, and you'll see results.

TIP

After I had set a goal of becoming a successful entrepreneur, I did whatever I could to generate feelings of positivity and success. I read inspirational stories of other business leaders, I smiled at my coworkers, and I enjoyed going to work every day (before I actually quit my job to focus on real estate). I felt those feelings of freedom, satisfaction, happiness, and abundance — and that's exactly what I attracted.

Meditating to Manage Stress and Risk

As the old Zen saying goes, "You should sit in meditation for 20 minutes a day, unless you're too busy; then you should sit for an hour." The busier we are, the more vital it is we take some time to find a bit of awareness, peace, and clarity. Meditation is a great way to do this.

REMEMBER

Meditation is about building an awareness of how you're feeling — what you're thinking, and what emotions and physical sensations you're experiencing at that time. It's a method of training and strengthening your mind, by bringing your attention to a particular something (like the breath or the body) over and over again. It's a very powerful way of rewiring your brain, making it easier to focus and achieve clarity and calm.

There are several different kinds of meditation, from simple mindfulness meditation (my favorite technique) to deeply spiritual and religious meditative practice.

Looking at the benefits of meditation

Our world is increasingly busy, noisy, and distracting. We're more connected than ever before, which is great, but it can also mean we're constantly "on." With our phones regularly pinging with emails, messages, and social media alerts, it's getting harder and harder to switch off.

True peace and calm, without any form of distraction, is precious. Without it, we become disconnected from how we're feeling and what's going on inside us. And that can be a really negative thing. Meditation can, therefore, help you carve out time to reconnect with what's going on inside.

Physical and emotional benefits

REMEMBER

Meditation has been proven to combat stress, anxiety, and depression. It has also been shown to boost positivity and vitality and promote feelings of calm. I find it makes me feel more positive and more connected to the present moment. And interestingly, I find that the physical and emotional benefits of my morning meditation stay with me all day.

Meditation helps me regulate my emotions and gain composure, regardless of what's going on around me. It gives me the training and skills needed to deal with stressful situations throughout the day — not just those brief, blissful few minutes in the morning when I'm meditating, but *all day.* I'm definitely calmer when I've meditated in the morning.

Don't get me wrong, meditation doesn't make me a saint, and people still get on my nerves at times, but it certainly helps me take a second, breathe deeply, and respond to difficult situations more calmly.

Business-related benefits

Reducing stress and anxiety is obviously beneficial in any context, but there are other benefits that will drastically help to boost your performance in a business context, including improved concentration and memory, and greater emotional intelligence.

Meditation also enhances creativity. Research suggests we come up with our most important breakthroughs and insights when we're in a more relaxed, meditative state (have you ever come up with a great idea just as you were drifting off to sleep, for instance?). This is because, as studies have shown, meditation induces states that promote both *convergent thinking* (generating a solution to a particular problem) and *divergent thinking* (a way of thinking that helps to generate lots of new ideas).

MEDITATION IN THE WORLD OF BIG BUSINESS

With all these benefits, it's easy to see why interest in meditation has grown significantly among business leaders over the last couple of years. In his book *Mindful Work,* David Gelles tells the story of Steve Jobs meditating on the floor backstage before addressing a large audience of Apple fans at a conference in 1981. He was just 26, yet Jobs was cool, calm, and focused before addressing the crowd. In the early '80s, the idea of a CEO meditating was pretty far out there, but, these days, it's becoming more common for CEOs to practice meditation and for companies to invest in mindfulness and meditation training for their people. Google and Ford are just two blue-chip companies that encourage their senior executives to practice meditation and mindfulness techniques.

TIP

I find meditation is a particularly helpful technique for getting to the root of things that may be bothering me and, by clearing my mind of distractions, coming up with potential solutions or ways forward.

So, if you're wondering how meditation can help you become a better real estate investor, ask yourself this: How can being calmer, more focused, and more creative *not* help you?

Making meditation work for you

Turn to Chapter 17 for a simple mindful breathing exercise that you can do anytime, anywhere. There, you'll also find a more business-focused meditation that you can try before an important meeting to focus your mind.

TIP

For now, here are my top tips for getting the most out of meditation:

>> **Meditate regularly, ideally every day or every other day and at the same time of day.** Regular practice is the key to getting the most benefits. I find that meditating in the morning sets me up properly for the day ahead, but you may prefer to meditate at night or take ten minutes out of your lunch break. Carve out a space and time that works for you.

>> **Get properly set up before you start by switching off your phone and telling your loved ones not to interrupt you while you're meditating.** They can cope without you for five or ten minutes.

>> **Meditate in a quiet place, in a comfortable position.** You can sit cross-legged on the floor if you like, lie flat on your back, sit in a chair, or whatever works for you. I meditate sitting upright in a giant beanbag chair!

>> **Use meditation alongside the other success-building techniques set out in this chapter, like positive affirmations and visualization.** For example, I like to review the goals on my goal list before I meditate. I also say my affirmations immediately before meditating, to help ingrain those positive thoughts deeper into my subconscious. This cocktail of "success techniques" is incredibly powerful when mixed together.

>> **Be patient with yourself.** Meditation isn't an easy thing to master if, like me, you have a busy mind that's always pinging between thoughts. And it's not a quick fix. It takes practice to master meditation and see the benefits, and this is where doing it regularly really helps. You know the old saying that it takes 21 days to form a habit? I'd say the same is true of meditation. It takes quite a few sessions before you begin to feel like you're doing it properly and really start to feel some benefits. So, I recommend you commit to doing it for a while before assessing how it's working for you. If you haven't tried meditating at least 15 to 20 times, then you haven't "tried meditation" at all.

>> **Try listening to guided audio meditations.** People don't often admit it, but meditation can be a bit, well, boring at first. The first few times I meditated, I found it quite dull, and my mind wandered off in all sorts of directions. That's why I turned to guided audio meditations. With guided meditations, a voice guides you through the practice, bringing your thoughts back to the meditation, which makes them great for the inexperienced. As you get more experienced, you'll be able to meditate on your own, without anyone guiding you.

>> **If your brain needs a little something to focus on to stop it from wandering off, you may find it helpful to repeat a simple mantra or affirmation while you're meditating.** One saying I find helpful is, "Calmness washes over me with every deep breath I take."

>> **Do some mini meditations throughout the day.** These will help you maintain a sense of calm no matter what's going on around you. So, if you get a spare moment, just use that time to sit quietly, breathing deeply and becoming aware of how you're feeling. A mini meditation can be as small as just one breath! There is no excuse not to take a second to be calm and bring yourself into the present moment.

REMEMBER

There's no rule that says meditation only counts if you do it for 30 minutes, or an hour. Even just one minute can help restore a sense of calm in a busy day. I find this is a particularly useful thing to do when something stressful or unexpected arises, or if I'm faced with a tricky problem. It may seem counterintuitive to take a minute to focus on breathing when all hell is breaking loose around you, but it'll help you respond in a more thoughtful and constructive way.

2

Money, Money, Money

Learn about traditional ways to finance real estate investments.

Come to grips with valuation methods.

Move beyond traditional mortgages and discover creative ways to fund your investments.

portfolio

» **Looking at a range of traditional finance options, like mortgages and bridge loans**

» **Understanding the nuances of overseas finance**

Chapter 6

Weighing Traditional Finance Options

You can finance your real estate investments in lots of different ways. A traditional mortgage is typically the first method people think of, but it's not the only route to buying property. Understanding and maximizing the wide range of finance options is what enables serious real estate investors to expand their property empires.

REMEMBER

Leverage is a financial term that you'll hear investors throw around a lot. It essentially just means using borrowed money to increase your returns. The concept of leverage is an important one to understand if you're looking to really grow your real estate portfolio — and fast.

In this chapter, I explore the traditional finance options that most people are fairly familiar with — mortgages, bridge loans, and the like. However, if these options are beyond your reach (for example, if you have next to no money for a down payment on a traditional mortgage), don't despair. Turn to Chapter 8 for some more creative ways to finance your real estate ambitions.

First, let's go back to basics and look at why finance, or the ability to use leverage successfully, is such a critical part of growing your portfolio.

Finance as a Key Element of Success and Growth

Think of how a regular business grows from a small startup to a large multinational. Rarely do the business owners have the cash to fund the necessary expansion themselves — and even if they did, they might have other uses in mind for their cash. (That villa in Saint-Tropez isn't going to buy itself, after all!) Businesses that really want to grow seek external investment to fund their expansion.

REMEMBER

In a similar way, finance, or more specifically, leverage, is your path to growth and building real wealth.

Seeing the link between leverage and growth

The best way to demonstrate the importance of leverage is with a simple example. Say, thanks to a large inheritance, you have $200,000 that you're looking to invest. You want to use that money to generate a solid income and create capital growth (growth in value) for the future that will serve as a retirement nest egg.

You can use that money to buy a $200,000 house outright, that you rent out, generating a monthly rent of, say, $1,000 (just to stick with a nice round number). Then, when you retire in 20 years, you have the option of selling that property for a tidy profit. Let's say the value of real estate in your area is doubling every 20 years, so you can sell it for $400,000. Not bad!

But what would happen if you applied the concept of leverage to that inheritance? In this case, you can buy four $200,000 properties by putting down a 25 percent down payment (that's $50,000) on each house and taking out a 75 percent loan-to-value (LTV) mortgage on each house to cover the remaining cost.

With each property earning $1,000 a month in rental income, you're generating significantly higher returns than you would have with just one property (granted, you have mortgage payments to cover, but you're still making a higher profit each month). Then, when you come to sell 20 years later, after the mortgages are paid off, if each property has doubled in value, you pocket a cool $1.6 million instead of $400,000. Now *that's* a nest egg.

REMEMBER

This demonstrates how finance is key to growing your real estate portfolio and your wealth. Figure 6-1 also neatly demonstrates the link between leverage and growth.

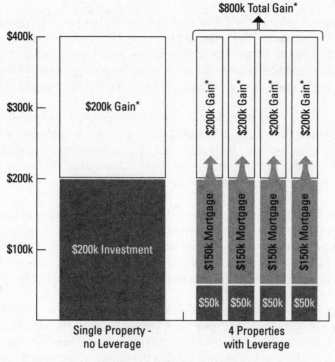

FIGURE 6-1:
Growth with leverage.

Single Property -
no Leverage

4 Properties
with Leverage

*Based on 100% growth in 20 years

Let's not forget that you can also leverage existing property itself to finance future growth. In other words, you can borrow against your already owned property (through secured loans, second-charge loans, releasing equity, and so on) to release funds for further investment. This is what makes property particularly attractive as an asset class: The larger your real estate portfolio, the more options you have for using leverage to fund future growth because you'll have more assets (properties) to secure the loans against.

Understanding the full range of finance options

Understanding the full range of finance methods and products is a huge part of investing successfully in real estate. For me, it's right up there alongside choosing the right investment strategy — it's that important to success.

REMEMBER

If you can get a really good handle on finance, you'll have a serious advantage over other real estate investors. Understanding and maximizing finance can be your competitive edge.

Without money, it's difficult to get a foot on the property ladder. So, if you don't fully understand the financing methods and products that are out there, all you can really do is spend your own money. And from a business point of view, it's hard to get agents, sellers, and potential business partners to take you seriously if you don't understand what sort of financing might be available to you.

TIP

But if you grasp both the concept of leverage as an investment strategy, and the different financing options available, not only do you know what's realistic for you as an investor, but you're also able to move much more quickly and secure appropriate finance when great opportunities arise. This ability to move fast can be a big differentiating factor in real estate success.

For example, mortgages take time to arrange and may not even be an option for the type of investment opportunity you have in mind. So, when you need to move fast or you're looking at a not-so-standard project, a bridge loan may be a suitable short-term option. I talk more about bridge loans in the section "Assessing a Range of Traditional Finance Products," later in this chapter.

But even a simple mortgage isn't as straightforward as it sounds. There are still lots of nuances to get your head around, such as the *term* (length) of the loan, fixed or variable rates, the *LTV percentage* (what percentage of the property's value you can loan up to), and the value of the property. I explore these factors and more in the next section, "Considering the Main Finance Factors."

TIP

It's a good idea to learn about these finance products and other means of financing investments (see Chapter 8) before you embark on your real estate journey. This is one area where learning on the job can cost you a lot in wasted time, wasted fees, and wasted opportunities.

Considering the Main Financing Factors

When taking out a loan (whether that's a mortgage or another kind of loan) to fund a real estate investment, there are a number of factors to consider before you find the right product for you. Always work with an experienced and reputable broker who will be able to guide you through the various options and what's best for you in a particular circumstance (see "Finding the Right Product For You" later in the chapter).

REMEMBER

For the most part, the following considerations apply to the various real estate–related financing products available:

- » The value, type, and condition of the property itself

- » Whether you want a fixed-rate or adjustable-rate mortgage

- » The length of the loan (for example, 1 year, 5 years, 25 years, and so on)

- » The LTV ratio (what percentage of the property value you borrow)

- » Whether to go for interest only or repayment

- » The lender's fees and other associated fees

Looking at the property itself

Obviously, the underlying asset (the property you're buying) is the first deciding factor in what options are available to you and whether a lender will actually lend you any money.

For instance, as a UK investor, I can't secure a standard residential mortgage on a derelict property or a property with no kitchen or bathroom because they're deemed uninhabitable. So, if a fantastic investment opportunity arose, but it fell under those criteria, I'd have to look beyond standard mortgages to fund the project.

Other considerations that the lender will take into account include whether the property is actually worth the amount that you're borrowing (if you default, can the lender recoup its losses from the sale of the underlying asset?), that it's well built and structurally sound (dry rot, for example, will rule out most mortgage lenders), and, if an investment property, whether the property will actually produce the income you predict.

TIP

When considering the asset itself, it's really important to develop a thorough understanding of real estate appraisal or valuation. This subject is covered in detail in Chapter 7.

Deciding between fixed-rate and adjustable-rate loans

There are lots of different types of mortgages and loans available for property, but you'll almost certainly have to decide between two categories: fixed rate or adjustable (variable) rate.

Fixed-rate loans

With a fixed-rate loan, the rate of interest that you pay remains constant, or fixed, for a certain duration, regardless of what happens with overarching interest rates. This fixed interest rate can be for the whole life of the loan or for an introductory period only (for example, fixed for the first five years of the loan).

REMEMBER

There are both advantages and disadvantages to fixed-rate payments:

>> **On the plus side, your monthly payments will always be the same for the duration of the fixed period, which brings some welcome certainty.** Knowing exactly what you need to pay each month is great for cash flow planning and is often considered a low risk.

>> **You'll generally be paying a higher interest rate than you would with an adjustable-rate loan unless the interests rates rise above your fixed rate.**

>> **If interest rates fall and stay low for a long period of time, you can be stuck with much higher monthly payments than adjustable-rate payments.** You can, of course, refinance and switch to an adjustable-rate mortgage in the future, but that that takes time, effort, money, and likely a substantial fee from the lender for ending the loan early.

Adjustable-rate (or variable) mortgages

With this type of loan, the interest that you pay varies over time. It can vary in line with a fixed economic indicator, like the national base interest rate, or it can vary in line with the lender's standard adjustable interest rate (usually at least a couple of percentage points above the base rate to account for the lender's profit margin).

REMEMBER

Here are some of the pros and cons of adjustable-rate loans:

>> On the sunny side, you'll generally pay a lower interest rate than you would with a fixed-rate loan.

>> If interest rates fall, your payments will, too.

>> You'll have less certainty in terms of what you'll be paying each month because interest rates can rise or fall out of your control.

>> If interest rates rise, your payments will increase accordingly, so you'll need to plan for a buffer.

WARNING

Adjustable rates can vary wildly from lender to lender, so always do your homework on what's available across the whole market. A good, independent mortgage broker will be able to help you with this (see "Finding the Right Product for You" later in the chapter).

Which type of mortgage is right for you will depend on a number of factors, including your personal risk profile (see Chapter 2), the likelihood of interest rate rising or falling, and how long you intend to hold the investment.

TIP

As a general rule, if I'm only planning to hold a property for up to a few years, I usually wouldn't bother fixing the rate. But if it's a long-term investment, I may prefer to limit my exposure to market fluctuations by fixing the rate. Turn to Chapter 4 for more on planning for interest rates and market fluctuations.

Looking at the length of the loan

How long do you want the loan for? In part, the term of the loan will depend on what type of loan it is. Bridge loans, for instance, are very short term. But standard mortgages could be anywhere from 10 years up to 30 years in some markets. Where I live, in the UK, a 25-year term is about standard for most residential or buy-to-let (buy-to-rent) mortgages.

REMEMBER

The right term for you will also depend on how long you intend to hold the investment for, your personal and financial goals (such as wanting to be mortgage-free before retirement age or before your children go off to college), and how much you can afford in monthly repayments.

A long-term loan, like a 25-year mortgage, means you'll pay lower monthly repayments, because you're spreading your payments over a longer period of time. Conversely, with a 10-year mortgage, your monthly payments will be much higher.

WARNING

You may think that a longer-term loan is riskier for you as an investor, because, without a crystal ball, you don't know what your situation will be in 20 or 30 years. But the reverse can actually be true. Short terms are attractive in the sense of paying off the debt quicker, but a shorter term can potentially put you at financial risk because your monthly payments will be a much bigger drain on your cash flow. What will you do if you lose your main income source or if a rental property stands empty for six months and doesn't earn you any money? You should only go for shorter-term loans when you're certain you can afford the higher monthly repayments.

In many cases, lower monthly repayments over a longer period of time are a safer cash flow option — plus, it means you can free up that much needed cash flow for other projects or to build your passive income. And very often with a longer-term loan, you still have the option of paying the loan off sooner (albeit it, sometimes, with an early repayment charge).

Finding the right loan-to-value balance

In the normal course of purchasing property, a buyer puts down a deposit or down payment and borrows the rest of the money needed to buy the property. Therefore, how much of a down payment you have is another key factor that determines the types of products available to you.

Understanding loan-to-values

The LTV is the ratio of the loan as a percentage of the market value of the property. For example, if you want to buy a $250,000 apartment and you have a $50,000 down payment, that's 20 percent of the value, meaning you need a lender that will offer you a loan with an 80 percent LTV ratio (assuming no other costs for simplicity's sake).

REMEMBER

Generally speaking, the most attractive mortgage terms come at the lower end of the LTV range. So, if you're making a large down payment of, say, 50 percent, you'll have your pick of great products to choose from, with attractive interest rates and lower fees. But if you've only got a 15 percent down payment, your range of choice will be a lot more limited, and you'll have to pay more in interest and, probably, fees.

In turbulent financial times, lenders tend to raise the drawbridges and massively tighten up on LTVs. For example, in the UK prior to the last financial crisis, borrowers could get their hands on mortgages with LTVs of 95 percent and even 100 percent pretty easily. Then all hell broke loose, and suddenly 75 percent LTV mortgages became the norm because banks needed to reduce their risk and exposure.

Therefore, it's not just about how much money you have to play with. Wider market factors will play a role.

REMEMBER

In the early days of their real estate portfolios, when cash flow is tighter, many investors need to take advantage of LTVs that are as high as possible to keep their down payments low. But even if you had a mattress full of cash, there might still be an argument for borrowing as much as you can comfortably afford if the income from the property warrants it.

Again, this is where leverage comes into play. In other words, you may prefer to take a higher LTV in order to make the most of your free capital, and use it to invest in multiple properties, not just one.

Finding the money for a down payment

In general, most investors go down the conventional route of making a down payment or deposit with their own capital and borrowing the remaining amount. So, how can you find the capital to fund your investments?

Common sources of capital include

>> Tapping into your savings

>> Releasing equity from your family home

>> Leveraging existing real estate investments by pulling equity from elsewhere in your portfolio

>> Making use of second-charge loans (see "Assessing a Range of Traditional Finance Products" later in the chapter)

>> Investing with other people's money (a great strategy for those with little or no capital behind them — turn to Chapter 8 for more on this)

TIP

If all these options elude you, consider opportunities to take control of a property instead of taking ownership. I explore this as a strategy in Chapter 8.

Weighing up repayment versus interest-only loans

When you think of a typical mortgage, what you're actually thinking of is a standard repayment loan (the loan is broken down into monthly repayments, with added interest). By the end of the loan term (whether that's 10 years, 25 years, or whatever), you've repaid the debt and interest in full.

REMEMBER

As the name suggests, with an interest-only mortgage, your monthly repayments cover just the interest on the loan. At the end of the interest-only term, you still owe the same amount of money as you did at the start — and you're still expected to repay that amount.

Why in your right mind would you choose an interest-only loan? Well, in certain circumstances, it can make good financial sense. For one thing, your repayments are significantly lower with an interest-only loan. So, if your margins are tight, paying just the interest means more profit in your pocket upfront.

REMEMBER

Particularly in the early days of your real estate portfolio, interest-only mortgage payments can help you generate a much healthier cash flow in the short and medium term. You can refinance to a standard repayment mortgage further down the line when your portfolio is better established. Or, you can sell the property at the end of the interest-only term, repay the original loan amount from the proceeds, and pocket the difference as profit. Naturally, this relies on the property market going one way (up!), which in itself can be a risky strategy unless you have a crystal ball.

WARNING

Interest-only loans should not be considered a route to funding otherwise unaffordable property (investments that you couldn't afford with a standard repayment loan). Interest-only is a means to improving cash flow, not over-stretching yourself financially.

Interest-only isn't for everyone. If your appetite for risk is low, you're likely to lean toward a standard repayment loan, and that's fine. Your choice of interest-only versus repayment may also be affected by the type of investment you're making; the interest-only option is far more commonly available on residential mortgages than commercial mortgages, for instance.

Taking fees into account

At the risk of sounding like a country song, finance don't come for free. It costs folks like you and me. So, whenever you're seeking traditional finance, you need to factor in the range of costs before you decide whether an investment is affordable for you.

Typical costs may include

>> **Loan application fee:** Usually, you have to pay this fee even if your loan application is rejected.

>> **Appraisal or valuation fee:** The lender needs to be sure that your property is actually worth the money it's lending you, so the lender will send out an appraiser (or surveyor, in the UK) to verify its value. On large residential properties or commercial properties, this fee can run into the thousands. Turn to Chapter 7 for more on valuing real estate.

>> **Credit report fee:** Lenders want to know you're a solid investment and that you aren't likely to default on the loan, so they'll carry out a credit check and charge you for the privilege. (See the sidebar "Keeping an eye on your credit report.")

>> **Fees for third-party assessments or structural surveys:** The lender may require an expert inspection in certain circumstances. For example, in the United States, it's common to have a licensed expert inspect the property and confirm it's free of termites.

WARNING

Fees can be well hidden in loan paperwork, so be sure you fully understand what you're agreeing to before you sign on the dotted line.

KEEPING AN EYE ON YOUR CREDIT REPORT

Any loan is subject to your credit rating. How easily you'll be able to obtain finance and how favorable the terms will be both depend on how good your credit history is.

Lenders would much rather attract borrowers with a good track record of paying their bills and making repayments in full and on time. So, if you have a poor credit history, finance (if you can get it) will cost you much more. Even getting a great broker on your side is easier when you've got a good credit score.

This is why you should always keep an eye on your personal credit report. This can be done easily online through a credit bureau like Experian or Equifax. You may have to pay a small fee, especially if you want to check your report regularly (which I highly recommend), but you'll get a surprisingly detailed picture of your credit history, including your previous addresses, associated people that you've got financial links to, whether you've ever missed a repayment or bill, and who has carried out credit checks on you in the past.

Lenders will look at your credit history before they loan you any money, particularly on a big loan like a mortgage. So it's vital that you monitor your credit report regularly, but especially closely in the months before you apply for a mortgage. I recommend logging in every month or two to check that everything is as it should be, but there'll be a limit on how many times you can check your credit report for free. For example, you may only be able to access a free copy of your credit report once a year; after that, you have to pay. However, in my view, this cost is well worth it, especially if you're about to apply for financing.

That's because mistakes can happen on your credit report. I've experienced this myself. One time, after selling a property, my company paid off the property's mortgage in full. Naturally, we stopped making mortgage payments after that. However, the mortgage company took a while to update its records properly and tried to take a mortgage payment the following month. This showed up as a failed payment on my credit history, which may have affected future financing applications. Luckily, after I spoke to the mortgage company, it rectified the mistake and had the failed payment removed from my history. But if I hadn't checked my report, I would never have known!

Naturally, in addition to checking your credit report regularly, it's also important to build a good credit history. You can do this through responsibly using and paying off credit cards and smaller loans; always paying your bills, mortgage payments and other repayments on time; and swiftly dealing with any mistakes on your credit history by contacting the credit agency in the first instance and the lender (in my case, a mortgage company) if they're the ones at fault.

And where you have genuine problems or blemishes on your credit history, don't despair. Some lenders are more flexible than others, so a credit blip doesn't automatically rule out future credit. Be upfront with your mortgage broker and potential lenders about credit hiccups and explain the circumstances behind them.

Assessing a Range of Traditional Finance Products

A whole plethora of financing options is available, opening up a world of exciting real estate opportunities. The most common and useful of the traditional options are

>> Standard residential mortgages

>> Commercial mortgages

>> Bridge loans

>> Second-charge loans

>> Land and development loans

Getting a standard residential investment mortgage

This is the type of finance most of us have come across. Even if you're a novice real estate investor, chances are, you used a similar mortgage to buy your family home. So, it's no surprise that standard residential investment mortgages make up the bulk of financing products out there.

There are literally thousands of different types of mortgages available (each with differing lengths, LTVs, and other factors, as outlined in the previous section).

REMEMBER

You're probably not going to be living in the property you buy (because you'll be renting it out or selling it for profit), so you'll have to get a mortgage that's specifically designed for investors. These are commonly available and go under names like *buy-to-rent mortgages* or *investment mortgages.*

In the UK, there are also specific mortgages available for houses in multiple occupation — properties where rooms are rented out individually as opposed to the whole house being rented as a single let (see Chapter 13).

Applying for an investment-type mortgage can be slightly more complex than a regular mortgage where you'll be living in the property. With a regular mortgage, the lender essentially needs to know that you earn enough to repay the loan and that the property is worth the purchase price. But with an investment loan, the lender may also want to look at income projections and, sometimes, your history as a landlord.

TIP

Treat your mortgage application like a business plan, where you're making a strong business case for investment. A good mortgage broker will be able to help you prepare the relevant paperwork and present a compelling case (see "Finding the Right Product for You" later in this chapter).

Seeking a commercial mortgage

As your real estate portfolio grows, you may start getting into bigger properties or different types of properties. This means you may need a commercial mortgage, rather than a standard residential mortgage.

REMEMBER

Commercial mortgages aren't just for commercial buildings, like office blocks and warehouses. Depending on what country you live in, a commercial mortgage can be an excellent choice for a large residential property. For example, I've used commercial mortgages to fund apartment blocks and large house in multiple occupation properties.

Some high street lenders offer commercial mortgages along with residential mortgages, but you may be better off seeking out a specialist commercial lender. Your mortgage broker will be able to help you assess this.

In my experience, commercial lenders tend to offer slightly lower LTVs than you may get on a residential investment mortgage. At the time of writing, LTVs of around 60 percent seem to be pretty typical in the UK for commercial mortgages, whereas on a normal residential mortgage for a rental property, 75 percent is standard.

REMEMBER

Commercial lenders will also certainly want to look at the property's *income* not just its straightforward bricks-and-mortar value. So be prepared for the lender to delve into your overall business model and proposition. On the plus side, this focus on income means that commercial properties can often achieve a higher investment valuation or appraisal. Turn to Chapter 7 for more on this subject.

Using a bridge loan

When you need to move fast and a regular mortgage isn't an option, a bridge loan can be a useful short-term option.

REMEMBER

A *bridge loan* is a short-term loan, typically for up to one year only, that's designed to provide temporary finance until the borrower can sell the property, secure longer-term financing, or free up cash flow (for example, by selling another asset). It's literally a bridge to tide you over temporarily until you can find better finance or for opportunities when you can do a quicker deal.

How does it work? Well, a bridge loan is a bit like an interest-only loan, but with some key differences. For one thing, you don't usually make monthly payments; you just repay the loan at the end of the year (or however short the term is). And interest is normally taken upfront. So, if you took out a $1 million bridge loan at 10 percent interest, the lender would take its 10 percent interest at the start, giving you just $900,000. Then, at the end of the loan period, you'd repay the full $1 million.

REMEMBER

As you can probably glean from that example, bridge loans are an expensive option and should only be considered under certain circumstances. But, on the plus side, they can be secured very quickly compared to a traditional mortgage, and you'll usually see much higher LTVs. With a bridge loan, you could potentially get up to 100 percent of the value of the property.

WARNING

Clearly, bridge loans aren't for everyone. You need to be very certain of your investment opportunity and that you can do what needs to be done before the end of the bridge loan period. If you haven't secured longer-term finance in that period or freed up cash flow, you'll be stuck with a hefty repayment and no means to repay. And bridge loan providers aren't exactly shy about recovering their money if borrowers can't pay promptly.

However, under certain circumstances and with the right investment opportunity, a bridge loan can be a good temporary solution. Here are some examples where it can work:

>> **If the money for a down payment on a new property isn't yet liquid (it's tied up in another property and the sale is still going through):** Bridge loans allow you to buy while you're in the process of selling another property so you won't miss a cracking opportunity.

>> **If you buy a run-down building that a standard lender won't lend on:** You could get a bridge loan for six months and renovate the property to a standard where it's mortgage-able through a traditional lender.

>> **If your investment is a development project and the current bricks-and-mortar value of the building is too low to secure the mortgage you want:** With a bridge loan, you can finance renovations, increase the value of the property, get it income generating, and then get it revalued by a standard lender.

>> **If you're asset-rich but cash-poor and you don't have enough income to meet a traditional lender's affordability calculations:** A bridge loan could mean you can get an investment set up and earning a regular income, making you a more attractive prospect to lenders.

If you're considering a bridge loan, you'll almost certainly need to go through a niche bridging provider rather than a household-name lender. A good, trustworthy, independent broker is worth his weight in gold here. He'll help you find a reputable, regulated provider.

Taking out a second-charge loan

A standard mortgage is essentially just a really big secured loan, secured against the property that's being purchased. This debt, the mortgage, is registered against the property and is known in technical terms as a *first charge* (because it's the primary debt registered).

A *second-charge loan* works in the same way. It's a debt that's secured against the property, but because it's the *second* charge it has less precedence than the first charge (main mortgage).

So, if you defaulted on your mortgage, your mortgage lender would take control of the property and sell it to recoup its money. If there was also a second-charge loan secured against the property, the second-charge lender would be repaid only after the first-charge lender got its money back. The second charge is lower in the pecking order, if you like.

For example, say you only had a 10 percent down payment on a house. Your mortgage lender will loan you 75 percent of the value of the property, so you still have a shortfall to make up. A second-charge lender can lend you the remaining 15 percent needed to purchase the property.

If you default and the property is sold at auction for 80 percent of its value, the first-charge lender gets back its 75 percent in full. But that leaves just 5 percent for the second-charge lender. The second-charge lender has lost the rest of its money.

Second-charge loans are riskier for the lender because there's a higher chance that the lender might not get its money back. Therefore, expect to pay higher interest rates and fees on a second-charge loan.

Getting land and development loans

Most of the loans I've covered up to this point are based on purchasing an existing property that can be easily appraised to reach a bricks-and-mortar value. But what if you're building an apartment block on a scrap of land or you're knocking down an old cowshed to build a house? In that case, you need to look at alternative financing.

For development projects, you can seek both a *land loan* (to cover the initial purchase) and a *development loan* (to cover the build costs). These loans are generally available through both traditional and specialist lenders. When the development is finished, the loans get rolled into one loan called a *term loan.*

As with any kind of specialist lending, expect to pay higher interest rates and fees for this kind of loan. Typically, you get both the land and development loans through the same lender, but you may get a better overall deal if you went with two separate providers; for example, you may get much more attractive terms on the development part of the loan through a lender that specializes only in developments. Talk to your broker to find the best route for you. Often using one lender is easier because it will have the whole picture of what you're trying to accomplish with the deal and can assess the risk more effectively.

The development part of the loan will often be drawn down in stages, meaning the bank will release funds a bit at a time, and only if it's satisfied that the project is running on track. The bank may appoint a surveyor or appraiser to monitor your build and assess how much money you can get at each phase of the build.

Essentially, you really need to stay on track and on schedule to get your hands on the development funding. If you're running over, the bank may not release the next phase of the funding, meaning you may have to go back to the bank to renegotiate the loan or arrange a separate valuation to reassess the value of property.

LOOKING AT LOAN GUARANTEES

To reduce their risk, some lenders may require a *personal guarantee* (PG) from you, on top of the underlying asset that the loan is secured against. That means, if you default on the loan, the lender won't just repossess the property; it'll also be able to come after any of your other assets to recoup its losses. Guarantees like this are particularly common in a real estate investor's early days, or if you're purchasing a property through a business name and the business doesn't have other assets.

If you can avoid loans with a PG requirement, that's obviously preferable. Personally, I don't have a problem giving a personal guarantee if it's absolutely required, but I'm an experienced investor and I know what I'm getting into. I'm comfortable with it in certain situations and if it suits my personal risk profile. Always be aware of what you're signing up for, and if a PG is involved, you'll need to be absolutely confident in your business model, numbers, and ability to deliver the project.

Sometimes a property can go down in value before it goes up. For example, if I take a perfectly usable office block and rip it apart to turn it into luxury apartments, it'll be worth less as a shell than it was when I bought it (as a perfectly good office!). You need to be aware of this if funding is released based on meeting certain valuations. Get your build costs right and always build in a contingency.

Turn to Chapter 9 for a more in-depth look at developing properties.

Finding the Right Product for You

Throughout this chapter, I mention several considerations for seeking finance and various different finance options. So, how can you put this into action?

Here are my top tips for finding the best kind of finance for you:

>> **Get a great independent mortgage broker as part of your dream team (see Chapter 3).** You can go direct to lenders if you want, but if you're serious about really growing as a real estate investor, I highly recommend working with a broker. Not only will she help you identify funding options, but she'll help you deal with all the paperwork and present a compelling, professional application.

A personal recommendation or referral is a good way to find a trusted broker. You may also want to speak to multiple brokers before making your final decision. If you do talk to multiple brokers, decide which one is right for you before you agree to any paperwork. You don't want to be submitting multiple mortgage applications and having multiple credit checks done at the same time through different brokers because this will negatively affect your credit rating in itself.

>> **Work with your broker to find the most appropriate lender and product** *for you.* For example, just because you're buying residential property doesn't automatically mean you want a standard residential investment (or buy-to-rent) mortgage. If you're buying an apartment block or larger rental property, a commercial mortgage may be your best bet.

>> **Remember that even the best broker in the world is only as good as the information you give them.** You should still do your own homework, have a solid business proposition, understand your chosen market well, and understand appraisal methods (see Chapter 7). The broker's job is to help you find the best finance, not tell you how to run your business!

>> **Work hard to keep your credit history squeaky clean (see the sidebar "Keeping an eye on your credit report").** When you have a great credit history, you stand a much better chance of attracting more favorable credit terms and more loan options.

>> **Network with local real estate investors and agents (see Chapter 5).** You can really benefit from their knowledge and experience with various lenders.

Dipping into International Finance versus Domestic Finance

If you're investing overseas, whatever country you're investing in, there will be a similar range of finance products to those outlined in this chapter. However, whether these are available to you as a foreign investor, someone who doesn't live in the country you're buying in, is another matter entirely.

REMEMBER

As a foreign investor, you may find it harder to access traditional finance, like a mortgage. This is because lending is all about assessing risk. And, as someone who doesn't live in the country you're borrowing in, you're a higher risk prospect.

Think about it: If I'm a bank in the UK, do I want to be chasing down someone who lives in New Zealand for an overdue mortgage payment? Even though there's an underlying asset that the debt is secured against, it's still easier for me to assess and work with borrowers in my own country.

There are ways to increase your chances of securing overseas finance. The best course of action is to pull together as big a down payment as possible. As a foreign investor, you're much more likely to get a mortgage with a 50 percent LTV ratio than a 90 percent LTV ratio.

TIP

When seeking finance overseas, you really need an advisor who knows the local market you're considering buying in and the full range of options available to you out there. Always seek a reputable local mortgage broker when considering overseas options.

Circle back to Chapter 2 for advice on weighing what you can afford when buying overseas, as well as alternatives to seeking overseas finance.

investors

» **Understanding the main property valuation methods**

» **Knowing which valuation method is most appropriate for your investment**

Chapter **7**

Understanding Property Valuation

It stands to reason that if you pay too much for a property, your investment will be off to a poor start. Likewise, being unable to achieve the right sale price for an investment because you didn't value it properly is bad for business. Either way, your cash flow suffers.

REMEMBER

Property valuation, or real estate appraisal, is a critical component of real estate success. Getting it right is as important as choosing the right investment strategy, getting to know your market, and treating your real estate portfolio as a business (see Chapter 3).

In this chapter, I look at why valuation is such an important piece of the real estate puzzle and explore the three main ways property is valued or appraised. I also take a brief look at the types of people typically involved in appraising and valuing property.

But first, let's explore what valuation means in practice.

Defining Value and Real Estate Valuation

Value is easy, right? It's the price you pay for a property? Well, it's not quite that simple — price and value aren't always the same thing.

REMEMBER

Real estate appraisal or *property valuation* is the process of determining what a property is actually worth. This may or may not be the same as its price.

Appraisers go under different names depending on where you are in the world; *real estate appraiser*, *property valuer*, and *chartered surveyor* are the most common names. I use the terms *appraiser*, *valuer*, and *surveyor* interchangeably throughout this chapter.

Comparing price to value in more detail

A property's *price* (how much the property costs to purchase) can be very different from its *value* (what the property is worth). For example, a property may actually be worth in the region of $300,000 but the seller may have an inflated idea of its value and insist on putting it on the market at $350,000 — or he may have been guided to set the price high by an especially greedy agent who wants a higher commission.

A buyer with a firm grip on valuation will understand that $350,000 isn't a fair market comparison (a concept I revisit later in this chapter) for that property, and refuse to cough up. But an unsuspecting and inexperienced investor could fall into the trap and end up overpaying.

There are a number of reasons why a buyer may gladly pay a price that's lower than the property's value. The buyer could, for example, be buying a property from a family member, who is cutting her a favorable deal and pricing lower than the market value. Or it could be a distressed sale where the property is priced lower than it's worth for a quick sale, or perhaps it's being sold at auction and the bidding doesn't reach the expected levels.

A buyer may also be willing to pay *more* than a property's market value in order to secure a particularly attractive investment in a highly competitive market. That's right, sometimes an investor may have arrived at her own valuation that's higher than the comparative market value, maybe because she plans on changing the use for a niche high-income strategy (like short-term rentals, for example).

REMEMBER

If, when you're valuing a property, you're using a different valuation method from the person doing the appraisal, you may well arrive at a different value. That's not necessarily a cause for concern, as long as you're sure of your own numbers. I look at the different valuation methods later in this chapter.

Understanding the purpose of appraisals

In general, appraisals or valuations are used in a number of contexts, from dividing up assets during a divorce to taxation. But for the real estate investor, valuation is used to determine

>> How much you can borrow to purchase a property (because appraisals inform mortgage loans)

>> How much you should reasonably expect to pay for a property

>> How much a property could generate in ongoing income (where income is the investment goal)

>> How much you could sell the property for after adding value (where capital growth is the investment goal)

Valuation is particularly important in real estate because each property is different. As an asset class, property is unique. When you buy two shares of stock on the same day, both shares are identical. But that's not the case with real estate.

REMEMBER

Even two properties on the same street can be very different. In fact, even two houses next to each other, even if they're both identical in size and layout, will vary a great deal in terms of condition, fixtures, and fittings and presentation. Their value will differ accordingly.

Valuation is also necessary because most people fund their investments through some sort of financing, like a mortgage. And when you're borrowing the money to buy a property, the lender will want to know that the property is worth what it's loaning you. If you default on the loan, forcing the lender to foreclose on the property and sell it, the lender wants to know that there's enough equity in the property to get its money back. In this way, real estate valuation protects the bank, as well as you.

Looking at factors that influence value

So, what kinds of factors impact a property's value? The key factors are

>> **The size of the property:** For example, it makes sense that a four-bedroom, three-bathroom house will be worth more than a two-bedroom, one-bathroom house in the same town.

>> **The condition of the property:** This is key because it's how so many investors add value to a property. By renovating and improving a property, even if you're not doing major structural remodeling, you can increase its value in a relatively short amount of time.

>> **How the property is (or can be) used:** For one thing, a commercial property will be valued differently from a residential property (see "Looking at the Three Main Valuation Methods," later in this chapter). What's more, various usage restrictions may also impact the value. For example, if zoning restrictions mean it's impossible to turn a commercial property into a luxury block of apartments, then that restriction may impact how much buyers are willing to pay.

>> **The property's location:** Compare a four-bedroom, three-bathroom house with a smaller house in the same town and it makes sense that the bigger house is worth more. But things get foggier when you bring different locations into the mix. Compare that generous family home in Des Moines, Iowa, with a studio apartment in Midtown Manhattan and the smaller property is likely to be worth more. That's because different locations are more desirable and valuable than others. Additional local factors like a nearby, highly rated public school or great transportation links can also drive up a property's value.

>> **Supply of property:** A few years ago, there was a lot in the real estate news about Bulgarian apartments. Investors were piling into the country in droves, and new apartment buildings were being thrown up left, right, and center in coastal and ski resort towns. The result? A market that ended up with way more supply (new-build apartments) than demand (actual buyers) and apartment blocks sitting empty and unsold. Compare that with, say, a sought-after coastal village location in Cornwall, in England's beautiful West Country, where supply of properties is relatively low. Because few properties come onto the market, their value is higher than if there was a deluge of available property.

>> **Demand for property:** Think back to the tiny studio apartment in Midtown Manhattan, and you can see how being in a buoyant real estate market, like New York, can impact a property's value. In a market where there's a wealth (pardon the pun) of motivated buyers keen to purchase property, combined with plenty of money to buy, demand goes up — and with it, market value.

Knowing who values real estate

So, who has a hand in deciding a property's value? Depending on the circumstances, the following people may all be involved in the process at some point:

>> **Sellers:** Plenty of sellers do their own homework on what their properties may be worth before they put them on the market. And, at the end of the day, it's the seller who weighs the agent's recommendation and agrees on the final price.

>> **Buyers:** Informed buyers do their own research and analysis, and reach their own conclusions on the fair price for properties.

>> **Real estate brokers and agents:** Any good real estate broker or agent knows her market inside and out, and she'll have a really good handle on the likely value of a property. That said, it's not uncommon for an agent to quote a higher valuation to get a seller's business (and a juicier commission), even though this can result in an overpriced property languishing on the market for longer than it needs to. So, when an agent gives you a valuation, do your own homework to determine whether that's a correct and fair price for your market.

>> **Professional appraisers, valuers, or surveyors:** Whenever you're seeking funding to buy a property, the lender will send a professional appraiser to value the property. (By "professional," I mean that many countries require appraisers to be qualified and certified.) Depending on the lender and type of funding, you may have some flexibility to appoint the appraiser yourself, or choose from a shortlist of the lender's appraisers (this is not unusual on a commercial mortgage in the United Kingdom). Many times, though, the lender will simply appoint its own appraiser, and you'll have no say in the matter. Either way, you'll ideally have the option of being present at the valuation (see "Making your own valuation case," later in the chapter).

WARNING

Be aware that a lender-appointed appraiser may not have a ton of experience in your type of investment; for example, he may specialize in standard residential properties rather than income-generating rentals. Find out more about the difference — and why it matters — in the section "Looking at the Three Main Valuation Methods," later in this chapter.

Seeing Why Valuation Is Fundamental to Property Success

Why is it so important to understand value before you buy, build, or develop? The obvious answer is, you don't want to pay more than a property is worth. But there's more to it than that.

REMEMBER

Personally, I've found that understanding valuation has enabled me to work out exactly what I should be paying for my investments and seek appropriate funding that matches that value. But it has also allowed me to realistically judge the income potential of various investments and maximize my resources on every investment.

Understanding enough to maximize your investments

You don't have to learn about valuation to the level of a chartered surveyor or certified appraiser. It's what they're trained and paid for. What's more, one way or another, you'll probably have a professional appraiser involved in every real estate transaction you make. Whether the mortgage lender has appointed an appraiser to assess a property's value before lending to you or whether you've hired your own appraiser, every transaction will be guided by what the professionals say.

REMEMBER

The goal here isn't to learn about valuation to the extent that you don't need professional help with appraisals. Absolutely not! But even though a professional will be involved, it's still important to understand how the appraiser arrives at her valuation.

And when you understand what the appraiser is looking at, you can give supporting evidence to help her value the property as accurately as possible. This can be particularly helpful when you're seeking a certain amount of funding from a lender. Also, understanding the end value of a development site is vital because it allows you to backward-calculate what you should be paying for the land or site in the first place — before you make an offer! You do this by taking the end valuation estimate and subtracting the estimated developments costs (including any agency, broker, legal, or other fees and costs); that leaves you with the land value and profit margin.

Knowing the difference between yield and return on investment

When it comes to working out the ultimate value of an investment, there are two key indicators you need to know:

>> **Gross yield:** Gross yield is an indicator of how well a property performs as an income-earning investment, making it a good way to compare investments. Expressed as a percentage, gross yield is calculated by taking the estimated gross income (so, before taxes and expenses) and dividing it by the purchase price.

>> **Return on investment (ROI):** ROI is, in very simple terms, a measure of what you put in versus what you get out. Like gross yield, ROI is expressed as a percentage, and it's calculated by taking the gross income and dividing it by the cost of the investment (for example, the cost of acquiring the property and any development costs).

The two indicators are different, so you absolutely need to consider both when you're weighing an investment. For example, an investment can deliver a fantastic yield, but if you have to put in a lot of money to get the investment up and running, the ROI will be lower.

For an example of these indicators in action, turn to Table 8-1 in the next chapter. However, it's important to note that acceptable yield and ROI will differ from project to project and from investor to investor.

Considering how valuation methods may affect your financing

Understanding valuation is all about gathering the right information to help you make the right decisions and find the right deals for you. This includes finding the right kind of finance. (Circle back to Chapter 6 for more on traditional finance options, like mortgages.)

REMEMBER

Different lenders will use different valuation methods. When you understand the different valuation methods, and how potential lenders may value a property, you can make smarter decisions on which lender or finance option is best for you.

Valuation affects your financing in two key ways:

>> **How much you can borrow is reliant on the underlying value of the asset (property) you're buying.** Both the overall loan amount and the loan-to-value ratio (see Chapter 6) can potentially be influenced by the property's value.

>> **Choosing the right finance option may come down to which valuation method the lender uses (more on that coming up).**

REMEMBER

Here's an example from my own portfolio: On one of my recent investments, it took me three different valuations on the same building to get the correct valuation needed for a loan. Why? The first two valuers were basing their valuation on the market comparison approach (see "Looking at the Three Main Valuation Methods," later in this chapter). That may be appropriate for a standard residential property, but this was a huge rental property, with each of the nine bedrooms already rented out to separate tenants. For a residential property, it was producing a very high income — something that isn't taken into account with the market comparison approach to valuation.

The third appraiser, however, looked at income when valuing the property, as opposed to how much similar properties were worth in the area. As a result, he arrived at a much fairer representation of the property's value as an income-generating investment.

If I had stuck with the first two valuations, I wouldn't have secured the funding I needed to buy that fantastic investment. But because I understood that an income-focused valuation was more appropriate for a property of that size, I was able to get a fair appraisal and secure a suitable mortgage.

REMEMBER

To demonstrate just how important this difference in valuation methods is, the first two valuations valued the large rental property at around £500,000 (around $638,000). But the third valuer, who looked at the property as a business, valued it at £750,000 (around $956,000). This is a fairly extreme example, in my experience, but it shows how valuation can seriously affect your financing.

Recognizing that appraisers are risk averse

A qualified appraiser or surveyor has to be able to justify his valuations. In other words, his valuation needs to be able to stand up in court in the event of a dispute or if a bank sues him for valuing an asset incorrectly.

REMEMBER

Therefore, risk is a factor that any professional appraiser or surveyor has to take into account. If his risk is high — because, for example, the property has no fair comparison and is difficult to value accurately — he'll be extra cautious in his valuation to protect himself (or his professional indemnity insurance) and mitigate his risks.

Plus, some valuers are just more cautious than others. So, inevitably, different valuers can arrive at different valuations, even if they're using the same valuation method. Often, the differences are pretty small, but not always.

For example, I had two apartment-block buildings valued on the same street a year apart. The first property was valued (and shortly after sold) at £2.35 million (about $3 million). Twelve months later, the second property was valued at just £1.9 million (around $2.4 million) by an incoming buyer's bank. Both buildings were identical in size and use, and the local real estate market was gradually going up, not down. So, why was the second property valued so much lower? You may be thinking that perhaps the second property was in a worse condition, but here's the clincher: Both properties were developed by my company, both to the exact same standard. So, what was the differentiating factor? The second surveyor was simply a lot more cautious than the first, even though I made a solid valuation case (discussed in the next section).

REMEMBER

Appraisers are often cautious by nature, and they need to mitigate their own risks when they look at a property. But there are things you can do to help an appraiser understand and value a properly more easily (see the next section).

Making your own valuation case

TIP

The value of a property can come down to the valuer on the day. But whether you're buying, selling, or refinancing, there are a number of practical things you can do on the day of the appraisal to help your valuation go as smoothly as possible:

>> **If you have the option of appointing an appraiser yourself (see "Understanding who values real estate" earlier in the chapter), choose someone you've worked with before.** You want someone you trust to give a fair appraisal, who knows you as an investor and understands your specific product or investment model.

>> **If the appraiser is being appointed by your lender, join the appraiser on the day of the valuation.** Someone has to give the appraiser access to inspect the property so make sure it's you.

>> **Before the valuation, put your own thought into the value of the property.** Do your own research and create your own pack of evidence, including (where appropriate) comparable properties and their values, rental comparables, and details of any other selling points or benefits over other similar properties the valuer may be looking at.

>> **Share your evidence and research with the appraiser to back up your case.** You can do this in person, if you're present at the property with the valuer, or send over supporting evidence via email, ideally in advance of the inspection visit so the valuer has an idea of what he's valuing before he gets there.

Some valuers will be delighted to receive your evidence, because it cuts down how much work they have to do. I've literally had some surveyors poke their heads in a few rooms in a property, and write their entire reports based on my research! Others, of course, will sincerely thank you for the information and then never look at it. (But that doesn't mean you shouldn't try.)

>> **Whatever you do, don't hand over your evidence in an "I can do your job better than you" kind of way.** Unless you really want to put the valuer's nose out of joint, you're far better off phrasing it as something like, "Hey, I know the area really well, so I've pulled together some comparable evidence that may help you with your own research."

>> **Where you have access to the property before the valuation (if you're the seller), make sure it's clean, well presented, and being shown in its best possible light.**

>> **If you aren't satisfied with the appraisal given, and you feel it significantly undervalues your property (therefore, potentially jeopardizing your financing), try presenting your evidence to the lender directly or hiring an independent valuer to give a second opinion.** This strategy is particularly helpful if the original valuer has used a valuation method that you feel isn't appropriate for the property being assessed (see the next section).

Looking at the Three Main Valuation Methods

There are several different methods used to value property, but here are the three most common methods:

>> **Market comparison approach:** Compares the property being valued with other similar properties that have recently been sold in that area

>> **Income or investment approach:** Looks at how much income the property being valued is already generating or could potentially generate

>> **Cost approach:** Looks at how much it would cost to build an equivalent property

Each valuation method is independent of the others, meaning an appraiser will mainly use only one approach rather than a combination of all three approaches to determine the value of any one property. The method used may be dictated by the lender in question. And, as my earlier examples show, each approach can arrive at quite different valuations, so it's important to know which valuation method your chosen lender is using. Different valuation methods are used for different situations.

I have sometimes seen more than one valuation figure quoted in reports, particularly for commercial mortgages where the market comparison (or bricks-and-mortar) valuation is used as a fallback if the investment valuation use of the building changes (for example, a paying tenant leaves and the income reduces to zero until a new one is found).

That's not to say that one approach is better than the others — only that one approach will be more applicable or appropriate for a certain property than the others. You need to understand the differences between each approach, and know which approach the appraiser is using for your investment.

In the following sections, I walk you through each method in greater detail.

Market comparison approach

If a total novice wanted to roughly work out the value of his home before putting it on the market, what would he do? He'd go online and look at how much similar properties nearby (ideally on the same street) sold for. "Well, honey, the Jeffersons at number 59 sold their home six months ago for $280,000, and they only had a single garage, not a double like ours. So, our house is bound to be worth a bit more." That, in a pretty crude nutshell, is how the market comparison valuation method works.

Also known as *market value approach* or *bricks-and-mortar valuation*, *market comparison* is a valuation method that's based on local comparables — in other words, how much similar, nearby properties have sold for recently. It's the most common valuation method and the one typically used by mortgage lenders to assess residential properties.

Identifying common considerations for market comparison valuations

Your average market comparison valuation will define a property's value by looking at prices of properties on the same street or prices of other properties of a similar size and condition from the local area. The value will be adjusted according to variances like the size, specification, and condition of the property being valued. Other variables may also be factored in, such as supply and demand in the local real estate market at that time or the availability of financing.

In addition, appraisers who are appointed by a lender may also be constricted by the lender's valuation criteria, which may lean toward the lower end of comparables in order to reduce their risks as much as possible. Therefore, the inherently cautious nature of lenders and appraisers means you won't necessarily get the valuation you hoped for. Just because the house down the street sold for $280,000 doesn't mean you'll get the same valuation.

Of course, no two properties are exactly alike. Properties A and B may be the same size and on the same street, but Property A may have a beautiful view of rolling hills, while Property B may have a rather uninspiring view of other houses. But maybe Property B has been stylishly renovated, while Property A is straight out of the 1970s, complete with peach satin drapes and brown shag carpets. That's why appraisers try to find a few comparable properties to help them determine a fair market value, not just one or two.

Recognizing the limitations of market comparisons

If there's one sticking point with the market comparison approach it's this: To get an accurate valuation, you do a good number of comparable properties. That's fine for a standard residential property, like a single-family home or an apartment, where there are lots of similar properties to look at. But when you start to get into bigger, unique properties, finding enough accurate comparable market data is challenging.

WARNING

Although it's a straightforward valuation method to understand, the market comparison method isn't always the best judge of value. Remember the huge nine-bedroom rental property I mention earlier in the chapter? Although it was a residential property, the market comparison approach just wasn't reliable because there weren't any similar nine-bedroom rental properties nearby.

In that example, the first two valuers, who were using the market comparison approach, had to look at larger properties elsewhere in the town. But that wasn't a fair comparison because the location of my investment property was far more desirable. Essentially, the property was unique in that market, meaning the market comparison approach just wasn't a reliable indicator of value, so these valuers took a cautious approach. For that investment, the income approach was much more appropriate.

Income or investment approach

Instead of looking at the bricks-and-mortar value of a property, this valuation method treats the property as an income-producing business.

Focusing on income not comparables

REMEMBER

The *income approach* or *investment value approach* to valuation assesses the value of a property as an investment. Also known as *commercial investment valuation*, this method is commonly applied to commercial properties like offices, but it may also be used for income-producing residential properties, such as rentals or blocks of apartments.

At its heart, the income approach is based on the understanding that the higher the income potential of a property, the more an investor is willing to pay for it. A property's income or investment valuation can be higher or lower than its market comparison value — in my experience, it's often (but not always) higher.

Understanding how the income approach works

The best way to describe how this valuation method works in practice is with an example. The example is based on a UK investment: a small block of four apartments.

Let's say each of the apartments is rented out for £750 per month. That's a gross annual rental income of £36,000. Now, based on her appraisal of the property, the UK valuer will apply two concepts to arrive at an income-based valuation of that property:

>> **Discount:** A discount that's applied to the *gross income* in order to establish a realistic picture of the *net income.* A discount of 15 percent to 25 percent is typical on a UK income valuation, but it depends on a number of factors, such as the quality of the property, how strong the rental market is right now, location, costs, and how likely it is that one or all the units can stand empty without tenants for a period of time (the void period). Basically, the lower the discount, the better the property. But let's say the discount applied to our £36,000 annual gross rental income is 20 percent. So, our estimated *net* income is then £28,800.

>> **Yield:** The return on investment the investor can expect to receive, expressed as a percentage. To determine the yield, the valuer will look at comparable properties, local rental incomes for similar apartments, demand in the local market, and so on. In a busy town with lots of renters, the yield will be better than in a rural setting, with lower demand from renters. Let's say the yield on our example investment is 7 percent.

To calculate the income valuation, the valuer will take the discounted *net* rental income (£28,800) and divide it by the yield (7 percent). The income-based value of that block of apartments is therefore £411,429. Valuers will usually round the figure down as well.

TIP

Don't be shy about calling a couple of local surveyors and asking what sort of yield they're currently applying to your type of investment property in your area. It's part of my process when I'm evaluating the potential of an investment deal because the end value is so important.

WARNING

Although this example gives a useful overview of the concept of valuing based on income. The nuances of the income-based approach will depend on which country the investment property is located in. For example, in the United States, a revenue multiplier or *capitalization rate* (rather than yield) is applied to net income. Always research the income valuation method that's used in your particular market.

Cost approach

The third approach to be aware of looks at neither income generated by a property nor local comparable properties.

REMEMBER

The *cost approach* is used to establish the cost of replacing the building being valued. It's widely used for insurance replacement purposes (so, if the building burned down, how much would it cost to replace the building on that spot?), but it can also be a useful method for brand-new buildings, proposed constructions, and unique properties that don't have local comparables and don't generate an income.

When using the cost approach, an appraiser will look at the estimated value of the land, as well as the cost to replace the building as new (minus depreciation, such as wear and tear).

Knowing Which Method Is Best for You and How Much an Investment Is Worth

Remember that each of the three main valuation methods set out in the previous section serves a different purpose. So, it's not a question of working out which method is better than the others — instead, it's about determining which approach is most suitable for *your* property.

Evaluating on a case-by-case basis

First and foremost, the most appropriate method will depend on the property that's being valued.

For example, on a large rental property, like the nine-bedroom rental I mention earlier in the chapter, the market comparison valuation was significantly lower than the investment or income valuation.

REMEMBER

But on the flip side, a rental studio apartment in London may be valued much more accurately using the market comparison approach — even though it's an income-generating investment. Given the sky-high prices in London, even a tiny studio apartment can sell for upwards of £400,000 (about $510,000). Yet, if it was valued using the income approach, earning a monthly rent of £2,000 (about $2,550), the property may only be valued at around £275,000 (about $350,000), using the same 20 percent deduction and 7 percent yield as described earlier. In this case, a straight market comparison approach could give a more accurate reflection of value. It would, however, come down to what yield and deduction a valuer is applying when valuing using the investment valuation method, so check that first.

Doing your own appraisal research

TIP

Here are my top tips for compiling your own research on how much a potential investment may be worth:

>> **Consider taking an online course on real estate appraisal to develop a deeper understanding of the valuation methods outlined in this chapter.** Understanding valuation in detail makes you a better property buyer. (Turn to Chapter 17 for more on tapping into online education resources.)

>> **In general, get to know comparable prices in your local market.** Constantly check out online agents and never walk past a real estate agent's office without looking at prices! Set new listing alerts for your chosen investment criteria on all the major real estate portals.

>> **When it comes to evaluating a specific property, compare it against similar properties that have sold recently in the same area to arrive at a market comparison valuation.**

>> **Do some basic calculations using the income valuation approach to see if that produces a higher valuation.** If the property is already being run as a rental, the seller should happily give details of current earnings and expenses. You can assess whether the current rent that's being charged is right for the market by looking at other rental listings in the local area and speaking to agents. Calculate the investment valuation with this data and compare this against the market comparable valuation. Which is higher?

>> **When making an offer on a property, if you've arrived at a lower valuation than the sale price, make a well-prepared case for your lower bid that's packed with reason and research on why you believe the property is worth X instead of Y.** You can use your newfound knowledge of valuation methods as a fantastic negotiating tactic on relevant deals!

TIP

If a lender is appraising a property as part of a loan arrangement, you may not have a say in which method it uses to evaluate your investment property. However, if you disagree with the method the lender has used, and you feel it undervalues the property, it's well worth seeking a second opinion through an independent appraiser.

Special Considerations for Valuing Property Abroad

The considerations I set out throughout this chapter still apply to overseas real estate, but there will be various nuances to understand within your chosen investment country. This is where your dream team of agents and advisors (see Chapter 3) is worth their weight in gold. They will already know the local peculiarities of valuation, and they can give you a helping hand as you learn the market for yourself.

WARNING

Be aware that a number of different factors (from the subtly different to the wildly different) will apply from country to country. For example, if you're looking at buying an investment property in rural France, and you intend to develop the property so it earns an income, you'll need to know that the local village or town mayor has a say in what changes you can make to the property. So, if the valuation you have in your head is dependent on making certain changes, you need to get friendly with the mayor — and fast!

TIP

Generally speaking, the following tips are important when you're grappling with valuation in an overseas market:

>> **Take extra care to understand the valuation nuances of your chosen country before you invest in it.** For example, which valuation method is most likely to be used in the country?

>> **Learn as much as you can about the local market comparables.** Do your research online. Talk to local valuers and agents to really get to know the local market. Build and nurture your dream team!

>> **If possible, be there to meet the valuer on the day of the appraisal, and present your own evidence, just as you would for an investment in your own country.**

Chapter **8**

Looking at More Creative Financing Options

When most people think of real estate investment, they think of the traditional route to buying property: You put down a down payment (25 percent of the purchase price, for instance) and take out a mortgage to cover the rest. With this traditional financing route (see Chapter 6), you must have money for the down payment. In other words, you still need some level of capital to get a foot in the door.

And even if the mortgage market changed and 100 percent mortgages became readily available, you'd probably still need some capital to make changes to the property and get your investment up and running.

Either way, this overarching requirement for capital is a big barrier to entry, leaving people with limited funds feeling like they'll never become real estate investors. This chapter aims to break down that barrier to entry by looking at other, more creative ways to raise funds.

REMEMBER

The idea that you need lots of capital to invest in real estate is a big misconception. There are multiple ways to build a real estate portfolio, and using your own money is just one of them. So, if you're short on capital, don't automatically count yourself out of the game. Read on, and you'll discover how to progress beyond the traditional financing options and get a little more creative when you're raising capital.

You Down with OPM? Investing with Other People's Money

Like many investors, I started my real estate journey funding my investments with my own cash. I used savings to adapt my own home and make an additional rental bedroom, turning the property into a house in multiple occupation, or HMO (turn to Chapter 13 for more on HMOs). That was my first investment. When it came to funding my second investment, I managed to refinance that first property to gather the money I needed.

Then that was it. I hit a brick wall — or rather, a capital wall. With those two investments up and running, I had pretty much run out of investment capital. I was eager to grow my portfolio, and as my expertise was growing I was spotting more and more great opportunities — I just needed to find better ways to finance them. Struck with a serious case of FOMOOP (fear of missing out on properties), I began looking at more creative financing options. That's when I discovered the theory of investing with other people's money (OPM).

Introducing the concept of OPM

So, what exactly is OPM and where can you get your hands on it?

REMEMBER

As the name suggests, OPM is the process of investing using money that isn't your own. Learning to harness OPM is a powerful way to expand your portfolio, or fund real estate investments when you have little or no capital to play with.

OPM can be institutional money (from a bank) or private money (from an individual). Strictly speaking, a mortgage is part-OPM, because you're buying the property largely using the bank's money.

Key sources of OPM may include

>> Traditional institutional lenders (for example, taking out a bank loan)

>> Joint venture (JV) partnerships

>> Private, external lenders

>> The good old Bank of Mom and Dad

>> Friends and acquaintances

>> Crowdfunding sites

Looking at OPM as a route to real estate success and wealth

Stuck at investment number two and keen to progress further, I very quickly realized that if I wanted to really grow my real estate business, I needed to learn how to use OPM successfully.

As a fast learner, I was already immersing myself in real estate by going to networking meetings and property shows (see Chapter 5), and I noticed at these events that partnering up with investors/using OPM came up time and time again as a critical part of growing a large real estate portfolio — and personal wealth.

Based on what I'd learned from immersing myself in the industry, I partnered up with a JV investor to fund my next project. It turned out to be one of the smartest business decisions I ever made, enabling me to begin to expand my portfolio and fulfill my ambitions.

TIP

Investing with OPM can be a one-off occurrence, or it can lead to surprising long-term partnerships. Always stay open to future possibilities, and cultivate every investment relationship as though you intend to do business together again in the future.

For example, my initial JV partner and I went on to build a highly successful property business together, and we remain business partners to this day. Although we started working together using my JV partner's funds (see more on this topic in the next section, "Joining Up with a Joint Venture"), we went on to secure funding from other investors as we grew. In this way, harnessing OPM has been absolutely critical to our success.

REMEMBER

Throughout this chapter, I primarily focus on JV partnerships and private lending as the main OPM financing options. Bear in mind that these OPM opportunities can come about with people that you already know (such as a parent or friend) or with third-party investors that you don't yet know (but soon will). Either way, whether you're best buddies or business partners only, the same basic principles that I set out in this chapter will apply.

Likewise, you may have one OPM source that you return to time and time again, or you may access several OPM sources throughout your real estate career. Again, the same basic best practice principles apply.

Joining Up with a Joint Venture

My first foray into creative real estate financing was with a JV, and it's an option I recommend to any serious real estate investor.

REMEMBER

Technically speaking, a JV is defined as a business enterprise that two (or potentially more) parties undertake, while still retaining their separate identities. In other words, you don't necessarily form a company together (although that's often used as the investment vehicle), and you aren't bound together in any way beyond the scope of the deal at hand. A joint venture agreement is well worth drawing up detailing the terms of your deal (see "Dotting the I's and crossing the T's with a joint venture agreement," later in this chapter).

Knowing what's involved in a joint venture

In practice, a JV can be anything from teaming up with a pal to a formal business arrangement with an external investor. It can be an equal 50/50 partnership in terms of effort and financial input, or it can mean one partner provides much more cash and/or expertise than the other. JVs are entirely flexible, and there's no one-size-fits-all approach.

REMEMBER

A key part of successful JV-ing is that each party brings something of value to the table, and that the outcome is mutually beneficial for both parties. I'm a big believer in win–win relationships in business, and never is this more important than in a JV. A great JV means both you and your JV partner benefit, and you both make some sort of positive contribution toward achieving the stated end goal. It's the simple theory of two (or more) heads is better than one!

In real estate terms, this could mean one JV partner provides the money, while the other (you, in this case) provides the expertise and does the legwork on the project. You benefit by getting another project off the ground — another feather in your real estate cap, if you like. You're able to grow your portfolio, develop your experience, and enhance your wealth. Meanwhile, your JV partner benefits by getting a positive return on her financial investment for very little effort.

WARNING

With a JV, your reputation and, therefore, your ability to do business in the future are on the line. So, it's vital that you deliver the agreed positive outcome (whatever that may be) for your JV partner. If you lose your partner's money, your reputation will be tarnished and future opportunities will be closed to you, so you must always, *always* treat your JV partner's money as preciously as your own (if not more so). You shouldn't enter into a JV partnership unless you're extremely confident in your numbers and your ability to deliver the intended outcome.

Looking at examples of joint ventures

Here's how a JV might shape up in practice with some simple hypothetical examples:

>> **You contribute the expertise and manage the project, while your JV partner contributes the funds.** This is perhaps the most common JV approach in real estate, and it forms the primary focus of my JV guidance in this chapter (in other words, I'm assuming that you're investing with limited funds and you're seeking a JV partner to help get a real estate venture off the ground).

>> **Your JV partner may contribute an asset rather than money.** For example, you may know a landowner with a plot of land that he wants to develop, but he lacks the knowledge and time needed to manage such a project. You can handle all aspects of getting permission to build, managing the build, and even selling or renting the property at the end. You then share the profit or income from the development between you. This option is more common than you may think — I'm regularly offered deals by landowners who want me to develop their land.

>> **You partner with a construction company or builder to develop a plot of land together.** For instance, you can buy the land (or it may be land that you already own), and they could fund and complete the build.

>> **You could even combine two JV approaches in one project.** For example, you could do a JV with a landowner who has land to develop and a contractor who can build on that land. You then sit in the middle and oversee the project, without injecting any of your own cash or assets.

As you can see from the last example, JVs can get pretty creative. This is why I love property: There's no limit to what you can achieve — if you have the determination, creativity, time, and knowledge, you don't have to be constrained by a lack of funds.

TIP

Don't be afraid to think outside the box when it comes to JVs. Just ask yourself, "How can I find win–win scenarios for me and potential JV partners?"

Understanding why people would invest in you

"But surely a wealthy investor wouldn't want to help me or invest in me. If it's such a great deal, wouldn't they just do it themselves?" This is something I hear from novice real estate investors all the time.

Apart from being a really negative mind-set (circle back to Chapter 5 for more on how mind-set is critical for success), it's also not true. There are lots of reasons why potential JV partners would consider working with you.

REMEMBER

Different people are at different stages of their lives and investment cycles. This is where great opportunities lie — connecting with people in a different cycle from you.

For example, your potential JV partner may well have a background in real estate and have made (literally) a boatload of cash from his own real estate projects. So, sure, he could do a deal himself and keep all the profit. But maybe he's reaching the end of his real estate career and he's looking to step back from the day-to-day minutia of managing a portfolio. Maybe he wants to spend more time on that boat he worked so hard to afford!

In this way, he's in a different cycle from you. You may be just starting out, hungry to build your portfolio and personal wealth. You'll put in every spare hour you have to make the project a success. He, on the other hand, no longer wants to put in 100 percent of the effort for 100 percent of the spoils. At this stage of his cycle, he's just happy to receive a healthy return on his investment with minimal effort.

Or your JV partner may have such a big portfolio, he simply doesn't have time to take on another project personally. But he's happy to invest financially and sit back and take the returns. Sometimes, a low-risk, low-effort investment is just what an investor is looking for.

TIP

Most people have that nagging voice in the backs of our minds telling us all the reasons why we're not worthy. Don't listen to it! Positive thinking is a big part of success in real estate (indeed, any part of life). So, instead of wondering why on earth someone would invest in you, focus on your strengths and all the positive things you bring to the table: drive, energy, knowledge of your market, and so on. Then go out there and find people who value those characteristics!

Finding the right joint venture partner

So, where are all these willing investors hiding? Is there a club where they all hang out? A secret handshake that'll get you in?

Unfortunately, it's not that simple. Finding suitable JV partners is perhaps the biggest hurdle to overcome in the early days of building your portfolio and reputation. And there's no doubt that it's more difficult for inexperienced real estate investors to secure financing through JV partnerships. It's a little bit like a chicken-

and-egg scenario; you need to demonstrate your expertise to get people to invest in you, but you can't build your expertise without their investment!

TIP

It makes sense to start with people who already know you. People who already know how brilliant you are. People who already know that when you set your mind to a goal, you don't stop until you achieve it. People who already trust you. Those people are a good starting point. They may be friends, family members (many a real estate entrepreneur got their start thanks to the Bank of Mom and Dad), or pillars of the local community. When you start putting yourself out there, you may be surprised who you find who's interested in backing you.

The larger your network and the deeper you immerse yourself in the real estate world, the easier it will be to find JV partners. *Remember:* Your network is your net worth!

In addition to nurturing your existing contacts, you also need to be continually building and enlarging your network (see Chapter 5). This may involve

>> Going to networking meetings

>> Attending national and regional property shows and conventions

>> Joining online property groups

>> Tailoring your LinkedIn profile to show your real estate skills and expertise, and then connecting with likeminded individuals on the platform

>> Utilizing other social media platforms like Facebook and Twitter

>> Writing articles on LinkedIn and contributing to online property forums and groups to demonstrate your expertise (investors are frequently watching in the background, so there are always opportunities to impress)

>> Creating a professional website, building your list of email contacts, and sending regular engaging updates (providing a valuable resource that helps grow your personal profile)

>> Interning or volunteering with investors and real estate companies (agents, developers, and so on)

>> Continually monitoring the market so that you can recognize good deals with they arise

TIP

Be patient. When you're just starting out, it may take time to find the right JV partner for you. But there are good people out there, actively looking for people to invest in. Don't give up. Keep a positive mindset and always dream big!

Creating a compelling business proposal for potential joint venture partners

Having found a great investment opportunity and a potential JV partner to work with, your next step is to create a compelling business proposal to present the deal in its best light and convince the potential partner to invest in you and your project.

In essence, your business proposal is about selling the deal itself, and selling you as a partner. The overarching goal is to show this person that the deal is a sound investment and that her money is safe with you.

When you start out, you may want to tailor your proposal and business model to each individual investor you're approaching. Then, as you get bigger and your expertise grows, you'll probably develop a more standard JV brochure or prospectus that could go out to multiple investors. That's the position my company is in now when we approach investors.

In the following section, I walk you through what you should include in your proposal or prospectus.

Selling the deal

Any potential JV partner isn't just weighing whether she wants to invest in you personally — she's also weighing whether the deal itself is worth investing in. Largely, this will come down to the numbers.

You'll need to present a well-considered, thorough, and compelling financial case for investing in your project. This can be broken down into three main components:

>> **Acquisition costs:** This includes all the costs related to obtaining the property/land, such as purchase price, taxes, legal and professional fees, and so on.

>> **Development appraisal:** How much will it cost to build or renovate the property? I always tend to be conservative on costs to give myself a bit of a buffer. It's always a good idea to build in a contingency.

>> **Exit or outcome of the project:** Are you going to sell the property and divide the profits, or are you going to rent it out? What is the expected return on investment? As with the costs, it pays to be conservative. You want to show that you're being realistic about what's possible, not "Well, this is what we could earn if the market grows 10 percent, the property breaks the ceiling price for this street, and we spin around three times while rubbing our noses!"

Table 8-1 provides an example of a simple deal calculation, including acquisition costs, development costs, yield, and return on investment (ROI). It's based on developing a property to sell. (Read more about yield, ROI, and developing properties to sell or rent in Chapter 9.)

TABLE 8-1   **Sample Deal Calculation for Approaching JV Investors**

Example Deal Acquisition	
Item	Amount
Purchase price	£250,000
Loan amount (@ 70% loan-to-value)	£175,000
Acquisition and Development Costs	
Item	Amount
Deposit (30%)	£75,000
Land tax (SDLT in the UK)*	£10,000
Legal fees and disbursements	£950
Survey	£700
Development costs	£20,000
Total acquisition cost	**£106,650**
Estimation of Outgoings per Month	
Broadband	£20
Gas	£30
Electricity	£50
Water	£25
Council tax	£127
TV license	£11
Property insurance	£30
Management costs	£0 (self-managed)
Total Monthly Outgoings	**£293**

(continued)

TABLE 8-1 *(continued)*

Ongoing Returns	
Mortgage loan rate	4.50%
Monthly mortgage repayment	£656
Expected monthly rent	£1,700
Net profit per month (after outgoings but before tax)	£751
Gross yield (ratio of gross income vs. purchase price)	8.16%
ROI (ratio of net income vs. total acquisition costs)	8.45%

*UK rate at the time of writing. Always check applicable rates in your target country.

Note: *This table assumes zero void periods and a self-managed investment. Net profit in this example is before tax (but includes the deduction of outgoings).*

REMEMBER

Good investors are "exit-led," meaning they won't do a deal unless they're very clear on what that deal's exit goal is (in other words, what the satisfactory conclusion would be). This could be the profitable sale of the property after renovation, or it could be refinancing the finished property, giving the investor her expected return or share of the profit, and keeping the property for yourself for its long-term rental income. Alternatively, if your JV partner is more interested in long-term income than a fixed return, you could share the ongoing rental income between the two of you. In any deal it's vital to consider multiple exit options if things don't go according to plan. Multiple exit options reduce your risk and give an investor more comfort because you've thought of multiple possible outcomes.

Selling yourself

It's always worth including an "About the Developer" section in your proposal that sells you as a potential partner. This can be a brief bio that sets out your experience and skills and makes a case for why someone should invest in you.

REMEMBER

You need to present a professional front to potential investors. Therefore, in addition to selling yourself in your proposal, you also need to employ basic marketing principles outside of the proposal. That means

>> **Having a proper website:** Your website doesn't need to be particularly extensive — just a basic blurb and contact details is enough to start with — but it absolutely must look professional and have a dedicated URL (for example, www.yourname.com).

>> **Having professional business cards**

>> **Having a proper business email address:** So many people email me seeking investment just using their personal Gmail addresses. It looks cheap (and, to be brutal, lazy), which doesn't inspire confidence. If someone can't be bothered to set up a proper business email address, where else might he cut corners? Instead of emailing potential investors from your Hotmail or Gmail account, shell out for a professional email like yourname@yourname.com.

Turn to Chapter 3 for more on marketing yourself as a real estate investor.

Dotting the I's and crossing the T's with a joint venture agreement

Having found someone willing to invest in you and agreed on who'll do what and how you'll you split the rewards, it's really important to formalize your JV partnership with a contract. This cuts any risk of ambiguity.

SO, HOW SHOULD YOU SPLIT THE REWARDS?

Every deal is unique and every investor is unique, so there's no general rule for how to divide the returns from an investment.

Ultimately, it's a negotiation. The goal is a win–win scenario for both parties, with no one out to screw the other party out of his just rewards. So, when you're preparing your business proposal, think about the person you're approaching and what would be a good return for him. What sort of split would attract him to the deal?

Obviously, as with any negotiation, 50/50 is a good starting point when thinking about how to divide the returns, but that's not necessarily what you'll end up agreeing on. For example, your JV partner may bring experience as well as money to the table, and he may expect to be compensated for that accordingly. Perhaps a 60/40 split in his favor is fairer. Likewise, 90/10 in your favor is potentially feasible, if your partner is totally hands-off and if it still represents a great return on his investment.

REMEMBER

Always get a proper JV agreement drawn up, even if you're partnering with friends or family. A good lawyer or attorney will be able to help you prepare a JV agreement, stipulating the following:

>> How much each party is contributing financially at the outset

>> What's expected of each party (division of labor, or what each party will be doing to achieve the intended outcome)

>> How the returns will be distributed between both parties, usually as a percentage

>> When parties can expect their money (and returns) back

>> What happens if either party wants to exit the agreement and get his money back earlier

>> The notice period for exiting the agreement (it's a good idea to build in as much of a notice period as you can, potentially giving you time to complete the development and sell the property)

WARNING

You may think this kind of agreement is overkill when your investor is a loved one, like your mom or your brother. But, in fact, partnering with family as opposed to a business acquaintance can be more, not less, tricky, particularly when it comes to navigating day-to-day involvement. That uncle who you thought would be totally hands-off? He may end up sticking his nose into every facet of your refurbishment, until you find yourself arguing over flooring options in Home Depot. A JV agreement means everyone is clear on his or her responsibilities.

TIP

If friends and family are your best financing option for now, but you're concerned that a JV partnership may strain your relationship, consider approaching it as a private lender agreement rather than a JV partnership. That way, the person is a lender, not a partner in the project. You can find more on private lending in the next section.

Securing Private Lending

Private lending is similar to a JV partnership in that you're teaming up with an individual or business entity (as opposed to a bank) to fund your project, but there are some critical differences.

REMEMBER

Private lending is a loan agreement rather than a partnership arrangement. That means the lender is loaning you a set amount of money for a set amount of time for a set amount of interest. Rarely does the lender get any share of the profits from the project, as she would with a JV — instead, her return is the interest that you pay. Also, the lender will usually have zero control over how the project is managed day to day, unlike a JV where the partner may get involved in the nitty-gritty a bit more and signing off on major decisions.

Private lending is a just like a traditional mortgage or secured loan, in that the loan will likely be secured against the property in question in some way. This gives the lender some level of security — if you default on the loan, she can take charge of the property (or the company holding the property) and sell it to recoup her money.

Finding and approaching private lenders

Unlike a traditional mortgage or loan, with private lending you go directly to a lender rather than a bank. These lenders can be

>> High-net-worth individuals

>> Investment companies

>> Property funds

>> Family offices or trusts

There are intermediary agents who can match those seeking funding with investors, but I prefer to approach people directly because it cuts out the middleman and gives greater control.

TIP

Here are my top tips for sourcing leads for private lenders:

>> **Use your existing network.** Maybe that independent financial advisor you know from your local networking ground has a potential investor among his clients. Would he be willing to make an introduction?

Similarly, your mortgage broker may not have direct experience of private lenders, but, like others in your network, she may be able to make useful introductions.

>> **Encourage others in your real estate network to keep you in mind and make introductions.** Attorneys, real estate agents, anyone who deals with

investors on a regular basis can make a valuable introduction. As a sweetener, you can even offer a referral or "finder's" fee for leads that pan out.

>> **Head online and market yourself and potential investment opportunities through LinkedIn groups, property forums (like ours at** www.propertyforum.com**), direct mail, and so on.**

>> **Consider paid marketing and advertising on property websites and forums as a way to increase your reach and draw investors to you.** I've found advertising to be a great way to pick up new contacts I wouldn't otherwise have met. Read more about marketing in Chapter 3.

REMEMBER

When approaching private lenders, just like approaching JV partners, it's a good idea to prepare a compelling proposal that "sells" you and your opportunity. You can do this by following the guidelines set out in the JV section, earlier in this chapter — but remember that you won't need to offer a ROI or profit share, because you'll be paying interest instead.

As your portfolio grows and you become more established, you can do what my company does and prepare a glossy brochure to send to private lenders.

Putting it all in writing

Just like when you take out a mortgage, you'll need to sign a formal loan agreement when you borrow from a private lender. This will set out how much you're borrowing, how it'll be repaid, when it'll be repaid, and at how much interest. It should also set out what happens if you're unable to make repayments and what happens if you want to repay early.

REMEMBER

Even if your private lender is a friend or family member, it's really important to formalize the loan with a proper contract.

A good attorney who specializes in financial agreements will be able to draw this up for you. Your regular family lawyer is probably not the right person for the job.

WARNING

The financial industry is under increasing scrutiny and regulation, particularly when it comes to certain financial products (like loans) and types of investments. So be sure to have your attorney check that your private lending arrangement complies with the regulatory requirements in your country.

Crowdfunding Your Way to Real Estate Success

Crowdfunding, or peer-to-peer lending, is an emerging finance method in real estate and a growing number of real-estate-specific crowdfunding companies are lending to investors.

REMEMBER

I'm not talking about putting your development opportunity up on Kickstarter. Instead, I'm talking about going to crowdfunding platforms that specialize in lending for real estate projects and that tend to be run by experienced real estate investors. There are hundreds of these platforms out there, including big names like Fundrise (www.fundrise.com), RealtyShares (www.realtyshares.com) and CrowdProperty (www.crowdproperty.com). A simple Google search will bring up lots of options, or your broker may be able to help you find the right crowdfunding lender for you and your project.

Think of a crowdfunder as like any other kind of lender, but slightly more flexible. This means they may be open to more niche strategies and projects than your average lender. However, just like a regular lender, a crowdfunding company will have a set loan-to-value (LTV) ratio they can lend, meaning you usually can't secure 100 percent funding through crowdfunding. And just like a regular lender, you'll have to pay interest on the money you borrow.

WARNING

As with any area of real estate, always do your due diligence before you jump in. Ensure that the platform is regulated by the financial regulator in your country, and check out reviews from previous customers.

Getting Control of a Property Instead of Owning It

Think of the typical path of a real estate investor: You buy a property using a mortgage (or perhaps some other form of finance, as outlined in this chapter), and then you own it. Hooray! But, in fact, you don't really own the property until the debt is repaid. Until then, the bank or lender owns it. Yet, because you (not the lender) control and manage the property, you're still able to make money from it, even when you don't own it outright.

REMEMBER

Therefore, instead of thinking of real estate investing in terms of *ownership*, it can be much more helpful to think in terms of *control*. Getting control of a property can be just as good as owning it, at least in terms of generating income in the short and medium term. After all, what is it you're trying to achieve through property? Money? Freedom to be your own boss? Greater security for you and your loved ones? That can all be achieved through controlling or managing property.

TIP

Two great strategies for controlling a property instead of owning it are rent-to-rent (see Chapter 11) and lease options (see Chapter 12). Both boil down to managing a property that you don't own, making money for you and the property's owner. And, best of all, both require very little in upfront capital.

You can also find other ideas for making money through property in Chapter 18.

Applying Creative Financing Strategies Overseas

In theory, the creative financing strategies that I outline in this chapter can be applied anywhere in the world. There's nothing stopping you from teaming up with a JV partner in Spain or finding a landlord in Canada who's open to your employing a rent-to-rent strategy in his property. As always, it's a case of finding the right partner (lender, landlord, and so on) and the right project in the right market for you.

REMEMBER

With traditional mortgages often being difficult to access for overseas investors, creative financing strategies can be a good route to funding foreign investments.

That said, language barriers, lack of local knowledge, geographical distances, and even time-zone differences can all make it harder to source and execute these creative financing options abroad. And, in the case of a JV partnership, you'll need to be very realistic about what exactly you're bringing to the table.

If it's a development in Spain, for example, and you're based in the United States and have little knowledge of the Spanish property market, what exactly is your contribution? Will you really be able to manage the development on a day-to-day basis when you're not in the country? Think carefully about whether it's a realistic option for you at this point in your real estate career, and remember that you must treat any partner's money more preciously than your own.

WARNING

As with any business or financial deal, you must always have a crystal clear idea of what you're getting into. This is more important than ever when you're seeking funding in an overseas market. Use your common sense and follow some key rules:

» Always team up with local independent financial advisors, brokers, lawyers, and translators — people you trust and who will work in your best interests. You can find more on building your "dream team" in Chapter 3.

» Do your due diligence on potential JV partners and private lenders.

» Wherever possible, work on word-of-mouth recommendations from trusted contacts.

» Have contracts translated into your native language by an independent, professional translator.

3

One-Off and Shorter-Term Income Strategies

IN THIS PART . . .

Add value and generate profit by developing properties.

Source property leads or become a retained buyer's agent to earn money selling property information.

» Sourcing great development opportunities

» Managing development projects like a boss

Chapter 9

Developing Properties

I n Chapter 4, I explain that smart real estate investors don't rely on the market to make money for them. In other words, they don't rely on a booming market and rising housing prices to deliver a healthy profit into their laps. Instead, they proactively find their own ways to generate a healthy return on their investment — usually by adding value to it.

REMEMBER

Property development is a great example of this in action. Whether it involves building a property from scratch or improving a building that already exists, property development provides a vast array of opportunities to add value and generate profit.

I started my real estate journey with rental properties. And although these properties delivered stable long-term income (see Chapter 3), I was also keen to diversify my portfolio (see Chapter 4) with some shorter-term strategies. That's when I got into developing properties. Years later, my business has successfully completed a wide range of development projects, from straightforward, single-tenant refurbishments to whole blocks of apartments, and everything in between.

It's important to note that this chapter isn't a nuts-and-bolts, step-by-step description of how to revamp or build a property — that would take an entire book in its own right. Instead, it's an investor's guide to property development, including the essential thought processes that precede a project, plus how to oversee a project and keep it on track.

Knowing What Property Development Means

Property development is a broad umbrella. It covers everything from a light sprucing up of a small property (new carpets and a fresh coat of paint, for example), a substantial remodel of a family-size house, the conversion of an office to residential apartments, to buying a piece of land and building a new build block of apartments on it. What's more, property development can mean developing a property to sell for capital growth, or it can mean developing a property to rent for long-term income.

REMEMBER

Underneath the specifics lies one critical defining characteristic: Property development is about *adding value*. Ultimately, it doesn't matter whether you just revamp the kitchen to make a tired family home more desirable, or you get really creative and change the use of an office block to luxury apartments. Either way, you're adding value to maximize the return on your investment.

Broadly speaking, adding value falls into two major categories or approaches:

>> Physically improving a building (by refurbishing it, for example) or plot of land (usually by building on it) to increase its value.

>> Changing the use of the building to increase its value. Examples of this include turning a family home into a house in multiple occupation (HMO) and renting out individual bedrooms to professionals (see Chapter 13), changing a single-tenant property into student accommodation (see Chapter 14), or turning a block of apartments or offices into serviced accommodation (see Chapter 15).

When most people think of property development, particularly when they're in the earlier stages of their real estate careers, they think of the first bullet point: physically improving a building or site. So, that's what I focus on in this chapter. If you're interested in changing a property's use and running it as a business, for example, as serviced accommodation, turn to the specific chapter for that strategy (see Part 4).

WARNING

Hopefully, it goes without saying that you shouldn't try to build a huge block of apartments as your first development project. Calculating costs and timing accurately can be really difficult when you're first starting out, and this can lead to costly mistakes.

TIP

Always start with smaller, simpler projects — projects that require less budget and time, where you're less likely to make expensive mistakes. You can gradually build your expertise and knowledge as you go, and progress to larger projects over time.

In this chapter, I assume you're starting fairly small, so I focus on smaller-scale developments where you'll be making improvements to an existing building.

Deciding Which Development Strategy Is Best for You

What's your end goal? What are you going to do with your finished property: Sell it or operate it as a rental property? What's the target audience for the property: families, young professionals, vacationers?

Before you buy a property and start gleefully knocking down walls, you need to know the answers to these questions.

Understanding why you need to think about the end before you start

You may think successful real estate development is mainly about buying property cheap, doing it up in an effective (and cost-effective!) way, and then selling it for a profit. Not quite. Your chosen exit strategy — and how well you can execute that strategy — has a dramatic impact on the success of a development project.

REMEMBER

The most successful property investors are exit led in their decisions and almost always have multiple exit options, not just one. Not having an exit strategy is like a football team heading out onto the field to play without having a game plan in mind. You can't just wing it — not if you want to win! You must always have the end goal or exit strategy in mind before you start sourcing the right property for that strategy — and certainly before you actually *buy* any property.

That's because the way you develop the property will depend entirely on your chosen end goal. An apartment that's going to be rented to students or low-income-housing tenants will probably be developed very differently from one that's aimed at young professionals. Students and low-income-housing tenants will expect lower-spec fixtures, fittings, and appliances, for example; students need desks in their bedrooms; you'll want to put in cheaper carpets that can be replaced more regularly; and so on.

Likewise, if you're developing a house, is it going to be sold as a family home, or is each bedroom going to be rented out individually (see Chapter 13 on HMOs)? If it's the latter, for example, you can convert the dining room into an extra bedroom to maximize your rental income. But if it's going to be sold as a family home, you'll need that dining room.

TIP

Make sure you're clear on your end goal before you source the right property. Almost every decision you make from here — project finances, layout of the property, overall finish, presenting the property, and so on — will be impacted by the exit strategy.

Looking at the main exit options

As you may have guessed, your main exit options are

>> **Selling the property outright:** This option may work for you if you're looking to generate capital growth or cash in the equity gain you've added in a relatively short space of time. Be sure to talk to your financial advisor about the tax implications of selling the property and pocketing the profit.

>> **Holding onto the property and renting it out for longer-term income:** This option in itself can be divided into many different options, such as running the property as an HMO (see Chapter 13), renting to young professionals, renting to students or low-income-housing tenants (see Chapter 14), providing serviced accommodation (see Chapter 15), or running it as a vacation rental if it's in a desirable vacation spot (see Chapter 16).

TIP

Even if you're looking to free up capital for future real estate projects, you don't necessarily need to sell the property. You can retain the property as an investment (renting it out to earn an income), and refinance or release equity (if there is enough of it) to free up capital for other projects.

Weighing which option is right for you

Which specific strategy is best suited to you as an investor? Only you can answer that question, but here are my tips for weighing your options.

>> **Identify your passion.** What interests you? If retaining and managing properties really isn't your bag, then turning developments around for sale is likely to be more suitable for you.

>> **Think about your goals as an investor and as an individual.** Find out how goals impact your investment decisions in Chapter 2, and turn to Chapter 5 for tips on how to identify and commit to your goals.

>> **If you're going to be renting out the property, consider what sort of target audience you really want to work with.** If I'm being honest, providing accommodation for student or low-income-housing tenants doesn't really appeal to me, and it's not something I've spent a lot of my time on. But maybe you're passionate about providing comfortable and affordable accommodation to people in need. Or maybe after years in education, you know the student market really well and you're ideally placed to meet the needs of student renters. When you really know your market, you're in the best possible position to tailor your product to that market.

REMEMBER

There's money to be made in each exit option and each real estate strategy. The key is to pick the right path for *you*, and play to *your* passion, *your* interests, and *your* strengths.

Keeping your target audience in mind

The best products are those that are tailored to their audience, designed firmly with the end user in mind. So, in real estate, just as in business, offering a product that's too generic can be a big mistake. In other words, developing a property so it appeals to lots of different audiences can lead to it falling between the cracks and not appealing to anyone.

Having decided on your strategy, you need to think about who the property is going to be aimed at. Whether you're selling it or renting it out at the end of the development, who is your intended audience? Who will be pulling up in the moving truck, hanging their hats in the hallway, and unpacking their boxes in the kitchen? A family with children (or a couple aspiring to have children in the near future)? Or busy young professionals who'll be sharing the space?

TIP

If you aren't sure which target audience is right for you, and you don't have a passion for a particular demographic, try talking to local sales agents and rental agents to get a feel for what's hot and what's not in your area. Talk to at least five local agents (always gather a range of opinions rather than rely on one or two) and ask each of them about the biggest target market in the local area. You can also look at demographic data, such as the local town or city's website and national demographic statistics.

REMEMBER

Like your overarching strategy, your target audience will inform lots of decisions you make along the way, from how many bedrooms your property should have to what sort of flooring is most appropriate. So, it's important to immerse yourself in your chosen target market and do plenty of research to understand your audience's needs.

First things first: View plenty of similar local properties that are aimed at the same target audience (whether that's family homes, apartment shares, student rentals, or whatever). Then, try to answer the following questions:

>> **How big does the overall property and individual rooms need to be to satisfy that market?** For instance, do busy young professionals who are addicted to the Grubhub app on their phones really need that big fancy kitchen?

>> **How many rooms do you need?** A desirable family home, for example, will need ample dining space and more than one bathroom. Don't forget outside space, too.

>> **What sort of specification and finish does your audience expect?** Will they expect stainless steel appliances and marble countertops, or do they not really care what the refrigerator looks like as long as it keeps the beer and leftover pizza cold?

>> **What sort of sale or rental price can you expect?**

>> **What's the best location for your audience?**

Giving yourself multiple exit options

Plans change. Circumstances shift. And markets can never be counted on to stay the same. So, although you should absolutely pick an exit strategy and target audience and work toward that end goal, it's also a good idea to have a backup plan in mind. Having a backup plan reduces your risk and gives you flexibility in case your circumstances change or the market shifts.

WARNING

Giving yourself multiple exit options makes good business sense in any scenario. But if you're investing with other people's money (OPM), it's especially important to ensure that you have a backup exit option in mind. After all, you have a responsibility not to lose your investor's money! If you want to cultivate strong relationships with investors and build a sound reputation as a developer, don't let yourself get caught out by unforeseen circumstances. You can find more on investing with OPM in Chapter 8.

So, what do I mean by a backup exit option? Say your intended goal is to sell the property for a profit. If your local real estate market takes a nosedive, you want to have the option of retaining the property and renting it out, thereby earning a stable income until the market recovers. That's your backup exit strategy.

Just as with your primary exit goal, you'll need to keep your backup plan in mind from the project's early stages. That way, you can develop the property in a way that works for either scenario and keep your options open. If you need to go back and make expensive changes down the line because your primary strategy is no longer applicable, your profit will be hit hard.

TIP

Unless I'm specifically targeting students and low-income-housing tenants, I tend to develop properties to a fairly high specification — so, that means nice kitchens and bathrooms, high-quality materials throughout, and so on. It's a spec that works for the goal of selling the property, but it will also attract quality tenants in case I need to rent the property out for a while. Although this approach costs more, I've found that it's worth the slightly higher spend to reduce my overall risk. Instead of making the mistake of not developing for a specific target market and creating a product that doesn't really appeal to any buyer, I *am* developing for that specific target market *but* with an alternative exit option as a backup — and those are two very different things.

Sourcing Development Opportunities

Whether you're developing to sell or developing to rent, sourcing the right property in the right location is a critical part of success. Source the wrong type of property (or an otherwise good property in the wrong location), and it doesn't matter how much value you add or how beautiful the finished product is — you may struggle to sell or rent it out at the price you want.

Assessing the property itself

When it comes to the property you buy, regardless of your end goal and the type of property you're looking for, what you're ultimately looking for is an opportunity to add value.

REMEMBER

Great opportunities to add value can be found in

>> Properties that haven't been well maintained or are generally unloved, perhaps because they've stood vacant for a while or have elderly owners.

>> Properties that are cosmetically dated but otherwise structurally sound (so a fresh coat of paint, new flooring, and new kitchen and bathrooms would work wonders) — you'd be amazed how many potential buyers can't see past the cosmetic features of a property.

>> Properties where the internal space can be reconfigured to better suit modern life (for example, turning two small pokey rooms into one light, airy open-plan space).

>> Smaller properties that have the potential to be extended, either by converting a loft or garage, or with space and planning precedent to expand the footprint.

>> Properties that aren't really suitable for the local demographic, where there's an opportunity to change its use (for example, by turning a large single house in a city center into separate apartments).

When you're just starting out, look for factors that may lower the value of a property — meaning you have a better chance of buying it at an attractive price — but that aren't huge, scary issues. A dark, unappealing kitchen can easily be brightened up with a coat of paint, large doors that open onto the garden, and new appliances. But a massive subsidence issue? That's not an easy, quick, and, crucially, inexpensive fix.

Deciding on the right location

Regardless of your end goal, choosing the right location is all about your target market.

REMEMBER

In addition to looking at the property itself, you must assess its location and how suitable it is for your intended audience. So, if your end goal is to sell a high-end family home, then a townhouse on a busy, inner-city street, with no off-road parking and no garden is unlikely to attract a premium price among that target audience — even if your end product is stunning. However, a quieter out-of-town location, with good local schools, is likely to be much more attractive.

On the flip side, young professionals may be turned off by that out-of-town location, particularly if there's not much in the way of nightlife and transport options. You're better off opting for a city-center location, or an affordable, up-and-coming location on the city's outskirts that has plenty to do and great transport links.

Finding the best properties (before anyone else)

There are two main ways to find great properties that are ripe for development and beat your competitors to the punch:

>> Sourcing properties through agents

>> Sourcing properties yourself

Sourcing properties through agents

Picture this scenario: A local sales agent has a great property come her way — it's structurally sound, in a good location, but in need of some refurbishment. Sure, she can advertise that property on the open market, and spend hours shuffling around behind time-wasters on viewings. Or she can call up one of her contacts, a serious local developer who she knows is actively seeking opportunities like this. If her contact is interested, the agent benefits from a quick sale (which is good for her reputation) and an easy commission.

That developer contact she calls? You want that person to be you.

REMEMBER

You really want to be sourcing properties *off-market* (before the property is advertised to the wider market). That way, you avoid going up against other buyers (particularly competitive developers like yourself), and you don't end up in a bidding war. If you're the first person an agent calls, you get a head start.

So, how can you get local agents to put your number on speed dial?

>> Get to know the agents in your target area.

>> Make it clear the types of properties you're looking for and in what sort of areas.

>> Spend time cultivating your relationships with agents and regularly touch base to ensure you stay at the front of their minds.

>> Build a good reputation and track record for yourself as an investor. Prove you can commit to deals and complete deals, so they know your word is good and you're no time-waster.

>> You could even offer a referral fee to get agents calling you before something goes on the market.

TIP

In addition to local real estate agents, there are lots of other professionals who can give you valuable property leads. Local architects, accountants, financial advisors, building contractors . . . all may know someone with a property to sell. You can always offer introducers a finder's fee for deals that pan out.

And if all else fails, you can employ someone to act as a buyer's agent for you, which means she'll actively go out and source properties just for you. Find out more about buyer's agents in Chapter 10.

Sourcing properties yourself

This is by far my preferred method for sourcing properties off-market. Most of my best deals have come from properties I've sourced directly myself.

In the world of property, pretty much everything is for sale. It just depends on the price and the terms and whether the deal is viable or not. So, if you've always had your eye on that neglected house in the neighborhood, even if it's not up for sale, the owners may still be open to doing a deal.

Here are my favorite ways to source properties directly:

>> **Identify specific properties that are of interest to you, and contact the owners to see if they'd be willing to sell.** If the owner lives in the property, you can drop off a letter or simply knock on the door to strike up a conversation. If the owner doesn't live in the property, you can either ask the tenants who the landlord is or ask them to pass on your contact details. Alternatively, you can look at government land registration data to find out who owns the property.

>> **If there's a particular area or street with plenty of suitable properties, you can put flyers on telephone poles saying that you're looking to buy property in the area.** The following text can be adapted for this:

> I'm a private investor looking to purchase three-bedroom houses in the Farm Park area. If you're thinking of selling your property, avoid expensive agent fees, and come to us direct for a quick sale at full market value. Contact Wallwork Property at 01234 56789 or email info@wallworkproperty1234. com for more information.

>> **Place an ad in the local newspaper or shops to generate leads using wording similar to that listed in the preceding bullet.**

Having identified a suitable property and made contact with the owner, you then need to approach him with a well-considered offer for the property.

Do your research to work out the market value of the property (see Chapter 7 for more on valuation), but keep in mind that if you're going to be adding value and making money on the property, you may be able to pay a little more than market value. That would certainly sweeten the deal for the seller and perhaps help make him consider selling now, as would the prospect of cutting out real estate agents and saving on fees!

When sourcing properties yourself, you really need to look like a professional investor, not some random weirdo turning up on the doorstep. This means having a proper website, letterhead, business email address, and business cards. It's difficult to get people to take you seriously if you don't come off as a pro.

Financing Your Development Projects

In Chapter 6, I looked at the main, traditional financing options, such as mortgages. One of the key options for development projects is development finance.

Understanding how development financing works

Development loans are a good option for property developers, because these kinds of products not only help you fund the original purchase (whether that's land or a property in need of refurbishment), but also provide finance to carry out the refurbishment or construction.

Looking under the hood of development financing

REMEMBER

Like a regular mortgage, development finance is basically a secured loan. However, unlike a standard mortgage, development finance typically breaks down into two portions:

>> **A land loan,** which contributes to the original purchase, whether it's land or a run-down property — at the time of writing, a standard loan-to-value (LTV) ratio on these types of loans is around 50 percent of the value, but some specialist providers will go up to around 70 percent to 75 percent.

>> **A development loan,** which covers the cost of the refurbishment work or construction — depending on the provider, you may be able to get up to 100 percent of the cost of the development/construction funded.

You can usually get both portions from the same lender, although you should explore all your options to see whether it works out better to get one portion from one lender and the other from a different provider. Development finance is available through some traditional lenders, as well as specialist providers, and a good independent broker will be able to help you assess the merits of different providers across the whole market.

WARNING

It's important to note that fees and interest rates on development finance are usually higher than they would be on a standard mortgage, which makes sense because the risk is higher for the lender. To further manage their risks, some lenders may ask you to provide details of your development experience, or demonstrate that you have an experienced team in place. Sometimes further security is required, such as a personal guarantee. Always take professional advice to help weigh the risks of any particular loan based on your own deal and personal circumstances.

Getting your hands on the development funds

REMEMBER

The development or construction part of the loan is almost always drawn down in stages. In other words, the lender doesn't hand over a check for $50,000 and send you skipping off to complete your development. You'll get the money in installments, in arrears, as you complete certain phases of the build or refurbishment project. Critically, these installments will only be paid out if the project is on track.

So, in essence, with development finance, you're funding the building work yourself upfront, and the lender pays you back after you've completed various stages.

Naturally, this means you must maintain a tight hold on both your project schedule and your cash flow. And it also means you should be prepared for your lender to monitor progress on your project closely, possibly sending out an official surveyor or valuer to conduct site visits at regular intervals.

WARNING

With development finance, cash flow is king! You need to be really on your game when it comes to managing your build, keeping in mind when exactly money will be paid to you. Many development projects stall because the developer runs out of cash and can't afford to pay the builder to complete the next phase. Yet, the lender won't release the next installment of money until that phase is completed. It's a nightmare, catch-22 situation, and one that you never want to find yourself in.

Knowing whether you need a development loan

If your development project is relatively small and doesn't require a big budget, then a development loan may not be the best option for you.

REMEMBER

Because development loans come with higher fees and interest rates, you'll need to consider whether it makes more financial sense to go for a regular mortgage, rather than a development loan.

If yours is a larger development that will take quite a sizeable spend, or if you're building from scratch on a plot of land, then a development loan will almost certainly be the best option for you. However, on smaller projects, it's less clear cut.

Always shop around and work with a good broker to consider all your options. He'll be able to advise you on the best way forward based on the amount of money you're looking to raise and the type of project you have in mind.

TIP

As a basic rule of thumb, I'd say projects with a development cost of less than $33,000 (about £25,000 at the time of writing) are probably better suited to a regular mortgage. That's because a regular mortgage will cost you less in fees and interest than a development loan — and with that sort of budget, it's relatively easy to finance the development cost yourself or through other more traditional forms of finance.

Looking at other ways to fund your development projects

If development finance isn't right for your project, or if you're unable to secure a regular mortgage (for example, if your property is unusual or you're employing a niche strategy), then you'll want to look at other alternatives for funding your development.

These include

>> **Releasing equity from property you already own.**

>> **Using personal savings:** This is usually only an option for funding the build costs rather than the purchase, unless you're a Rockefeller!

>> **Using personal loans or credit cards:** This is an expensive way of paying for building work, but it's one that many developers have called upon at one time or another. Just keep in mind that it's best as a short-term measure only, due to the higher interest rates involved.

>> **Turning to private lending or a joint venture:** Private lending could come from an investor or from friends and family. In a joint venture, you generally enter into a more formal business arrangement with an investor. See Chapter 8 for more on both these options.

WARNING

>> **Bridge loans:** Bridge loans are expensive, and they're only really for investors who are very confident in their business model and their own ability to complete the project successfully and on time. But if other avenues are closed to you, a bridge loan can provide a useful temporary option until you can complete the development and refinance through more regular means. Turn to Chapter 6 for more on bridge loans.

Working out how much it's going to cost

You have to work out your budget carefully before you secure finance. How much it's all going to cost will inform both the amount of finance you need and which type of finance is most appropriate.

At a very basic level, your budget will break down into three areas:

>> **The cost of buying the property:** Don't forget to include all the ancillary costs involved in the purchase, like legal and other professional fees, and taxes. In the United Kingdom, stamp duty can really add up on a project, and in the United States, the so-called "mansion tax" equals 1 percent on properties sold for $1 million or more.

>> **How much it will cost to develop the property:** There's more on development costs coming up next.

>> **The estimated value of the property (either in terms of sales price or rental income) when the development is completed:** To gauge this, you'll need to thoroughly research your local market to see what similar properties, done to a similar spec, are selling for.

Figuring out what improvements are needed

Many properties simply require a light spruce to make them more attractive to prospective buyers. So, if the property has been a little neglected, redecorating can be enough to add value. But even with a simple project like this, it's still important to budget carefully.

REMEMBER

If the property needs a little more work than that, you'll want to focus your budget (and your time) on those improvements that will add the most value. After all, you're not going to be living in the property, and buyers will inevitably want to put their own stamp on the place, so there's no point spending time and money on nonessential upgrades.

Value–adding improvements to prioritize tend to include the following:

>> Fitting new kitchen cabinets and upgrading the appliances

>> Installing a new bathroom suite (or simply retiling to make a bathroom look fresh and new)

>> Adding new features that are particularly desirable right now, like French doors that open onto the garden

>> Landscaping the backyard (this can be as simple as tidying it up and replacing dead plants)

>> Improving the curb appeal at the front of the property (for example, installing a new front door, adding attractive landscaping, and freshly painting the exterior)

>> Creating off-road parking, where possible

TIP

Over time, as your experience grows, you'll be able to ballpark these figures yourself when viewing a property. But if you're just starting out, it's a good idea to have a builder accompany you on viewings to get a rough idea of costs. You'll get more detailed quotes further down the line (see the next section "Managing the Development"). For now, you just need a good enough idea to sort out your financing.

Managing the Development

You've sourced a promising property, you've arranged appropriate financing, and you're ready to start your project. So, what now? In this section, I look at what's involved in getting a development project underway and bringing it to a successful conclusion.

Knowing where you need professional help

You can't do it all yourself. Even if you're an extremely skilled jack-of-all-trades, personally handling every element of the build or refurbishment is probably not the best use of your time — not if you want to really grow as an investor and build multiple income streams (see Chapter 3).

You'll need professional help if you're going to complete the project on time, on budget, and to a high standard. The key professionals you'll likely work with are

>> Architect and/or planning consultant

>> Project manager

>> Building contractor and tradespeople

TIP

Successfully managing development projects is about building a great dream team around you, and ideally that same team will work with you on many projects to come. Turn to Chapter 3 for more on building and nurturing your dream team.

Working with an architect and/or planning consultant

If your project is a straightforward refurbishment, with no structural changes and no changes to the footprint of the building, then you probably won't need to hire an architect or planning consultant.

REMEMBER

However, if your project is more complex than that, you'll want to employ an architect to turn your vision into detailed drawings and plans. On large or complex projects, it's vital to have accurate drawings done before you start work — builders need drawings to work from, after all (and, in many cases, they won't even be able to give an accurate quote for the work until they've seen the plans).

Depending on the scale of your project, the types of drawings/plans that you may need include

>> **Existing and proposed floorplans for the interior.**

>> **Mechanical and electrical (M&E) drawings for the design and installation of plumbing, electrical, and other main services:** This is often as detailed as how many sockets will be in each room, what sort of lights you want in each room, location of switches, how many lights are needed in each room, and so on.

>> **Exterior elevations (again, existing and proposed), showing the features and design of the property's exterior and what changes are to be carried out there.**

If the changes you're making to the property require planning permission, you'll need to work with a planning consultant, or for more simple applications hire an architect who can work with you to apply for the appropriate permissions.

Working with a project manager

The project manager is the person who'll oversee the project as a whole, booking tradespeople and generally keeping the project moving along as it should.

When you're just starting out, you may prefer to act as your own project manager. That's what I did for my first few builds because I wanted to be more hands-on and learn about property development from the inside.

WARNING

Managing a big project can be a full-time job, so you'll need to weigh the pros (saving money, learning opportunities, and so on) and cons (time pressures, inexperience, sleepless nights!) of doing it yourself. As you get more established and take on more complex or larger projects, it's certainly worth hiring a professional project manager so you can concentrate on building your business.

Read more about keeping the project on track later in the chapter.

Working with builders and tradespeople

If your project is a fairly straightforward refurb, then you may prefer to complete some of the work yourself. You may, for instance, have a passion for landscaping or love decorating. If so, that's fine. But there will no doubt be areas where you need professional help. Structural changes, plumbing, and electrical should always be left to the pros, for instance — not least because they'll be insured for any blunders!

REMEMBER

When it comes to sourcing good builders and tradespeople, the basic rules for any dream team member apply (see Chapter 3). Word-of-mouth recommendations are a great way to source good people, but you should still check out reviews of the company online and ask to see some of their previous projects. If you're employing a project manager, he'll be able to help or manage this process for you. Your architect may also be able to recommend good contractors.

When it comes to organizing the practical building/trades stuff, you have two options to choose from:

>> **Work with a master or managing contractor, who'll run the build and manage all the subcontractors (plumbers, electricians, and so on) from start to finish.** You'll pay more for the privilege (perhaps as much as 10 percent or 20 percent more), and you won't learn as much about the development process, but you'll benefit from the master contractor's experience and knowledge (provided he's reputable and good!), and you'll have more time to concentrate on growing your business.

>> **You (or your project manager) employ separate builders and tradespeople for every element of the project, sourcing, booking, and overseeing the work yourself.** This can save quite a bit of money and is certainly a good way to learn about property development, but it can suck up a lot of your time.

As your portfolio grows and you take on more and more development projects, you'll build a team and find a method that works for you. I now have an excellent and proven dream team of project managers, external master contractors, and smaller tradespeople to call upon at any one time, depending on the scale and specifics of the project at hand. It's taken a while and I've had my fair share of poor-quality people, but it's worth it in the end.

Creating a detailed budget

You'll have had a ballpark development cost in mind when deciding on the project and seeking finance, but now's the time to really flesh out the details and create a thorough budget.

Pulling together costs

If you can build for less, that's more profit for you. So always shop around and get three different quotes for every substantial element of the project to find the best deal for you. Doing the legwork at this stage can really add value for you further down the line. Don't be afraid to try to negotiate a discount either!

The nitty-gritty of your budget will depend on the scale of the project and the specification that you're going for in terms of fixtures and fittings (which, in turn, will depend on your end goal and target audience), so there's no real rule of thumb to follow. However, to give you an idea of the types of costs to consider and budget for, Table 9-1 shows an example cost breakdown for the conversion of a large family home into a large multi-tenant HMO.

TABLE 9-1

Example Cost Breakdown for a Refurbishment Project

Item	Cost
Mains services connections (possible upgrades)	£1,100
Demolition, site preparation, and strip out	£800
Enabling works, ground works	£650
Waste disposal, including skips	£1,800
Drainage installation and upgrades	£750
Roof work and repairs, including guttering	£650
Carpentry, first fix	£1,750
Plumbing, first fix	£6,250
Electrical, first fix	£4,500
Fire alarm, first fix	£2,250
CCTV (more common for larger or commercial sites)	£1,500
Broadband Internet/phone line installation (often included in electrical)	£350
Drywall/plasterboarding	£2,500
Plastering	£2,300
Insulation (wall, ceiling, and floor, including acoustic flooring)	£3,250
Bathroom(s)/en suite(s) supply and fit	£5,500
Kitchen(s) supply and fit	£3,450
Carpentry, second fix	£2,500

Item	Cost
Plumbing, second fix	£2,500
Electrical, second fix	£3,250
Fire alarm second fix and fire protection measures	£750
Ironmongery supply and fit	£1,475
Windows (replacement or refurbishment)	£3,250
Painting and decorating	£4,100
Fixtures and fittings	£4,350
Exterior garden/landscaping works	£400
Bike and bin storage creation (often a planning requirement)	£850
Carpet supply and fit	£1,800
Appliances (oven[s], washing machine[s], dishwasher[s], etc.)	£2,250
Furniture (if being rented or sold furnished)	£4,500
Builders clean	£400
Contingency (about 10%)	£7,173
Total development cost	**£78,898**

Note: All costs are simplified to include labor and materials, although for further accuracy, these two elements should also be separated. All costs will vary depending on the type and size of your own project.

If you're planning on doing more developments in the future, it's well worth signing up for trade accounts with key suppliers of materials. It'll save you money (trade customers often get better prices than regular retail customers), and you'll get more favorable payment terms.

Building in a contingency

It's clear that you'll need to monitor your cash flow extremely well throughout the project, particularly if you're funding the project through development finance because you'll need to plan carefully for loan installments. But it also helps to build a contingency fund into your development budget at the outset.

The appropriate contingency depends on the scale of the project, the budget, and your risk profile. Ultimately, the bigger the contingency, the better, certainly in your early days, but 10 percent to 15 percent is a fairly standard rule of thumb. As you grow in confidence and experience, you may find you can get away with a smaller contingency of around 5 percent to 10 percent, especially on smaller sites. It's a trade-off between using the cash available wisely (because you'll likely be paying interest on it!) and maintaining a safety buffer for unforeseen circumstances or delays. For larger projects I tend to keep a larger buffer.

Creating a realistic schedule

In addition to creating a detailed budget, you'll also need to create a detailed schedule that shows the different stages and trades involved, how long each stage will take, and when it's supposed to take place. Figure 9-1 shows an example schedule for the same conversion discussed earlier, of a large family home into a multi-tenant HMO.

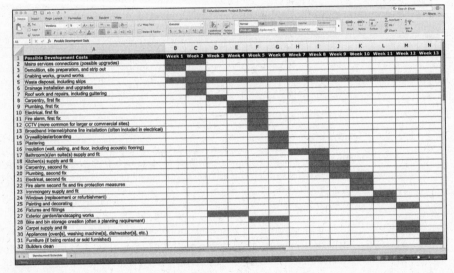

FIGURE 9-1: Example schedule for a refurbishment project.

There's a natural order to the work flow on a typical project, as illustrated in the example schedule. As a very obvious example, a plasterer can only come and do his thing after the walls have been built!

As you get quotes from builders and tradespeople, be sure to ask them how long they'll need to complete the work, but also ask them what needs to have been completed before they can start. This will inform the order of work and your overall schedule. Learning how the trades work together and overlap each other is a key part of successfully project managing a real estate development.

Microsoft Project is a really useful tool for planning a project schedule. In addition, I like to pad out or overestimate each stage ever so slightly to build that little bit of contingency into my schedules. You may want to do the same.

Communicating to keep the project on track

After the project is up and running, you or your project manager will need to keep a close eye on the project from start to finish.

Good communication is key to keeping a project on track. So, if one part of your project is running slightly behind schedule, and that means your plumber may have to delay his work by a week, you need to keep that plumber (and any other future trades) informed as you go.

The last thing you want is to lose good tradespeople because delays or changes to the schedule haven't been properly communicated. Similarly, if anything changes about the plans or specifications for the work (not ideal, but it does occasionally happen), you need to be informing everyone who needs to know as early as possible.

Most projects are a fluid process, and it's not uncommon for timing and costs to shift slightly as the project progresses. Therefore, it's vital that you continually communicate with your team and continually monitor and update your budget and schedule as you go along.

Preparing the property for sale or rent

Whether you're selling or renting the property, you want to present an attractive finished product that's perfectly tailored to your target audience. Most buyers (and renters, for that matter) will look at multiple properties before they make a decision, so you want your property to stand out from the crowd and make a great impression.

Selling buyers on a lifestyle, as well as a property

Before you list the property, consider *staging* or *dressing* the property to make it attractive. This means temporarily furnishing the property so it looks like a home rather than an empty property.

Dressing a property is an additional cost to factor into your budget, but it's usually money well spent. In my experience, it's much harder to sell an unfurnished property because people struggle to visualize how they'd use and live in an empty space. But when the property is beautifully dressed, you're painting a compelling picture of what it's like to live there. In essence, you're selling a lifestyle as much as a property — which, again means you absolutely need to know your target audience and what would appeal to them.

If you have zero flair for design, consider connecting with an interior designer as part of your dream team. Particularly if she specializes in presenting properties for sale, she'll have useful contacts for renting furniture at a good price, which cuts down the expense and hassle for you.

For larger projects, you may be looking to sell off-plan (before the project is completed). In this case, it's well worth having good-quality computer-generated imagery (CGI) drawn up to help prospective buyers visualize the end result. And if it's a multi-unit development, you could complete one unit first and present it as a "show home."

If you're renting out the property

For a rental property, you have the option of renting it out furnished or unfurnished. There are pros and cons to both, but in my experience tenants generally prefer the simplicity of a furnished property. You can also charge more in rent if the property is simply ready to move into.

One option may be to furnish the property but offer prospective tenants the choice to rent the property with or without the furniture. That way, you're able to market the property to a wider audience, and you get to present the property in a more attractive way (like buyers, renters like to see furniture in a space because it helps them visualize living in the property).

Five International Locations Where This Strategy Would Work

Development opportunities exist all over the world, making it hard to pinpoint certain locations over and above others.

In a way, the specific country, region, or city doesn't really matter. What's more important is that there's a strong demand for quality, developed property among your target audience.

Having said that, the following locations are enticing developers in my network and beyond:

>> **Spain:** A perennially popular choice, particularly among British investors.

>> **Dubai:** This high-end city in the United Arab Emirates has piqued my interest, but the rapid pace and scale of development means it's not for the fainthearted.

>> **Panama:** Popular with North American investors, Panama's strengths include affordable sale prices and a strong rental market, particularly in Panama City.

>> **United Kingdom:** Even in very mature property markets like Britain, development opportunities abound.

>> **United States:** Likewise, the U.S. property market is still rife with development gems. Focus on the fringes of bigger town or cities where prices are still sensible, but they're shortly going to benefit from their proximity to these already strong areas. Good transport links is also key to almost any real estate investment.

TIP

Focus on areas where you have a deep knowledge of the local market, with a target audience that you know well. These markets will always provide your best opportunities to be competitive and really add value.

Chapter **10**

Dealing in Property Information

I nvesting in real estate can sometimes feel like the old chicken-and-egg conundrum. You may find a great deal, but not have the capital to invest at that time. Similarly, you may have trouble getting people to invest in you (see Chapter 8) if you're unable to demonstrate your real estate credentials — yet, without tons of your own cash, you can't build up your expertise and experience unless people are willing to invest in you. Chicken and egg, see?

What's a cash-strapped but ambitious real estate investor to do? One option is to forget buying and selling the properties yourself (at least for now), and instead focus on trading in property information. What if you're already an experienced investor? Well, dealing in property leads can be a lucrative additional income stream worth considering.

REMEMBER

When you trade in investment property leads, you're essentially bringing together people who have an investment property to sell and people who want to buy that sort of property. As a strategy, it's ideal for anyone looking to be more hands-on and learn about the real estate industry firsthand. And, best of all, it requires very little capital to get started.

I know what you're thinking: "Isn't this just the same as being a real estate agent or broker?" The honest answer is, well, sort of. But as you read on, you'll discover that dealing in specific investment property leads is much more niche and specialized than what the average real estate agent does.

In this chapter, I set out what's involved in trading in real estate investment leads, and explore the two main ways to make money through property information.

Dealing in Investment Property Leads: The Five-Minute Lowdown

If you think about it, what's a real estate agent's product? What is he selling? He's selling property information. He attracts sellers who have a property they want to sell, and then markets that property to potential buyers. However, dealing in specific investment real estate *leads* isn't the same as becoming a traditional real estate agent (if that's your bag, turn to Chapter 18 for more real-estate-themed career paths).

There are obvious similarities:

>> As someone who sells property leads, you're essentially facilitating property deals behind the scenes.

>> You bring sellers and buyers together, and earn a commission for your troubles.

However, there are major differences:

>> Most real estate agents deal with all sorts of residential or commercial property, and some cover both sales and rentals.

>> When you trade in real estate leads, your focus is purely on sales of *investment properties.* Your aim is to find great deals that will appeal to other investors — people like yourself who are looking to make money through real estate. In this way, it's a bit like being a really, really niche real estate agent but with added knowledge around the investment side of things.

How does it work?

There are two key ways to deal in property information. At first glance, they look similar — indeed, they're closely related and, for many real estate entrepreneurs, one route tends to lead onto the other — but there are important differences.

The two routes are:

>> **Becoming a property finder or sourcer (not to be confused with a sorcerer or saucer, both very different things):** As a property sourcer, you start with the leads themselves (meaning you find people who want to sell their investment property), and then you try to market those leads to interested investors.

>> **Becoming a retained buyer's agent:** Crucially, a buyer's agent starts with the buyer, not the leads. So, you first find someone who's looking to invest in real estate, and then you go out and source the ideal investment property or properties for your client.

As you can see, the biggest difference is whether you start with the potential deals (properties for sale) or the buyer. How you go about sourcing the leads may differ depending on which role you're performing.

Generally, you start out on the sourcing side, purely because it's difficult to secure a gig as a retained buyer's agent when you're inexperienced and unproven. So, if this is your first foray into property leads, I recommend you focus on becoming an investment property sourcer in the first instance.

How can you progress from an investment property sourcer to a retained buyer's agent?

Over time, as you facilitate more and more deals, you may find yourself dealing with the same investor a couple of times. Then, one day, she may ask you to find a specific type of property especially for her. Bingo! You've secured your first client as a retained buyer's agent.

However, rather than ditch your role as a property sourcer at the first whiff of a retained contract, you may prefer to do a combination of the two roles. For example, you may have one or two clients for whom you act as a retained buyer's agent, but still continue to source other property leads on the side. This can be a great way to diversify your revenue stream (see Chapter 4 for why diversifying and creating multiple streams of income is important).

As markets shift and fluctuate, there are times when it's easier to find the deals, but less easy to find buyers. Other times, lots of investors are looking to pile into real estate, but it's not so easy to find the right deals because it's a booming market and all the best deals attract stiff competition. In this way, a blended approach can be a good way of riding out market fluctuations and keeping the income coming in.

Note that, in the United States, a buyer's agent is a licensed real estate salesperson and is, therefore, subject to formal accreditation, whereas in the UK, anyone with the contacts and skills can act as a buyer's agent. Always check the professional requirements for your part of the world. You may need to take an accredited course and sit an exam before you can act as a licensed real estate salesperson.

Is this strategy right for you?

Working as a property sourcer or retained buyer's agent presents some big advantages for aspiring real estate investors:

>> It's a great entry into real estate, allowing you to get to know your chosen market from the inside.

>> There's minimal startup capital required — all you really need is time, effort, ambition, and a willingness to learn.

>> You can operate from home, usually at times that suit you.

>> You'll become practiced at sourcing properties, identifying fantastic opportunities, and working out which deals are a good value — which stands you in great stead if you want to make your own investments in the future.

>> Over time, you'll build up a history of facilitating deals for buyers and sellers, and this track record may help you secure investment for your own projects in the future.

>> You'll also learn how to work with agents, sellers, and buyers successfully, build yourself a solid network of contacts, and learn how to market properties — all of which will help you in the future, if you move onto other real estate strategies.

>> It's a particularly good stepping stone to property development (see Chapter 9), because you'll quickly learn to spot great deals and have a readymade network of potential buyers.

But is it the right strategy for *you*? Perhaps a better question to ask yourself is, "Am I the right person for this strategy?"

Whether you're a property sourcer or a retained buyer's agent, or both for that matter, there are some key ingredients to success. So, if you already have or are willing to develop the following skills and characteristic, then there's a good chance that dealing in property information will be a great strategy for you:

>> **Good communication and networking skills:** You need to present yourself to both buyers and sellers as someone who can help them get the job done, and be great at building and maintaining useful connections.

>> **Boundless enthusiasm and willingness to put in the hours:** Particularly in the early days of sourcing leads, you'll probably need to spend a lot of time pounding the streets and doing your homework to find the right properties.

>> **Deep understanding of your chosen niche market:** You can find more on the importance of finding your niche later in the chapter.

>> **Awesome sales skills:** Selling yourself, selling leads, going all out to secure great deals for your clients . . . if you thrive on "doing deals," you'll absolutely love this strategy.

TIP

Dealing in property leads can be a useful first step into other real estate strategies, but it's not necessarily a temporary stopgap. Plenty of real estate entrepreneurs become very successful just through selling property leads, and it becomes their full-time, long-term business focus. In fact, I still own a business that acts as a niche investment agency and buyer's agency. It's a useful additional revenue stream in my portfolio, and it provides all sorts of excellent leads and opportunities for my other development companies. This agency also acts as my development company's main agent selling on our own developed investment sites, so it's a very valuable addition to my group's overall expertise and offering.

Generating and Selling Property Leads

There are two clear sides to being a property sourcer: First, you find the property leads; then you market those properties to potential buyers. In this section, I look at both aspects. But before you dive into the nitty-gritty of sourcing and marketing properties, there are some key questions to address:

>> What types of properties are you going to source — in other words, what's your niche?

>> How can you create value for your clients and differentiate yourself from the average traditional real estate agent?

>> How does the financial model work?

Let's look at each question in turn.

Finding your niche

Before you start trying to source properties, you first need to identify what specific type of properties you want to source so that you can really immerse yourself in that market. Dealing in property leads is a bit like becoming a super-niche real estate agent. *Niche* is the key word there.

You can always expand your area of expertise as your experience grows but, to start with, being niche is a good idea. It's easier to build your expertise and contacts when you have a laserlike focus on a specific market. It's also easier to focus your time and efforts and establish your reputation.

To find your niche, think about where your passion, interest, and expertise lie. For example, you may want to specialize in finding student properties that would make a lucrative investment for investors. Or maybe you like the idea of sourcing properties that would make great holiday rentals. The chapters throughout Parts 3 and 4 of this book set out some of the key strategies investors are interested in, so you may want to use these as inspiration.

If a certain strategy appeals to you, you can narrow down to the best location to source those types of properties. Ask yourself: Where's the best place to find the kind of properties I have in mind? So, taking student accommodation as an example, you can look at cities with a large student population or explore universities that are growing fast.

Perhaps, if you want to focus your efforts in your local town (as opposed to exploring other locations), you can flip the process and ask yourself: What's the best strategy to deploy in my chosen area? In that case, you could talk to local agents to unearth the most in-demand properties in your area.

In my view, education and knowledge should always come before action (circle back to Chapter 5 for more on real estate education). So, take your time to get to know your chosen market before you start properly sourcing properties. You can immerse yourself in your chosen niche by

>> **Viewing similar properties already on the market, just to get a feel for what makes a good deal and what doesn't.**

>> **Trawling property listings online, again to get a feel for available properties and their value:** The more you do this, the easier it becomes to spot a great opportunity when you see one. See Chapter 7 for more on valuing properties effectively.

>> **Getting to know local agents marketing the types of property you have in mind:** Talk to them about what properties they have on their books right now, and any current trends they've noticed.

>> **Doing your research on supply and demand in your chosen market:** For example, if the university is growing, are there enough student properties to go around? Is the university rapidly building its own housing for new students or are students left to fend for themselves in the local rental market?

Creating value for your clients by facilitating off-market deals

The Internet has revolutionized property sales, and most of us have whiled away many hours looking at property listings on the likes of Zillow (www.zillow.com) or Rightmove (www.rightmove.co.uk), from idly looking up how much the neighbors are selling their house for to nosing around properties we can't afford — we've all done it. This means properties are now advertised far and wide, as well as in the local real estate agent's office.

Plus, there are more and more online-only agents who offer to sell your property for a much cheaper commission. All this means that it's more important than ever to identify how you as a property sourcer add value for sellers and buyers.

REMEMBER

In Chapter 9, I mention how my most valuable development projects have come off-market, meaning I sourced them myself and they were never advertised on the open market (through a platform like Zillow or Rightmove). That kind of off-market scenario is exactly what you're looking for as a property sourcer.

In the most valuable off-market scenario, you have exclusive rights to find a buyer for the property. There's no agent involved, which saves the buyer money. And the property ideally never needs to be advertised on the open market — instead, you market it in a targeted way to investors, which adds value for both the seller and buyer. The seller benefits from her property being specifically marketed to serious investors, and buyers benefit because they don't have to work so hard to find the good deals.

If all you do is plonk the property on Zillow and wait for potential buyers to get in touch, what value are you adding for either party? None. Instead, you should look to add value by bringing sellers and buyers together in a more targeted way. You do the legwork to identify good investment properties and work hard to find suitable buyers who can move quickly. It's a win–win for both buyers and sellers.

TIP

Depending on your chosen strategy or niche, another good way to add value for both buyers and sellers is to really think about the potential end product and create a compelling pitch for investors. So, if you're sourcing properties that are ripe for development, you can get quotes for improvement works and package it all up as a well-thought-through proposal that sets out acquisition costs, development costs, potential yield, and return on investment. Now that's adding value.

Understanding the financial model

Like real estate agents, property sourcers earn their money through a percentage commission. Ordinarily, this would be paid by the seller — because you're working for the seller to help sell her property — at the time when the seller and buyer exchange contracts on the sale.

How much commission should you charge? It can vary, but in the United States, a commission of 6 percent is usually paid by the seller to the broker, and at times split with the buyer's agent; in the United Kingdom, a commission of 1 percent to 2 percent of the sale price is fairly standard. But, like most things in real estate, it's a negotiation. If you're adding additional value (for example, by getting quotes for improvement works), or if the deal you've sourced is particularly lucrative for the buyer, you can potentially negotiate a higher fee.

WARNING

Always get a proper contract drawn up by an attorney to secure your working relationship with the seller and protect your commission. This may include

>> Your fee, and when and how it'll be paid

>> Whether you have the exclusive right to market the property (this is ideal) or whether the seller is also working with other agents

>> How long you have to sell the property (for example, if there's no buyer within six months, the seller may have the right to terminate the agreement)

Sourcing valuable properties

You've chosen your niche, you've gotten to know your target market, and now you're ready to start sourcing properties. Awesome! Now we get to the really fun part.

Pitching to potential sellers

Before you proactively go hunting for suitable properties (and I get to that next), take some time to think about how you'll pitch your service to potential sellers. *Remember:* You're ideally looking for those off-market deals, meaning the property isn't yet up for sale and the owner may not yet know that she wants to sell. Your job is to get her thinking about the possibility of selling up.

It's vital you look like a professional company, not a random individual getting in touch out of the blue. So, before you reach out to any property owners with an unprofessional-looking personal Gmail address, get all the common-sense professional building blocks (pardon the pun) in place:

>> A simple yet professionally designed website, with a dedicated URL (like www.*yourname*.com)

>> A personalized business-appropriate email address (like *yourname@your name*.com)

>> An appropriate and well-thought-out profile on LinkedIn

>> Business cards (and maybe letterhead, too)

>> A simple flyer setting out what you do and encouraging potential sellers to get in touch

>> Maybe even a toll-free number for sellers to call (making it as easy as possible for leads to come your way)

When you approach the owner of a property, have a prepared pitch that you can deliver smoothly and without hesitation. As you'll see in the next section, "Finding property leads," you may be pitching in person on someone's actual doorstep, speaking to the receptionist of an office you're interested in, writing a letter, or putting a flyer through the door. Either way, you're looking to emphasize your expertise, identify clear benefits for the seller (how you can add value), and encourage her to follow up with you.

So, an example in-person pitch may be something like the following:

Hi, there. I'm an expert in student property in this area, and your property is exactly the kind of property that investor buyers are looking for. Have you thought about selling? By working together, we can maximize the value of your property and cut out expensive agent fees. Can I leave you some information about my business?

Or if you're posting flyers through doors it can include a similar blurb such as the following:

Wallwork Property are experts in student property in the Farm Park area. We have investor buyers who are actively looking for properties just like yours, so if you're thinking of selling, contact us to discuss what your property might be worth. We'll help you maximize the value of your property and avoid expensive agent fees by selling direct to motivated buyers. To find out more, contact Wallwork Property at 01234 56789 or email `info@wallworkproperty1234.com` for more information.

WHY WOULD A SELLER CHOOSE YOU OVER AN ESTABLISHED LOCAL AGENT?

As a niche investment agent or sourcer you'll be creating a business that's "international" because you'll be acquiring investment buyers from all over the globe. Therefore, you'll have much greater marketing reach than a local agent who just focuses on one small area. That's of value to a seller and a major unique selling point you can concentrate on when sourcing properties.

Also, as a property sourcer, you're mostly looking for those properties that aren't yet advertised on the open market, which means you have an ideal opportunity to get a foot in the door before the property owner has even spoken to an agent.

That's exactly what happened with Susie from Berkshire, England. When her only son left to go to university, she initially enjoyed having their three-bedroom family home to herself. Over time, it began to feel a bit big and empty, but it still didn't feel right selling — what if her son needed to move back home after university? Fast-forward a few years and, after her son had been backpacking, he ended up settling in Australia and marrying an Australian.

A flyer dropped through her letterbox the same week Susie learned she was going to be a grandmother. The timing couldn't have been better. She'd been thinking more and more about finally selling, and was now keen to spend more time in Australia, but hadn't got as far as contacting any agents. Would she consider selling her property, the flyer asked? Heck, yes, she would. And save money on fees? With a round-trip to Australia in her near future, of course!

Finding property leads

Sourcing investment properties is a numbers game. You may need to knock on 50 doors before someone says, "Actually, I have been thinking about selling." And you'll almost certainly source more properties than you sell.

Have you heard of throwing lots of things at the wall to see what sticks? It's a little bit like that, except you're focusing on specific types of properties rather than trying to source any old property. But, even within your niche, you may need to throw a lot of properties at the wall before you work out what sticks and what doesn't.

Because it's a numbers game, be prepared to invest plenty of time and hard work in the process of finding leads. Keep at it, and your hard work will eventually pay off.

REMEMBER

Here are some of the most effective ways to source property leads:

» Identify specific areas, streets, and even individual properties that would work for your strategy. Then knock on doors to talk to the owners. I've knocked on plenty of doors to canvass property deals before, and it really works.

» If you can't have a face-to-face conversation with the owner, you can pop a flyer or letter through the door inviting him to get in touch if he's interested in selling.

» If the resident isn't the owner, you can find out who owns the property either by asking the tenant or looking up the property on official land registry information.

» Build links with attorneys, financial advisors, surveyors, accountants, architects, and other professionals in your target area. Through their network, they may know motivated buyers and sellers who they can introduce you to (perhaps for a small, enticing fee!).

» Look for unloved properties or those that have stood empty for a while. The owners may be very motivated to sell to get rid of their "problem" properties.

» Contact owners of properties that have been on the market for a while already. They may have had to reduce their sale price to attract more offers. If they're nearing the end of their tether (and contract) with their real estate agent, they may be willing to try a different route.

» Use paid advertising, online and offline, to raise awareness among potential sellers in your chosen niche. Facebook advertising, for example, can drill down into incredibly specific target audiences, like homeowners who are over 55 in a certain geographic area.

» Post in relevant groups and forums online to establish your expertise in your target market. My website, Property Forum (www.propertyforum.com), is a great place to network and show your "peacock feathers" in the public domain.

» If your budget allows, host events in your target area to raise awareness of your business and help build your list of contacts.

» Keep in touch with previous sellers and buyers. Add them to your mailing list (with permission) and send occasional updates. Send a handwritten note of thanks when the deal is done. Ask for a referral or endorsement quote that you can use on your website and promotional materials. Send handwritten

Christmas cards and so on. When your business stays on their radar, they're more likely to recommend you to other buyers and sellers.

>> Even if a contact decides she's not ready to sell, don't give up on her completely. Check in occasionally and stay on her radar. If she changes her mind, you want her to contact you first.

Marketing the property to bring buyers and sellers together

You've sourced a great property and gotten the seller on board. Now all you have to do is find the right buyer.

Learning how to sell successfully

It's really important to think of yourself as a marketer and salesperson — not just in the sense of selling your deals, but also selling yourself and your business as an expert in your field.

The concept of "selling yourself" can be awkward. But everyone has to sell themselves at some point or another, whether you're selling yourself as the ideal candidate at a job interview or selling your boss on why you deserve a pay rise.

You need to wholeheartedly embrace the idea of yourself as a kick-ass sales person and employ some time-honored sales techniques to promote your property deals — and yourself!

What do I mean by time-honored sales techniques? For one thing, good salespeople really understand their target audience, so think about who you're targeting, what their pain points are, and how you can help them solve those problems. Assuming you're targeting real estate investors, a big hurdle for them is finding great deals and motivated sellers — you've already done the hard work by identifying suitable properties and getting the sellers onboard.

Another key part of selling is selling *benefits* not features. A car ad isn't selling the car's physical features, like the air conditioning, power steering, and fuel economy. Everyone would fall asleep. Instead, it's selling the lifestyle associated with that car, whether it's cruising along a beautiful coastline and getting frisky with your loved one on a deserted beach, or escaping the 9 to 5 and letting loose the outdoorsy, off-roading adrenaline junkie who lives deep inside, or taking idyllic family outings where no one ever gets carsick or asks "Are we there yet?" every five minutes.

Likewise, when you're selling the idea of a property to investors, you're not just selling the number of bedrooms, floor space, or new heating system. You're selling the benefits of that property for the investor. For example, you may pitch it as a hands-off investment that earns regular income while the investor spends precious time with her family.

Knowing where to market your properties

In the early days, you may have to do some paid advertising to market your properties and acquire buyers. You can use Google Ads and social media advertising to target your properties at specific web users.

You can also list the property on property investment portals and general sales sites like Zillow and Rightmove. Be warned, though, that some of these portals charge a hefty fee — and, as someone who wants to add value for your clients, you should never rely solely on these sites. If you can sell them off-market first, that's definitely the best strategy; many investment buyers shy away from "on market" deals.

TIP

Ultimately you're looking to build your own list of active investors so that you can sell properties entirely off-market. Here are some of the most effective ways to build your own list of buyers and market your properties in a more targeted way:

>> **Approach contacts you already have.** That ex-colleague who's retiring next month? You never know. He may be looking for an investment to bring him a healthy retirement income.

>> **Build trust and establish yourself online as an expert in your field by responding to questions on property-related social media groups and property forums like mine** (www.propertyforum.com). You want to build a name for yourself as the go-to person for your niche strategy in your target location, so be helpful and contribute to the conversation. Don't just yell about your amazing deals — it can come across too "salesy"!

>> **Consider writing blog posts to further establish your expertise.** You can publish the posts on your website, social media, and LinkedIn, and/or you can approach property forums to ask if they'd like occasional guest posts. Your articles should be helpful and informative, not a vehicle for shameless self-promotion. Property Forum (www.propertyforum.com) offers these kind of guest posts as I'm sure other useful relevant portals do, too, so get your message out there!

>> **Go to plenty of networking events and exhibitions or conventions that are relevant to your chosen market.** These events are a great way to meet investors.

>> **Begin to generate your own mailing list of interested investors.** When you meet people at networking events, ask if you can send them regular updates. Have a "Sign up for future updates" link on your website. If you publish articles, direct people to where they can sign up.

>> **Send out regular updates to your mailing lists to notify them of recent deals (remembering to focus on the benefits, not just the features).** But also send general updates, too. You want to establish long-term relationships with investors, not "sell, sell, sell" all the time.

>> **Use a customer relationship management (CRM) tool (see Chapter 3) to build and manage your own list of prospective buyers.** This will allow you to keep track of your contacts and note useful information, such as what sort of properties they're interested in, so that you can target your mailings accordingly.

Acting as a Retained Buyer's Agent

Many buyer's agents start out as property sourcers. Then, having built up connections with real estate investors over time, they begin to work for them directly to source properties that suit the investors' needs. This, in essence, is what a retained buyer's agent does: Source appropriate properties for their clients, and approach property owners to see if they'd be willing to sell to their investors.

Knowing what it means to be a retained buyer's agent

Let me address the *retained* part first. *Retained* doesn't mean you work for the buyer full-time, indefinitely, or that you automatically have an exclusive arrangement with him. You may or may not be the only buyer's agent he works with (some investors work with multiple buyer's agents at a time), and, indeed, you may work for multiple buyers at a time. Similarly, your arrangement can be a one-off project to find a specific property, or it can be a long-term arrangement where you source multiple properties over time.

Being retained just means that you have a written agreement with a buyer to go off and find the type of property he's looking for. It gives you a certain level of security, because, assuming you find the right property, you know you'll be getting paid. Plus, having a contract in place means you're able to act more formally for your client.

REMEMBER

So, how does it work? In a nutshell, you work for the buyer, not sellers. The buyer tells you what type of property he's looking for in what sort of price range (this is his *brief*), and you then go off and find properties that meet that brief. This means trawling the markets, canvassing property owners to see if they'd be interested in selling, conducting lots of viewings, and compiling a shortlist of the most suitable properties.

You're using your market knowledge, expertise and sales skills to source investments with great potential for your client. You're also saving him lots of time and effort by whittling down the number of properties he needs to look at to a small, manageable shortlist.

REMEMBER

Typically, you'll also support the buyer throughout the sale process, negotiating with the seller on his behalf, working with the attorneys, and overseeing the administrative side of the sale.

Understanding the financial model and agreeing terms with buyers

As you may expect, the financial model as a buyer's agent is similar to that of a property sourcer or real estate agent — meaning, you only get paid your full commission if you successfully facilitate a deal for the buyer. Ordinarily, this fee is paid when the buyer and seller exchange contracts on the sale.

Knowing what to charge

There's a lot of work involved in being a buyer's agent. You'll spend a lot of time trawling the market, going to viewings, and evaluating properties — and all this comes at a cost, both in terms of some financial outlay and your time. And at the end of it, you may not find a suitable property, or the buyer may not like any of the properties you shortlist for him.

Then there's the fact that each buyer is unique and has unique requirements. Some buyers may require a lot of hand-holding and guidance from you on the local market. Some may expect you to put together a very detailed pitch on shortlisted properties, including renovation quotes, floorplans, and potential yield or return on investment (see Chapter 7 for more on yield and ROI).

Meanwhile, other buyers may be experts and already have a very clear idea of what they're looking for, in which case you just have to find the properties that fit their predetermined criteria. It's all about creating value wherever you can for your buyers, in a way that works for both of you.

REMEMBER

With all this in mind, you have a bit more flexibility in how much you can charge as a buyer's agent — and it may be more than you would charge as a property sourcer. In addition, the fee can be a flat fee, a percentage of the purchase price, or both, depending on how you and the buyer prefer to work. Some buyer's agents charge a small upfront flat fee of, say £500 (around $635), and then a commission on the purchase price of up to, say, 2.5 percent. (Commissions may be higher in the United States, where buyer's agents are subject to licensing and accreditation.) At the end of the day, though, it's a negotiation. It's up to you to find a fair, win–win financial model that works for you and your client.

Sorting out the legal stuff

WARNING

Make sure you have a formal contract drawn up by an attorney that you can share with your buyers. Even if you know and trust the investor, it's really important to agree on the terms of engagement and protect your income. An agreement is likely to cover

>> Your fee for successfully finding the property (expressed as a percentage of the purchase price, a flat fee, or both), as well as when and how it'll be paid

>> The type of property the buyer is looking for

>> Whether you're working with the buyer on an exclusive basis, or whether the buyer is also liaising with other buyer's agents

>> What you can and can't do on the buyer's behalf

>> How long it'll take you to source the right property (for example, the buyer may have the right to cancel the agreement if you haven't found something suitable within three months)

Attracting buyers to your service

In terms of marketing and sales, you ideally want to be attracting serious investors to your service, so that you can build long-term relationships and work together on multiple deals. Unlike a property sourcer, you're not marketing properties as such (although your buyer may expect you to "pitch" properties that you've found) — you're selling yourself as a real estate expert.

REMEMBER

As a buyer's agent, you're selling yourself as someone who solves problems. Someone who saves the buyer time and effort. Someone who can spot great deals and separate the wheat from the chaff — so the buyer doesn't have to.

TIP

Because many buyer's agents start out as property sourcers, they often already have connections with real estate investors in their target markets. So, when it comes to attracting buyers to your service, your own network and list of contacts should absolutely be your first port of call. You can also advertise your service online and on social media to real estate investors, and work to build your own profile as an expert online, on property forums, and on social media. The ideas I set out in "Knowing where to market your properties," earlier in this chapter, will also apply to marketing yourself as a buyer's agent.

WHY WOULD A BUYER NEED A BUYER'S AGENT?

One question people sometimes ask is, "But why would an investor need a buyer's agent when she can just look for properties online?"

The answer to that is very simple: The best-value deals for investors are often to be found off-market. When a property hasn't been listed on the open market and advertised far and wide, an investor has much more scope to negotiate a good deal, without as many time and price pressures. That's because, when a property is advertised far and wide, if it's a good deal, there'll be lots of competition from other buyers, and a bidding war may erupt. But when the buyer has found a great property that hasn't yet gone to market, she can concentrate on the task of securing the best deal, without worrying about the competition.

That's one of the reasons so many investors choose to source properties direct for themselves — as in, identify suitable properties or streets and approach homeowners directly — rather than go to the local real estate agent or search online.

However, a really busy investor with a large portfolio may not have time to source each and every property they invest in. By working with a buyer's agent, they can have someone else do all the legwork and bring them a list of suitable properties. In this way, a buyer's agent creates real value for investors.

Sourcing properties effectively for your buyers

Generally speaking, my tips for finding property leads in "Sourcing valuable properties," earlier in the chapter, will help you to find suitable properties for your buyers off-market.

REMEMBER

However, the best option or options for you will depend on the buyer you're working for and their individual requirements. For example, your buyer may have a very specific geographic location in mind, even a specific couple of streets, in which case you'll be targeting property owners in that specific area to see if they may be willing to sell rather than advertising to a wider audience of property owners online.

It's also a good idea to build relationships with local real estate agents. Although you're primarily looking to source properties off-market, that's not always possible. Just because a property is already up for sale with a local agent, doesn't mean it's not a good deal. It may be exactly what your buyer is looking for. In that scenario, both you and the real estate agent can win; the real estate agent has found a serious buyer for her listing (it's obvious an investor is a serious buyer when the investor has gone to the trouble of appointing a buyer's agent), which makes her look great in the eyes of the seller, and you've still found a great deal for your client. If you've built a great relationship with the local agent, she may even give you the heads up on the deal before she starts mass-marketing it!

Five International Locations Where This Strategy Would Work

This strategy is kind of like being a very narrowly focused real estate agent, and there aren't many places left in the world where real estate agents aren't needed. So, in theory, this is a strategy that can be applied all over the world, depending on your goals, passion, and knowledge.

TIP

When looking at overseas locations, I'd say finding your niche and passion, and then drilling down into the right location for that niche is a better approach than choosing a location and then working out what sort of properties you can source. (And don't forget: Whether you decide to delve into an overseas market or stick closer to home will always depend on your chosen strategy, risk profile, and personal passions and ambitions. Circle back to Chapter 2 to work out whether overseas markets are right for you.)

Having said that, here are some niche-and-location combinations that could work well, depending on your skills and knowledge:

>> Sourcing holiday villas in Spain for time-strapped investors

>> Sourcing student properties in any of the big university cities in the United States

>> Sourcing house in multiple occupation (HMO) investment opportunities in the United Kingdom

>> Sourcing bed-and-breakfast businesses for retirees in France

>> Sourcing development opportunities for busy overseas investors in your home country

REMEMBER

The key to success is finding the right niche or strategy, the right location, and the right buyers. It's a bit like putting together a jigsaw puzzle: finding properties, buyers, and locations that fit snugly together.

4

Ongoing and Passive Income Strategies

Make money from properties you don't own, via rent-to-rent.

Earn money now and secure capital growth for the future through lease options.

Rent individual rooms to tenants, as opposed to the entire property, through a houses in multiple occupation strategy.

Discover the ins and outs of renting to students and low-income-housing tenants.

Incorporate serviced accommodation into your real estate portfolio.

Make money through viable vacation rentals.

Chapter **11**

Making Rent-to-Rent Work for You

When most people think of real estate investing, they think of the traditional model of buying a property and making money from it, either by selling it on for a profit or renting it out and earning a monthly income.

But do you actually have to buy a property to make money from it? Surprisingly, the answer to that question is no. As investors, we're primed to think of ownership as key to successful real estate investing, when, in fact, controlling or managing a property can be just as profitable in the short and medium term, especially when it comes to cash flow.

Think about it: What's your ultimate goal as a real estate investor? To make money through property? To create financial freedom for you and your loved ones? To be your own boss? To build a reputation as an effective, professional real estate entrepreneur? Rent-to-rent can help you achieve each of these aspirations, without owning the property in question.

REMEMBER

Rent-to-rent involves renting a property and then subletting it to other tenants. Because you don't need to buy the property to earn money from it, this strategy is ideal for investors with little capital.

Before we get started, it's important to address the fact that rent-to-rent can sometimes get bad press — often characterized by unscrupulous landlords cramming too many tenants into a property that's not big enough and overcharging them for the privilege. To be clear, that's absolutely not what I'm talking about in this chapter. Instead, I show you how to run a professional, ethical, and rewarding rent-to-rent service that benefits you, your landlord, and those all-important tenants.

Defining Rent-to-Rent: The One-Minute Rundown

Think of rent-to-rent as a specialist form of property management. You rent a property and, with the owner's permission, sublet the property to tenants whom you find and manage. You make sure the property is run well and keep everything ticking along so that the monthly rent keeps rolling in.

REMEMBER

Usually, you would rent a larger property and sublet it on a room-by-room basis (for example, a house in multiple occupation, or HMO, covered in Chapter 13), but you can potentially lease a smaller property and sublet it as a whole. It depends on your chosen approach and type of property — you can find more about types of properties and how they may be used in "Applying Rent-to-Rent across a Range of Properties and Strategies" later in the chapter.

But how do you make money from a property you don't own? You earn profit in the middle by managing tenants effectively and maximizing the property's rental income. For example, you might rent a four-bedroom house for $1,000 a month and sublet each of the bedrooms for $500 a month, bringing you a monthly revenue of $2,000. Even after you've covered the rent and bills of say $400 per month, there's still a profit of $600 left on the table for you each and every month.

As you can imagine, this makes rent-to-rent a great low-capital strategy, because you don't need a lot of startup money to secure a rental property. Read more about the rent-to-rent financial model, including startup costs, in "Margin in the Middle: Understanding the Rent-to-Rent Financial Model," later in this chapter.

To be clear on the terminology used in this chapter:

>> When I talk about the *landlord,* I mean the property owner or person or entity that you're renting the property from. They're your landlord.

>> You are also a landlord (strictly speaking, a sub-landlord) in the sense that you're subletting the property, but another description in this scenario could be *property manager* or more likely the *operator*. So, when I talk about the property manager or operator, that means you!

You may be wondering why a landlord would be willing to rent his property to someone who's only going to sublet it to others? If we take the example of the four-bedroom property, clearly the landlord can rent out each of those four bedrooms himself, and keep all that lovely profit for himself. But, in reality, many landlords want a simple, hands-off way to earn money from their properties; they don't want to be managing four separate tenants when they can be dealing with just one. That's where you come in.

TIP

The truth is, there are lots of reasons why a landlord would be open to a rent-to-rent strategy, and there are plenty of ways you can give a compelling pitch and sweeten the deal. I explore this later in the chapter (see "Sourcing the Ideal Rent-to-Rent Property"). Ultimately, your job is to find those willing landlords, work with them to add value (again, more on that coming up), and manage the property so that everyone wins.

Addressing Rent-to-Rent's Image Problem

We need to talk about the unsavory side of rent-to-rent. The bad press. The horror stories. The so-called "slumlords" who line their own pockets keeping vulnerable or desperate tenants in poor-quality, overcrowded, and sometimes downright dangerous accommodation.

There have been numerous stories in the press about tenants (often, but not always, migrant workers in expensive urban areas) living in cramped and poorly maintained accommodation. Ten or so people to a house with one bathroom. Tenants sharing rooms with other tenants. Stud walls being put down the middle of an already small room to create another rentable space. Tenants being housed in garden sheds even. Shoddy wiring. Mold. The list goes on.

WARNING

As with any strategy in this book, there are unscrupulous operators out there giving that strategy a bad name. The same is true of rent-to-rent. (Although, to be fair, plenty of terrible landlords are the property's owner, not a rent-to-rent operator.)

So when I talk about rent-to-rent in this chapter, what I'm really talking about is *ethical rent-to-rent*, not illegal subletting. That means you must be

>> **Offering properly managed accommodation that is desirable, safe, clean, comfortable, and of a reasonable size:** No garden shed nonsense here!

>> **Safeguarding and managing your tenants in the way that you would like to be treated yourself:** In other words, they're paying customers, and you're providing a service. Never forget that.

>> **Charging your tenants a fair market rate and paying the landlord a fair rent that reflects how the property is being used.**

>> **Getting consent from your landlord to sublet the property, and ensuring that your rental agreement accurately reflects this (see "Sorting Out Your Rental Agreement," later in this chapter):** In addition, it's a good idea to ensure that your landlord has permission from his mortgage lender (if any) to operate in the way you're planning. You can, for example, have a clause written into your agreement confirming that the landlord has permission to use the property in this way.

>> **Signing a formal rental contract with each of your tenants so that their rights are protected:** Again, more on this coming up.

>> **Operating within the regulations that apply to your specific business model (for example, HMO) and the laws of your country, state, or jurisdiction.**

>> **Acting as a responsible entrepreneur who's running a good, reputable business.**

Unscrupulous landlords prey on vulnerable tenants who have little choice but to accept what's on offer, but it's important to remember that a lot of not-at-all desperate tenants actively want to live in a clean, professional multi-tenant property, like an HMO. Particularly in cities, housing is expensive and not everyone can afford an apartment of his own. Renting a nice room, rather than a whole home, is an attractive option for today's young professionals. And not only does it make good economic sense, but it delivers all the social benefits of sharing with likeminded young professionals.

Therefore, there's an obvious need for this type of accommodation, and — dodgy operators aside — I believe rent-to-rent can, and should, be part of the solution. Delivering comfortable, affordable, well-run accommodation provides a practical answer to the lack of affordable housing.

Applying Rent-to-Rent across a Range of Properties and Strategies

When it comes to deciding how you want to deploy rent-to-rent, you need to decide what type of property you want to rent, and how you, in turn, will rent it out to other tenants. Both factors go hand in hand, and each factor will influence the other.

What types of property are suitable for rent-to-rent?

From large houses to studio apartments, rent-to-rent can, in theory, be applied across many different types of property in any area. It all depends on what you're planning to do with the property and your end proposed use strategy.

REMEMBER

For example, if you want to maximize rental income by renting rooms to individual tenants, you'll need a larger house or apartment — something with multiple bedrooms and potentially even spare reception rooms (for example, a dining room or office) that can be turned into extra bedrooms. But if you want to run the property as a single-tenant rental, then a smaller studio or one- or two-bedroom apartment will be easier to rent out.

In theory, rent-to-rent can also potentially be applied to commercial properties. For instance, you can rent an office and sublet smaller, serviced offices within that space (indeed, shared office spaces are becoming a popular solution in expensive cities like New York). Or you can rent a shop and sublet different parts of it to different businesses. The same is also true of an outdoor market trading area — you manage the site and attract and manage market traders.

Generally, though, rent-to-rent is more commonly applied in residential properties, which is an easier entry into property investment. For this reason, I focus on residential properties in this chapter.

What approaches can you take to sublet the property?

Rent-to-rent is an interesting strategy because it's often used alongside other, supporting real estate strategies.

What do I mean by that? Well, if you're renting the property on a room-by-room basis and you're in the UK, then the property may qualify as an HMO (see Chapter 13). In this case, rent-to-rent may be your primary strategy (because you don't have the capital to buy a property to run as an HMO), but your additional strategy is HMOs. That means you'll need to get yourself up to speed on the nuances of running an HMO, in addition to learning how to make rent-to-rent work for you. Both are essential if you're going to make a success of the project.

Similarly, if you're renting a small studio apartment and subletting it as an Airbnb on a nightly basis, then it's effectively being run as serviced accommodation (see Chapter 15). That means it's vital to educate yourself on the serviced accommodation strategy, as well as rent-to-rent. Essentially rent-to-rent is the mechanism to acquire control of the property in the first place; from that point on, it's up to you to run a successful rental strategy!

By now, you probably have a good idea of the most common rent-to-rent approaches, but let's look at them in a little more detail:

>> **Renting out rooms to individual tenants:** This may or may not qualify as an HMO, depending on the number of tenants and where you are in the world (see Chapter 13). The tenants may be professionals, students, or low-income-housing tenants. All three may be viable approaches in terms of making money, but some landlords simply don't like the thought of their property being sublet to students or low-income-housing tenants and will refuse you permission. So, when I talk about renting rooms to individual tenants throughout this chapter, I'm working on the assumption that you're aiming at professionals.

>> **Renting out the entire property as a single rental:** This can be on a night-by-night basis (like an Airbnb), on a short-term basis (such as renting the property on monthly or quarterly terms to professionals who are in the area for a short time only), or on a longer-term basis (the standard one- or two-year rental contracts that we're all familiar with).

Which approach is right for you?

I can't categorically tell you which approach will be most suited to you or which will make you the most money. It largely depends on your passion, your interests, the area you're looking to rent in, and your skills as a property manager or operator in your chosen field.

TIP

You'll need to weigh the pros and cons of each approach in terms of how they relate to you. For example:

» Running a studio apartment as a single rental to one long-term tenant is pretty easy in terms of finding and managing tenants and maintaining the property. But where are you adding value? You may struggle to make any real money with this approach because the existing landlord will be getting market rent already.

» Running that same small property as serviced accommodation, and renting it out on a nightly basis is certainly adding value because you're managing the property much more intensely. It's a higher-income model because guests are paying by the night, but your costs will be higher and it'll be a lot more work to run. A higher turnover of people coming and going creates more wear and tear, more cleaning, more general maintenance, not to mention the time involved in checking tenants in and managing them. You need to be sure you're earning enough to make this worthwhile.

» Taking a regular house renting to young professionals and turning it into an HMO (or other multi-tenant property, whether it counts as an HMO or not) also adds value because you're getting more tenants in there. Sure, it takes more work in terms of managing tenants and the property. Wear and tear will be higher than with a single tenant. But it's likely to be less work than the constant revolving door of tenants that comes with the serviced accommodation model. If you wanted to go all out, you can even convert the property to an HMO *and* operate a serviced accommodation model rather than renting to longer-term professionals. This approach would certainly maximize the property's potential, but don't underestimate the work required.

TIP

Your current circumstances (economic, relationship, and so on) may also dictate which approach is best for you. For example, I know of people who have used rent-to-rent as a way to rent a nice, big property for themselves, sublet the other bedrooms to friends, and have a ball living with their pals while living effectively rent-free because the profit they earn covers their own rent. It can also be a useful way to make moving to a new area less painful — you can rent a nice property, meet new people by renting out the other bedrooms, and quickly establish both a social circle and income stream in your new location.

In this way, although many investors use rent-to-rent as a business opportunity, for some, it's a way of making money from a place that they live in. Both are perfectly valid approaches, but one is likely to appeal more to you than the other. The thought of living with your tenants may be your worst nightmare! But it's how I started out in real estate, and my first two tenants are still my best friends today.

Exploring change of use in more detail

When we look at the different approaches for rent-to-rent properties, a key term crops up: *adding value.* In any real estate strategy, the surest way to make money is to add value.

REMEMBER

In rent-to-rent, adding value will typically mean changing the use of the property in some way. Renting the rooms out to individual tenants is a change of use because it's no longer a standard single rental. Likewise, renting the property via Airbnb is also a change of use, from a regular home to a serviced accommodation.

WARNING

Change of use is, therefore, a general term for running a property in a different way from how it's currently run. However, confusingly, *change of use* can also be used as a specific technical term for changing the way the property is categorized for planning or zoning purposes. It's important to know the difference and understand whether running the property in a different way means you're taking the property from one planning category to another.

For example, large HMO properties in England are no longer classified as standard residential properties, which means you need to apply for formal planning permission to run the property in that way. (Turn to Chapter 13 for more on the planning aspects of HMOs.)

Even if you're renting out the property on Airbnb, official planning permission may be required, depending on how often you're renting it out and where you are in the world. For instance, if it's rented every night of the year, it may no longer count as a residential property, which means you may need to apply for formal planning permission and be subject to much more complicated management regulations or licensing. You can find more on serviced accommodation in Chapter 15.

Change of use restrictions can seem like a pain, but it's important to understand the local authority's point of view. Local authorities use planning and zoning laws to control property in their area for the benefit of the community. If your local authority has concerns that your plans for the property may have a negative effect on the community (for example, lots of different people coming and going), it's understandable that they may want to either prevent you from running the property in that way or oversee what you're doing very closely to ensure it's well run and safe for your tenants. Good operators welcome and support sensible regulation, not just because we operate to the best possible standards anyway but because it helps keep out the rogue and poorer-quality operators. Just make sure you understand the regulations that apply to you and keep your standards well above them.

REMEMBER

It's a case of working with your local authority, and demonstrating that you're an ethical operator, rather than trying to work against them or fly under their radar and hope you won't get caught. And remember that every local authority and jurisdiction is different, so be sure to check with yours on what you can and can't do with the property and get the lowdown on which rules apply to you.

TIP

If it looks like formal planning permission may be required, and you're in the process of negotiating with the landlord, it's a good idea to make it clear that your offer is subject to planning permission being granted. That way, if your whole proposition is based on running the property as an HMO and you're denied permission to do that, you aren't stuck with a property you can't use in the way you intended.

Margin in the Middle: Understanding the Rent-to-Rent Financial Model

It's clear that the basic rent-to-rent financial model involves making money in the middle, between the tenants who pay you their monthly rent, and the rent you pay to your landlord. But let's unpack that simple notion in a little more detail, including startup costs, ongoing costs, and income.

Looking at the startup costs

While rent-to-rent is a low-capital strategy, there are typically some costs involved in getting the property up and running:

>> **Security deposit:** As with any rental agreement, you'll be required to pay an upfront deposit to give the landlord some security. Typically, the deposit is equal to one month's or six weeks' rent, although you may need to pay a larger deposit for a more commercial or longer-term contract or if the landlord has concerns about the wear and tear involved in a multitenant strategy.

>> **Deposit insurance:** Depending on what you can negotiate with your landlord, you can take out an insurance policy instead of paying the security deposit. The insurance policy covers the deposit, freeing up your cash flow for other things (such as improving the property or advertising for tenants). However, like any insurance policy, it's really important to read the fine print and check that the policy allows for rent-to-rent.

>> **Rent in advance:** One month's rent is pretty standard on any rental agreement, and it means that, going forward, you'll be paying your rent in advance, rather than in arrears. However, if you have your tenants in place on the same terms, they'll essentially be paying this for you anyway.

>> **Money for any improvements to the property:** Ideally the property you source will need very little money spent on it to get it up and running in the way you intend (see "Sourcing the Ideal Rent-to-Rent Property"). After all, it's not your property, so why spend money when you don't have to? However, depending on how you plan to operate the property, there may be some unavoidable costs to get started. For instance, if it's going to be a multitenant property, you'll probably want to fit locks on each of the bedroom doors. You may also be subject to certain health and safety requirements, such as fire doors, fire alarm, firefighting equipment, gas safety checks, and so on (see Chapter 13 for more).

WARNING

Don't be tempted to scrimp on mandated improvement works, particularly when it comes to health and safety regulations. As an ethical, professional operator, the safety of your tenants is a primary concern. Always check with your local authority on the regulations that apply to your property and chosen strategy.

All in all, you're probably looking at a couple of thousand bucks to get you started. But this is a short-term cost only. Providing you have tenants in place quickly, you'll have earned back these startup costs in next to no time.

Getting started on a shoestring budget

Remember when I talked about startup costs? (Of course you do — it was only a paragraph ago.) Well, here I'm going to argue that you can potentially get a rent-to-rent property up and running with almost no startup costs. I'm not saying it's the norm or that it's easy (you'll have to negotiate hard with your landlord, for one thing), but it is possible. Here's how.

TIP

If you don't have a couple of grand sitting around in your bank account to cover the deposit, first month's rent, and so on, don't despair. This is my tried-and-tested method for keeping startup costs to an absolute minimum:

1. **When agreeing the deposit and upfront rent with the landlord, ask to pay just a small holding deposit of, say, $200 upfront, with the balance of the deposit and rent to be paid a few days before you move in.**

You may need to offer a higher deposit or longer tenancy term to sweeten the deal, but, for now, the main thing is to keep your cash flow flowing and as little money down to secure the deal as possible.

2. **If any improvement works are needed, negotiate with the landlord to carry out and pay for these works on the basis that you're willing to sign an attractively long lease, so it's worth his while in order to secure you as a tenant.**

   Not every landlord will agree to this so either move on (remember sourcing the right property is a numbers game!) or do the works required in the first couple of months of taking control of the property using your initial rental profits. Ensure that all safety works are done before any tenants move in, though — that's vital.

3. **Agree on a move-in date that's ideally at least one month or six weeks away.**

   This works really well when you source a property that isn't yet available (the current tenants aren't due to move out for a month), so the landlord doesn't miss out on a month's rent.

4. **Agree with the landlord that you'll have regular access to the property before your tenancy starts so you can start showing your potential tenants around as soon as possible.**

5. **Start finding tenants immediately (learn how in the section "Finding Tenants and Managing the Property").**

6. **Having found good tenants and received their security deposits and first month's rent, pay the balance of your security deposit and advance rent to your landlord using your tenants' money paid to you.**

   And bingo, you're off, with very little money spent.

REMEMBER

This process isn't for everyone. You'll have to work really hard to find good tenants quickly and get their deposits and rent in a timely manner; otherwise, you'll end up letting down your landlord. (Not great when you're trying to build a reputation as a professional operator.) It can be stressful, too. And you'll have to be a great negotiator. But, done well, this is a good way to get control of a property with minimal money down.

Covering ongoing costs and earning an income from the property

Ongoing costs are as you'd expect for any property: utility bills, insurance, cleaning, and so on — plus there's the rent you pay to your landlord every month.

Like any business, your profit is the margin between your revenue and your costs. You ideally want this margin to be as comfortable as possible.

REMEMBER

Here's a breakdown of monthly income, costs, and profit for a fictional example, a large five-bedroom house that's being run as a multi-tenant HMO outside of London:

>> **Rental income from five bedrooms at £500 per room per month (including bills):** £2,500

>> **Rent you pay to the landlord:** £1,000 per month

>> **Other monthly costs to run the property:**

- **Electricity:** £100

- **Gas:** £100

- **Water:** £30

- **Council or city tax:** £150

- **TV license (applicable in the United Kingdom):** £12

- **Internet:** £30

- **Property insurance:** £35

- **Cleaner for the kitchens, bathrooms, and other communal spaces:** £205

>> **Total costs for bills and rent:** £1,662

>> **Money in your pocket at the end of the month:** £838

That's not a bad profit considering it's coming from a property that you don't even own. Your initial outlay for the deposit and first month's rent (assuming you even paid these out of your own pocket, instead of taking my "shoestring budget" approach) are covered within a few months, and the rest is capital for you to grow your real estate portfolio.

Many rent-to-rent operators manage multiple properties as a full-time business, so you can imagine how the income would add up over several properties. I know more than one landlord who has over 20 properties run like this — you can soon be earning a great living from it!

REMEMBER

Clearly this strategy is all about income, rather than capital growth. You don't own the property, so you won't have the option to sell it in the future and pocket the profit (unless, of course, you can negotiate the option to buy the property from the landlord at some point in the future — this is called a *lease option,* and it's covered in detail in Chapter 12). But what you will gain is income, cash flow, vital real estate experience, and the knowledge and expertise to manage properties and tenants with confidence. In this way, rent-to-rent can be a good springboard to other real estate investments (for example, owning your own HMO in the future).

That said, don't overlook the idea of maintaining rent-to-rent as an ongoing part of your real estate portfolio — it's a good way to diversify your income stream.

Sourcing the Ideal Rent-to-Rent Property (and Landlord)

Rent-to-rent isn't everyone's cup of tea. For one thing, it's typically more work in terms of finding and managing multiple tenants. You have to keep your landlord happy, as well as your tenants. And there's another key hurdle to overcome: It's often harder to source properties for a rent-to-rent strategy.

REMEMBER

Why would it be harder? It's more challenging because you're not just looking for a suitable property. A five-minute Internet search could find five potential properties in my local area that are suitable for a multi-tenant strategy. The problem is, of those five properties, there's no guarantee that any of the landlords would be open to my subletting the property. You're, therefore, looking for the ideal landlord, as much as the ideal property. I look at both aspects in this section.

Evaluating potential properties

You can't source the ideal property until you know what type of strategy you're planning to deploy. *Remember:* The strategy and property go hand in hand.

What type of property do you want?

If you're renting individual rooms, you'll naturally be looking for a larger property (usually a house, but there's no reason a large apartment wouldn't work). That's because you'll need to sublet multiple bedrooms to make the strategy work. Plus, a larger property will have the more spacious and desirable communal areas that quality tenants value (decent kitchen, multiple bathrooms, lounge or den, outdoor space, and so on).

A serviced accommodation model, however, will probably lead you to a smaller property (or larger block of smaller units together to maximize efficiency). Most travelers, whether they're business or pleasure travelers, travel in small groups (a solo business person, a couple, perhaps a group of three or four friends). So, a studio apartment or a one-bedroom apartment with sofa bed may be ideal for what you have in mind. Usually these kind of tenants or "guests" require fully self-contained accommodation, including a kitchenette.

What are you looking for in the ideal property?

TIP

When sourcing a rent-to-rent property, you need to evaluate the following characteristics:

>> **Location:** This will depend on your strategy. Professionals renting rooms in a multitenant house will want to be in or close to the city center for work. But if you're aiming at vacation rentals (see Chapter 16), you may want a property that's by the sea or in an idyllic rural spot.

>> **The condition of the property:** You're obviously looking for a property that needs as little physical work as possible to run it in the way you intend. You don't want to be doing major structural work on a property that isn't yours.

>> **Money needed to get the property up and running:** There's nothing wrong with spending a bit of capital to increase your returns, but, in my opinion, the ideal property will need little more than individual locks on bedroom doors and maybe a little inexpensive fluffing here and there to appeal to the target audience (repainting what was a child's bedroom in neutral colors, for instance).

>> **The amount of space available and potential number of tenants:** I'm not looking to cram lots of people in; I'm running a viable property management business in a sensible, ethical way. So, don't get greedy and reduce amenity space too much to make way for additional tenants. For example, it's not uncommon to turn a dining room or office into a rentable bedroom, but do you really want to do the same with the living room? Professionals sharing with other professionals often like a room to hang out and be sociable in. And that tiny shoebox bedroom? Will that really appeal to a paying adult professional? Maybe it would make a better TV room. You know your target market and what they expect, and if you provide the best accommodation possible, you'll keep your rent levels strong.

>> **Whether it delivers what your target audience is looking for:** If you're aiming at young professionals, they'll expect to see kitchens and bathrooms that are of a decent quality, and they'll definitely need more than one bathroom! Stylish neutral decor is another must.

Where should you look?

Some of the strategies in this book — such as developing properties (Chapter 9) and selling property leads (Chapter 10) — advocate sourcing properties off-market. This isn't one of those strategies.

For a rent-to-rent property, you can, in theory, target specific properties and knock on doors to see if the owner would be willing to rent it to you. But a better use of your time is sourcing properties through the open market (properties that are already listed for rent).

TIP

Here are my favorite ways to source rent-to-rent properties:

>> **Study online and agent listings in your target area.** Even when you're not actively in the market for a new property, keep regularly trawling through local listings and stay on the agents' mailing lists. It'll keep you in touch with your market and hone your skills at spotting terrific properties.

>> **Make friends with local agents so that they give you a call when a suitable property comes their way.** But always be upfront about your rent-to-rent intentions.

>> **Look for properties that are advertised as available to rent in a month or so.** If it's already standing vacant, the pressure is on to find tenants right away, but if the current occupants aren't vacating for a few weeks, you have a little bit of breathing space to get yourself sorted.

>> **Look at properties that aren't shifting, probably because they're not targeted correctly.** For example, that smart four-bedroom family home that's been up for rent for months with no takers? Perhaps in that location, not many tenants can afford to splash out on such a property (if they could, why would they be renting?). Perhaps demand in that area is for smaller, more affordable accommodation — in which case, you have a great argument for changing its use and renting individual rooms.

>> **You can potentially look at properties that are already being run as HMOs or multitenant properties.** I've made no secret of the fact that it's hard work managing lots of tenants, and some landlords get fed up and want out, quickly. You can offer to take the property off their hands and keep running it in the same way — if you're lucky, you may even be able to keep the same tenants.

>> **You could even look at properties that have been listed for sale, rather than rent.** If there's been little interest in the property, the owner may be open to your renting it from him. He gets to pay his mortgage, retain ownership of the property for future capital, and forget the stresses and strains of finding a buyer. This can be particularly attractive for an investor owner.

Finding a landlord who's open to rent-to-rent

You could find ten good properties, but nine of the landlords won't allow you to sublet. Maybe they just don't like the idea, or maybe they're concerned about the additional wear and tear that comes from using a property more intensely.

Getting permission

In addition to finding the right property, a critical part of the rent-to-rent strategy is finding a good landlord who is happy to rent to you, knowing that you'll be subletting the property and managing it under a slightly different use.

Illegal subletting is not a smart choice for a serious real estate investor, so you have to be open with potential landlords about how you intend to use the property and get their full permission.

Ordinarily, your landlord will be the owner of the property. However, in some rare circumstances, you may even be renting the property from a tenant, not the owner. (Effectively, they're subletting to you and you're sub-subletting to others — complicated but it does happen, although it's a little more common in the commercial office space world.) If your landlord is not the property owner, tread carefully. Do your due diligence to check that your landlord has permission from the owner to rent the property (this should be stipulated in your contract) and the owner is happy for you to employ a rent-to-rent strategy. Essentially, always make sure the owner is onboard with how the property will be used.

Making the case for rent-to-rent

Why would a potential landlord be happy for you to sublet her property to others? There are some compelling pluses for landlords, which may help you persuade her:

>> She only has to deal with you, not a revolving door of tenants.

>> She gets steady longer-term income that's almost entirely hands-off. Because you'll be running the property for her, she gets more money for less work.

>> She can save on agent's fees because you'll deal directly with her and manage the property yourself.

>> She never has to worry about *void periods* (when the property sits empty without paying tenants). You'll be paying the rent each month, and it's your job to cover any void periods. (Thankfully, in a multitenant property, even if one room stands empty for a while, you're usually still earning enough to more than cover the rent and bills.)

TIP

To further sweeten the deal and convince the owner to rent the property to you, you could

>> **Offer a monthly rent that's slightly higher than the market value for the property's current use (normally single tenant):** You'll need to be clear on your numbers (what rent you can charge, estimated costs) before you do this, but offering an extra $200 or so a month can be very attractive to landlords.

>> **Offer to pay a larger deposit than is required:** If she has concerns about the property being damaged because there'll be more tenants living there, this is a great option.

>> **Offer to sign a longer lease than normal:** This gives both of you some much-needed security. She knows she'll have a hassle-free income for a long period of time, and you know you can run the property in the way you intend without being asked to leave after 12 months. You can find more on tenancy terms in the section "Sorting Out Your Rental Agreement."

>> **Emphasize your credentials as a professional, ethical property manager (more on that coming up next).**

TIP

If you need to make any changes to the property to suit your strategy and target audience, always ask for permission, even if it's a minor change. You may even be able to negotiate with the landlord to cover some or all the costs.

Positioning yourself as a professional rent-to-rent operator

You're not just selling the idea of rent-to-rent to a landlord; you also need to sell yourself as a great person for her to work with. That means positioning yourself as a professional operator and an expert in your chosen strategy.

If you haven't already got a website, a professional-looking email address, and business cards, get these building blocks in place before you approach landlords. Otherwise, you run the risk of looking like an amateur.

TIP

Your goal is to demonstrate your credentials as an honest, ethical operator. Where possible, talk about your track record of managing properties and tenants to per-fection. And if you haven't got experience yet, sell them on your in-depth market knowledge instead. Show them how well you understand your chosen strategy, the local market, and any licensing, planning or regulatory issues that may apply to your strategy. Make it clear you're ready to run their property in a legal, safe, and professional manner.

Sorting Out Your Rental Agreement

There are two sides to this contract-related coin. First, you'll want an agreement with your landlord that fully reflects your relationship. Then, you'll need a separate contract with each of your tenants. Let's look at both types of contract in turn.

Agreeing the length of the lease and other terms with your landlord

What you're looking for is an open, honest, and harmonious relationship with your landlord, where he's supportive of your rent-to-rent strategy. Naturally, this relationship should be reflected in the contract.

WARNING

Make sure your contract with the landlord confirms that you have permission to sublet the property and change its use in the way that you intend (for example, renting it to multiple tenants). If the contract doesn't allow for subletting, you risk being evicted from the property.

Other key terms include

>> **Monthly rent:** Having looked at plenty of properties during the sourcing process, you'll already have a good handle on the fair market rent for this property. But it's not uncommon to pay a slightly above-market rent to reflect the fact that the property will be used in a more intensive way.

>> **Length of the contract:** A regular rental agreement is for one year, maybe two at most, but that's unlikely to give you the security you need to run your business, nor does that particularly sweeten the deal for the landlord. Get as long a lease as possible, ideally five to seven years.

TECHNICAL STUFF

In the United Kingdom, anything over seven years may require a commercial contract rather than a standard residential contract (called an Assured Shorthold Tenancy [AST] contract). In some situations, it's worth the hassle of a commercial lease to secure a longer tenancy, but you may equally want to keep it under seven years to make the contract more simple. Talk to your lawyer about the best type of contract for your circumstances.

>> **Whether either party can terminate the contract early, and under what circumstances.**

>> **The responsibilities of you and your landlord:** For example, you'll find and manage tenants, ensure the property is kept in a clean and tidy condition, and

maybe even undertake general maintenance and minor repairs. But if the expensive central heating system fails or a tree crashes through the roof, who is responsible for that sort of major repair work or insuring for it? (*Hint:* the landlord!)

TIP

You may also want the option to buy the property in the future after you've built up some capital, in which case, see if your landlord would be open to a lease-option clause. You can find more on lease options in Chapter 12.

REMEMBER

Always have your contract drawn up by a specialist real estate lawyer, preferably one who has experience with rent-to-rent and subletting strategies.

Having a tenancy agreement in place with each of your tenants

As a professional rent-to-rent operator, you'll also need a rental agreement with each of your tenants. This sets out your relationship and responsibilities, protects your interests as an operator, and protects your tenants' rights.

If you're running the property as serviced accommodation, it's a bit laborious to expect every guest to sign a one-night tenancy agreement. Simple terms and conditions should suffice. If you're using an online booking platform (like Airbnb), you may be covered by their terms and conditions. Find out more about this in Chapter 15.

However, if you're running the property as a multitenant rental, or even as a regular single-tenant rental, you absolutely need a written tenancy agreement in place for every tenant.

TIP

An AST agreement is my preferred form of contract in the United Kingdom, because it offers maximum protection both for you as a landlord and for your tenants. However, your lawyer will be able to advise you on the best contract for your circumstances and your legal jurisdiction.

So, what exactly should your contract cover? Turn to Chapter 13 for a detailed list of the standard terms that pretty much any rental agreement should cover.

Finding Tenants and Managing the Property

You've sourced your property, reached a harmonious agreement with your landlord on how you intend to run the property, gotten a handle on your financial model, and sorted out your contracts. Now you can get to the fun bit, the part that I find really rewarding: providing great-quality, affordable accommodation for your target audience.

Finding good tenants

Here are my tried-and-true methods for finding tenants:

>> **Advertising online through property portals:** Two good options are SpareRoom (www.spareroom.com) and Roomi (www.roomiapp.com).

>> **Thinking about where your target audience hangs out and putting up advertisement there:** For example, if you're targeting young professionals, your local co-working space or artisan coffee shop might let you pin an ad to the notice board.

>> **Potentially working with local rental agents to rent the rooms:** There's obviously a cost associated with this, but it can be a good solution to outsource this element if you're managing multiple properties.

>> **Spreading the word through your own network, particularly using social media.**

>> **When you already have some existing tenants, leveraging their networks and asking them to spread the word for you:** Who do you think they'd rather have renting the bedroom next door: someone they already know or a complete stranger? Perhaps offer existing tenants a small referral fee for successfully introducing a new tenant to you who ends up taking a room.

TIP

In your ad, be sure to include lots of information about the property and rooms, and include high-quality images. It also helps to sell the benefits of the property, rather than features. In other words, what lifestyle does this property offer them? (The answer may be living in a high-quality property close to cool bars and young professionals like them with one simple rent payment including all bills, taking the hassle out of renting.)

REMEMBER

As you deal with more and more tenants, you'll become a great judge of character (if you aren't already). But it's still important to carefully vet tenants and check their references. The detailed advice on vetting tenants in Chapter 13 will help you do just that.

Managing the property after your tenants are in place

As a responsible landlord, you have a number of responsibilities to uphold. For one thing, it's your duty to provide safe, clean, and well-maintained accommodation.

REMEMBER

Chapter 13 sets out a detailed list of landlord responsibilities, and this will apply to most rental scenarios. But what's unique about rent-to-rent is that it's not your property. That means it's more important than ever to be respectful and maintain the property really well. That may mean:

>> **Conducting more regular checks than a standard landlord might:** I recommend monthly checks.

>> **Paying for a cleaner to come once every week or two to clean the communal areas:** Young professionals, in particular, are generally happy to pay a little more in rent for the privilege of never having to clean someone else's hair from the drain. Keep the cleaner close to you because their regular visits can also act as an early warning sign for any maintenance issues or misbehaving tenants.

>> **Encouraging tenants to reach out as soon as any maintenance issues crop up:** A small thing that goes ignored can cause bigger problems further down the line.

>> **Giving the property a light spruce (a coat of paint and so on) at regular intervals provided this has been agreed on with the landlord.**

You also have a responsibility to manage tenants and step in when problems arise. That's not to say you need to referee arguments between Liz and Ben on whose turn it is to buy milk. Instead, if one tenant is causing a genuine nuisance — at the risk of sounding like an old man, it's often noise-related — you need to nip that problem in the bud or you risk losing good-quality tenants.

REMEMBER

Let's not forget that you're running this property as a business, and you're very likely committed to a pretty long lease. That means you really need to keep the property occupied with good, reliable tenants; otherwise, you'll struggle to keep up with your monthly rent commitments. One unoccupied room at a time is unlikely to break the bank, but if you're losing tenants left, right, and center because of one bad apple, that will hit your finances hard.

When problems arise, ordinarily, a frank conversation and verbal warning that the tenant is in breach of the rental agreement is enough to solve the issue. But if that's not enough, you may need to take action to remove the tenant from the property. Turn to Chapter 13 for advice on how to get that ball rolling.

Identifying Five International Markets Where This Strategy Would Work

Like many of the strategies in this book, it's hard to pinpoint specific locations where rent-to-rent would and wouldn't work. If you have the right property for your target audience, demand for that type of accommodation, and an amenable landlord, you can make rent-to-rent work pretty much anywhere in the world. *Remember:* It's the combination of the property, landlord, location, and your chosen strategy that makes one particular area work so well.

REMEMBER

In general, if you're planning a multitenant property, like an HMO, that's aimed at professionals, then any bustling urban center with high real estate prices should be suitable (because if they can't afford to rent or buy a place of their own, renting a room is the natural next step).

Here are just a few locations that fit that bill, with professionals flocking to these vibrant cities:

>> Paris

>> New York

>> Copenhagen

>> London

>> Melbourne

Chapter **12**

Leveraging Lease Options

In Chapter 11, I talk about the rent-to-rent strategy, where you rent a property and earn money by subletting it to tenants whom you find and manage. Rent-to-rent is a great strategy for earning a steady income from property — especially when you don't have the capital to buy — but as a strategy, it lacks any form of capital growth. Because you never own the property, you'll never profit from selling it at some point in the future, nor will you be able to leverage it to finance other investments.

Lease options deliver a powerful solution to some of these downsides. How? In addition to renting the property, you negotiate the option to buy the property in the future, and this option is written into your contract with the property's owner. That way, you get income now *and* potential capital growth for the future. It's no wonder, then, that lease options have become incredibly popular with investors.

However, when you're new to the concept, lease options can be tricky to get your mind around — the option to buy the property in the future adds a layer of complexity over and above the rent-to-rent approach. You'll need to reach a fair agreement with the owner of the property and ensure your arrangement is properly reflected in your contract. But before you can do any of that, you need to find the right kind of opportunity.

In this chapter, I cover all these elements and more, enabling you to approach lease options with confidence.

Understanding Lease Options and How They Work

The central concept of lease options is actually quite straightforward. So let's start with a simple definition: A *lease option* (sometimes known as *rent-to-buy*) is a contractual agreement where you agree to rent a property from its owner, with the right to buy it down the line. This strategy is closely linked to rent-to-rent (see Chapter 11) because, after you've taken control of the property, you rent it out and create an income from it. The main difference between the two approaches is that the lease option includes the option to buy.

REMEMBER

Depending on the wording of your contract, you should have the option to purchase the property at any point during the agreement (not just at the end). And *option* is the key word there; you're not obligated to buy the property at any point, you've simply secured the *option* to buy it. So, if the value of the property goes down, and you no longer want to buy it, you don't have to. All upside for you as an investor!

Breaking down a lease option into its component parts

There are two key elements to any lease-option arrangement:

>> **The leasing/rental element:** This means you pay a monthly fee to the property owner (your landlord) to rent the property, and, as part of this, you have the right to manage the property, rent it out to tenants whom you find and manage, and earn a profit in the process.

>> **The option to buy:** Here, you secure the option to purchase the property later. As part of this, you agree what price you'll pay for the property when (or if) you buy it.

Both elements will be included in your lease-option contract. Turn to the section "Negotiating the Deal and Contract" later in the chapter for more on lease-option contracts.

The agreement is between you and the property's owner, who is also your landlord. Yet, you're also a landlord because you're renting the property out to your own tenants. You can see how the terminology can get tricky! To clarify the terminology used in this chapter.

>> I use *owner* to describe the property owner (your landlord).

>> I use *investor* or *property manager* to refer to you, the person renting the property from the owner. Another term for this is *sub-landlord*.

Now that that's cleared up, let's address the biggest advantages and disadvantages of lease options.

Looking at the pros of lease options

If you've read other chapters in this book already, you'll notice that *win–win* is one of my favorite phrases. Successful real estate investing is all about the ability to spot and execute win–win scenarios. For me, lease options are a clear and shining example of a win–win opportunity.

REMEMBER

Here's why I think lease options make such great investments:

>> **You don't have the hassle of taking out a mortgage right now.** This is great for investors who simply don't have the down payment for a mortgage, or are concerned about taking on more debt at the moment (maybe they don't qualify for some other reason, like low income or previous bad credit).

>> **You can take control of a property and start earning money on it almost immediately.** And you can do so with relatively little cash down compared to a standard buy-to-rent investment where you have to fork over tens of thousands for a down payment.

>> **You generate a steady income from the property by renting it out.** In fact, the profit you make can be set aside to help with purchasing the property in the future — so you're effectively earning the down payment from the property that you intend to buy.

>> **The idea is that the property goes up in value over the time you're managing it.** So, when you purchase it, at the price you agreed upon years ago, you've generated instant capital growth. In other words, it's already worth more than you paid for it, even though you've only just bought it!

>> **You may even be able to increase the value of the property simply by the way you're running it.** For example, a property that's being run as an HMO (see Chapter 13), with rooms rented to individual tenants, may achieve a higher valuation than if the same property was rented to one household. Therefore, you'll be able to borrow more based on that increased value. You can find more on valuation in Chapter 7.

>> **If the market changes or you no longer want to buy the property, you don't have to.** Great, no downside! Your agreement comes to an end and you move on to the next project, having earned a decent income (or down payment on a different property) in the meantime. Win–win, see?

Weighing the cons

Although lease options offer lots of mouthwatering advantages, there are some risks to be aware of, most of which can be easily planned for.

WARNING

The biggest risks with a lease option are as follows:

>> **Even though you're paying rent each month, the owner could default on *his* mortgage.** If that happens, the property may be repossessed, meaning you lose out on your rental income (and your tenants are kicked out of their home), and you lose out on the potential to own the property in the future.

>> **As with any investment, the value of the property may go down instead of up, trashing your plans for all that lovely capital growth.** Remember, though, that you aren't obligated to buy the property.

>> **The property isn't legally yours until you've bought it.** So, spending money on the property (for maintenance and improvement works) comes with the risk that you may never get a return on that investment.

>> **The owner may default on the lease-option agreement and refuse to sell the property to you.** This scenario is mercifully rare, providing you enter into a fair agreement and both parties go into it with honest expectations. But if the owner is adamant that he no longer wants to sell to you, and you're adamant that you still want to buy, you'll have no choice but to hammer it out in court. The lawyers' bills alone may mean it's better to just walk away (depending on the deal, of course).

REMEMBER

There are ways to protect yourself against these risks, such as having it written into your contract that the owner will supply you with regular mortgage statements to show he's paying down the mortgage. For more on safeguarding your investment, refer to "Negotiating the Deal and Contract" later in this chapter.

There's another disadvantage to consider upfront: It can be much harder to identify lease-option opportunities and convince the owner that he should rent his property to you with the option to buy (as opposed to simply selling the property right now). I talk more about the benefits that lease options bring to homeowners in "What's in It for the Property Owner?" later in the chapter.

Deciding whether lease options are right for you

Much of the advice I've seen on lease options says it's too complicated a strategy, it's not for the fainthearted, and it's completely unsuitable for less-experienced investors. Personally, I largely disagree.

MATCHING STRATEGIES TO PEOPLE AND CIRCUMSTANCES

Finding great deals is all about understanding the other party's needs and goals, so that you can help them solve problems and create a win–win scenario that works for both of you.

In the United Kingdom alone, there are around 17 million homeowners, each of whom has his or her own unique circumstances, goals, and needs. A big part of successful real estate investing is learning to spot circumstances and opportunities, and then matching the right strategy to that situation. That's why I believe it's so important to understand a range of different property strategies — and, ultimately, it's why I wrote this book to give you access to that toolkit!

You may be talking to a contact who has very specific needs — for example, she wants to maintain ownership of her investment properties but needs to take a step back from the day-to-day management for health reasons — and think to yourself, "Wow, rent-to-rent is perfect for this scenario." Or say another contact has had trouble selling a particular property; you may find yourself thinking, "A lease option would really solve his problem." Or you may know someone with land to develop but no idea where to start, in which case, "I could develop that site in a joint venture (JV) partnership with her."

In my experience, it's this ability to spot such needs and think, "How can I meet this need or solve the owner's problem?" that's pivotal to building a successful, diversified real estate portfolio. And if you don't have a product or strategy that's right for that particular scenario, maybe you know someone else who does. Maybe you could pass on that lease-option lead for a finder's fee. Or act as a property sourcer and bring a seller and buyer together.

In essence, although some of the strategies in this book may not appeal to your skills or goals, don't discount a strategy altogether. You never know when you'll meet a contact for whom that approach may be perfect.

Because you need relatively little capital to get started with lease options, it makes a great strategy for investors who are in the early days of their real estate careers and haven't yet built up much capital. (That's not to say it's exclusively for beginner investors — far from it. As an experienced investor, I still regularly invest in or help others invest in lease options.)

However, you do need to go into lease options with your eyes wide open. Sourcing the right property can be hard work (as can negotiating with the owner, who's perhaps never even heard of lease options). And there are risks attached, as I've already mentioned.

So, is a lease option the right approach for you? Only you can answer that, and the answer will depend on your goals, your financial situation, and your skills. If you're willing to put in the hours and invest time in learning the strategy, and if you can run a property in a professional way, you have a strong financial model, and you have a good dream team around you (including a real estate lawyer, see Chapter 3), lease options may be a great way to grow your portfolio quickly.

Even if you decide you don't want to go down the lease-option route right now, or perhaps the market is too strong to convince owners of the merits of lease options, don't brush the idea off completely. Keep lease options in the back of your mind, because you never know when the ideal lease-option scenario will arise (see the sidebar "Matching strategies to people and circumstances").

Understanding the Financial Model for Lease Options

Unlike rent-to-rent (see Chapter 11), a good lease option will deliver a steady income as well as capital growth. When it comes to making money with lease options, there are three strands to consider:

>> **Earning profit from the rental income:** After you've received the rent from your tenants and paid the bills and your monthly rent, there's profit left over for you.

>> **Capital growth for the future:** When you come to own the property, it should be worth more than you paid for it.

>> **Selling on the lease option to a third party:** If for some reason you no longer want to manage the property or buy it, you can sell the option to another investor.

Let's look at each area in turn, and briefly explore the typical costs involved in lease options.

Earning rental income from the property

Your strategy for earning income from the property is essentially the same as with the rent-to-rent approach. So, if you haven't yet read Chapter 11, I encourage you to circle back and learn more about how the rent-to-rent income model works.

REMEMBER

In a nutshell, though, you make money by earning more in rent than you have to pay to the owner. The smartest way to do this is by changing the use of the property — most commonly from a standard single rental (rented to one tenant or household) to renting out individual rooms in a larger house or apartment. However, you can also change the use by renting the property out on a nightly basis, as serviced accommodation. You can find more on changing the use of a property in Chapter 11.

Let's look at a brief example: Say I rent a three-bedroom house from the owner for $800 per month. That's plenty to cover the owner's mortgage, so he's happy. However, I know it's possible to maximize the rental income by renting individual bedrooms, so I turn the dining room into a fourth bedroom and rent each bedroom out for $400 per month, including bills. That nets me $1,600 per month in rental income. After covering my rent obligations ($800) and bills for the property ($450), I'm left with $350 profit each month.

Earning capital growth on the property

Where lease options differ from rent-to-rent is the option to buy the property in the future. This is where your potential capital growth comes from. The best way to illustrate this is with a quick example.

REMEMBER

Let's continue with the example of the three-bedroom house. I agree to rent it from the owner for five years at $800 per month. The property is currently worth $150,000, and, because I don't anticipate buying it until the end of the tenancy period, I secure the option to buy it for $160,000. At the end of the five-year period, the property is actually worth $170,000. So, when I buy it for $160,000, as agreed, I've instantly generated $10,000 in equity. Now, I can sell the property on and take the profit, or continue to rent it out and earn income, or even leverage the property to finance another investment. Plus, thanks to my $350 monthly profit, I've already banked $21,000 from renting the property out for five years.

And what if property values in the area flatline and, at the end of the five-year period, the property is still only worth $150,000 — meaning it's not worth the purchase price I agreed for it? The short answer is, I don't have to buy it. I can simply let the option expire and hand the property back to the owner.

Sure, it can be disappointing for both parties when the arrangement doesn't end in a successful purchase. However, in this example, I've pocketed more than $20,000, and the owner has benefitted from five years of having his mortgage paid hassle-free — so it's hardly been a waste of time.

What's more, if the rental market is strong (which can happen when property sales take a nosedive), I can always negotiate to extend or start a new lease-option agreement, thereby continuing to earn a great rental income while waiting for the property's retail value to recover.

Selling the option instead of buying the property

If you don't want to buy the property and don't want to continue renting it out, there's still another opportunity to make money from the lease-option arrangement: You can sell the option to another buyer.

Continuing with the three-bedroom house example, let's say the property is worth $170,000, and I secured the option to buy it for $160,000. That's all well and good. Yet, my circumstances have changed and I no longer want to buy or operate the property (perhaps I'm focusing all my efforts on a new strategy, or I just can't generate the capital to buy the property as planned).

I can walk away, happy with the rental income I've generated. But I know that the property would be ideal for my contact, Jane Austen, and I also know she'd be very eager to buy the house for the agreed-upon price. In this case, I could sell the option to Ms. Austen for $5,000, and everyone benefits. I'll still be pocketing some profit, Ms. Austen gets a house worth $170,000 for the grand total of $165,000 (including the option fee she paid me), and the owner still gets to sell as planned.

Understanding the "consideration" payment

Now that I've covered the income and capital growth potential of lease options, let's look at the main costs involved.

REMEMBER

One of the most important costs involved is called the *consideration*. For the lease-option contract to be legally binding (at least in my legal jurisdiction, in England), some money needs to change hands between you and the owner. You, therefore, pay a fee to the property owner to secure the lease option. This fee is the *consideration* payment.

You need to negotiate the consideration with the owner as part of the lease-option deal, but, technically, the consideration can be as little as £1 (and this is often the case). You can find more on negotiating the consideration and other contractual elements in the section "Negotiating the Deal and Contract."

Considering ongoing costs

There are also costs involved in operating the property on an ongoing basis, including the following:

>> Monthly bills such as gas, electric, and insurance

>> Any management fees (if you employ a managing agent to look after the property for you)

>> Costs associated with finding and vetting tenants

>> General maintenance and upkeep of the property

When it comes to maintenance and upkeep, you should expect to cover the basic costs yourself. That will include keeping the property clean and well presented, giving it the occasional coat of paint, and carrying out any basic improvements that are necessary to appeal to your target tenants.

WARNING

However, because you don't yet own the property, be wary of paying for big-ticket upgrades and maintenance. If the roof needs replacing, for example, I would absolutely expect the owner to cover that sort of job. Who is responsible for carrying out (and paying for) maintenance and repairs should be stipulated in your contract.

In Chapter 11, I offer a more detailed discussion of the typical costs involved in a rent-to-rent property, including startup costs to get the property up and running.

Knowing What's in It for the Property Owner

Having come to terms with the basics of lease options and the financial model for you as an investor, you may be asking yourself one big question: Why on earth would a property owner agree to a lease option?

On the face of it, there aren't many advantages. The owner is committing to a sale price now, knowing that the value of the property may go up beyond that. And he's locked in to a contract with no realistic option to pull out of the deal (unlike you, who can walk away at the end of the tenancy if you want). That's why lease options are often portrayed as a last resort for property owners, suitable only for distressed sellers and the very desperate.

I disagree, though. Sure, when someone is seriously looking to sell his property, nine times out of ten he'd rather sell now than a few years down the road. He'd rather have the certainty and the capital to move on to another property. But that's not necessarily true for every property owner.

Perhaps it's an investment property (not the owner's home), and he'd rather have a hands-off investment than run the property himself. Maybe he's looking to retire, and he finds the idea of a steady retirement income very attractive. Maybe he's taking a midlife career break and backpacking around the world for two years — in which case, he'd rather the property was rented for two years, saving him two years' worth of fees on furniture storage, and then he comes back to a (pretty much) guaranteed sale!

REMEMBER

Scratch the surface and there are actually a number of reasons why an owner may agree to a lease option. After all, the advantages for him are as follows:

>> He gets guaranteed rent for the duration of the tenancy, with no void periods.

>> He gets his mortgage paid, hassle-free.

>> He only has to deal with you as the tenant, rather than a revolving door of different tenants.

>> He saves on management fees, because you'll be responsible for running the property.

>> He has a buyer lined up for the future.

Sometimes, sadly, an owner is in financial trouble and the idea of guaranteed mortgage payments is what seals the deal. This can be particularly true if the owner is in *negative equity* (owing more on the mortgage than the property is worth). Negative equity isn't necessarily a huge problem if you can afford to ride out the market trough and wait for prices to recover. But if the owner absolutely has to move (for example, for work), negative equity can be disastrous. With a lease option, he would at least be earning a secure rental income on the property, without having to manage tenants. It's important to remember that, with distressed owners, you are effectively helping to solve their problem! If the owner lost his job, for example, and can't pay his high mortgage, you can come in and save him from getting bad credit by taking over the mortgage payments effectively with your rent, allowing him to perhaps downsize to a smaller apartment and stop repossession. It should be a win–win scenario.

Sourcing Lease-Option Opportunities

Given that most property owners looking to sell would rather sell immediately than agree on a sale for the future, finding the right lease-option deal is as much about finding the right owner as it is about finding the right property.

In this section, I look at both aspects: the property and the owner.

Deciding what type of property you want and how you'll operate it

The right property for you will depend on your chosen strategy for operating the property. If you're renting individual rooms, for example, you'll want a property with multiple bedrooms. If you're renting the property out night-by-night via Airbnb, you may want a small apartment. Circle back to Chapter 11 for advice on how to source the right kind of property for your plans.

REMEMBER

The lease option is not really a real estate strategy in its own right; instead, it's the legal mechanism by which you take control of the property. You'll need to decide which strategy you'll employ to physically run the property and make money from it as well.

You can find guidance on some of the most popular real estate strategies throughout this book. For example, if you're going to run the property as an HMO, turn to Chapter 13. Or if you're going to rent it out to students or low-income-housing tenants, Chapter 14 will help you do that. Chapter 15 will apply if you're running the property as serviced accommodation. Or turn to Chapter 16 if it's going to be a vacation rental.

REMEMBER

Whichever strategy you choose, you must make sure the owner is onboard with your running the property in that way. To be clear, I'm absolutely not talking about illegally subletting a property without the owner's knowledge — you must always have permission to sublet the property and manage it in the way you intend, and this should be reflected in your contract with the owner.

For advice on managing the property on an ongoing basis, turn to Chapter 11 and/or the appropriate chapter for your chosen strategy.

Looking for motivated sellers who would be open to a lease option

You're not just looking for a property that suits your strategy, you also have to find the right kind of property owner to work with. This is a case of finding the right person, at the right time in his life — a case of finding someone who's motivated to work with you.

TIP

Win–win scenarios are what you're aiming for, so look for people with a problem you can solve (for example, someone who can no longer afford to pay his mortgage) or people who are looking to offload the work of managing tenants (for example, someone who's already renting the property but now wants to be more hands-off).

For example, the owner may be

>> In negative equity

>> Suddenly unemployed and unable to pay his mortgage

>> Getting divorced and unable to cover the mortgage on a single salary

>> Retiring to his second home and looking to earn hands-off income on his primary property (see, it's not necessarily all doom and gloom!)

>> Needing to move quickly (for example, for a great job opportunity)

TIP

Here are my top tips for identifying such motivated sellers:

>> **Look for properties that have been for sale for a while or that are clearly overpriced (and, therefore, won't sell).**

>> **Explore property markets that have seen big peaks and troughs in property prices.** If someone bought at peak price, and the market hasn't yet fully recovered from a slump, she may well still be in negative equity and may welcome a good offer.

>> **Drop flyers through doors in an area with a lot of distressed sellers.**

>> **Set up Google and Facebook ad campaigns (both platforms allow you to target very specific demographics if you want to), highlighting the benefits of having a mortgage paid hassle-free followed by a guaranteed sale.**

>> **Run ads in the local paper, shops, and other community spaces.**

You may also know investor-owners from your own network who may be open to a lease-option arrangement. For example, they may be

>> Running the property poorly (in which case, there'll be a high turnover of tenants)

>> Fed up with managing tenants or paying others to manage the property for them

>> Looking to take a step back and wind down their day-to-day involvement

TIP

If an owner gets in touch and you feel her property isn't right for you, don't discount it entirely. If it's a solid proposition (perhaps it's just not your field of expertise), it may be right for another investor in your network. If that's the case, there may be an opportunity to pass the lead on for a finder's fee.

Getting the owner onboard with a lease option

First thing's first, unless the property owner is a fellow investor, it's very likely you'll need to start by explaining what the heck lease options are.

WARNING

Don't scrimp on this. Yes, it takes time and effort to explain the whole concept, and you may still get a hard "no," but it's important that the owner enters into the deal fully aware of what he's getting into. The last thing you want is for her to feel like he's getting the short end of the stick and renege on the deal after you've gone to all the trouble of finding and settling in tenants — or, worse, try to claim that you hoodwinked him into it and took advantage of his lack of knowledge.

In addition to describing how lease options work, you'll also want to spend time selling the benefits for him as an owner (as discussed in "What's in It for the Property Owner" earlier in the chapter). Even if the owner is in dire straits and really needs this deal, you want his full support and cooperation for the duration of the agreement, and a stress-free purchase at the end — so make sure he's clear on the benefits and that these suit his needs.

Negotiating the Deal and Contract

For the most part, a rent-to-rent contract and lease option contract are very similar, so I won't repeat what I say in Chapter 11. Instead, in this section, I focus on the added complexities that you'll find in a lease-option contract.

In addition to the areas covered in Chapter 11, the key things you'll need to agree on with the owner and stipulate in your lease-option contract are

>> How much you'll pay in rent each month

>> How long the agreement lasts for

>> What price you'll pay for the property when (or if) you come to purchase it

>> That purchasing is an option, not a legal obligation

>> How much you'll pay as the *consideration* (upfront fee), if applicable

In this section, I cover each of these elements one by one.

WARNING

You don't want to be accused of mis-selling a deal to a property owner, so it's vital the owner fully understands the agreement and has taken proper legal advice. I would always recommend that the owner has his own lawyer, independent of yours. You could offer to pay their legal fees for the lawyer of his choice if the thought of paying for a lawyer puts the owner off.

You and the owner may also want to take expert advice on insurance requirements, any leasehold implications (if the property is an apartment, there could potentially be a restriction on subletting apartments in the building), and whether the lease-option agreement affects the mortgage on the property.

Your monthly rent

When it comes to deciding the monthly rent, there are three options to consider:

>> **Offering the going market rate for renting a property of that size and type in that area:** This option seems fair for both parties.

>> **Offering slightly above the market rate, if you need to sweeten the deal for the owner to secure the right property:** You may do this if you've really done your numbers and you're sure you can still make the profit you want.

>> **Offering a little less than the market rate:** This option may make sense if it's enough to meet the owner's needs (paying the mortgage every month and covering other costs associated with owning the property). You may be able to negotiate this option if the owner prefers to be hands off and values your managing the property even if it's for a little less monthly rent.

REMEMBER

You want to strike a deal that's attractive and beneficial for both parties. If you try to screw the owner out of a fair deal, you're only running the risk that he'll default on the agreement as soon as he can afford to, leaving you (and your tenants) in the lurch. Remember that you're looking for a long-term partnership here, and that's only possible when both parties are happy.

To strike the best deal for both of you, you really need to understand the owner's goals and needs. So, spend time getting to know him and understanding his motivations for entering into this deal. If all he wants is to cover his mortgage and expenses each month, and to not have to worry about the property for a few years, then that will obviously inform your rent negotiations.

REMEMBER

Always crunch the numbers carefully and make sure the rent you've agreed upon works for your financial model and leaves enough profit on the table for you at the end of each month. Expecting to turn a decent profit is entirely fair — after all, you're the one running the property on a daily basis, dealing with tenants, keeping the property in good order, and so on. It's only fair that you earn enough to be compensated for this time and effort.

The length of the agreement

Like a rent-to-rent agreement (or any type of rental agreement, for that matter), you need to agree how long you'll rent the property for. After this period of time, you'll then have the option to buy the property or hand it back to the owner. (Of course, if you wanted to, you could buy the property at any point during the agreement, not necessarily at the end.)

REMEMBER

Because you're looking to run the property as a business, you want the stability of agreeing the longest possible term. A longer agreement period also allows more time for *capital growth* (for the property to go up in value beyond the agreed-upon purchase price), and it gives you more time to accumulate rental income. Essentially, more time usually translates into more profit for you.

There's no rule of thumb on contract length — it all depends on your goals as an investor and the owner's circumstances, so it's entirely up to you to negotiate the most suitable length for both parties. It can be as little as 3 years, or it can, in theory, run as long as 10, 15, or 20 years.

For example, someone with a 20-year mortgage whose circumstances have suddenly changed may want certainty that his 20-year mortgage will be paid and have a guaranteed buyer at the end. In which case, he may be open to a very long lease. Certain longer leases may also attract land tax (Stamp Duty Land Tax in the United Kingdom), so double-check with your attorney before putting forward any offer to ensure your numbers don't leave anything out.

TIP

It's a good idea to have a break clause in the contract that allows you to hand the property back sooner if you want to. (For example, if it's a five-year lease, you may want the option to hand it back after only three years.) Ideally, this break clause will be on your side only. You don't want the owner to have the option of demanding his property back at any point.

The purchase price

A critical part of the negotiation is agreeing what price you'll pay for the property when (or if) you come to purchase it.

REMEMBER

Here, you're ideally trying to agree on a purchase price that's not too much more than the current market price, to give you the best possible chance of achieving capital growth. For example, if the house is currently worth $200,000 and you're entering into a ten-year agreement, then a purchase price of $215,000 may be appropriate. You're obviously banking on a couple of factors here:

>> The property will go up way beyond $215,000 over the next ten years, earning you instant equity when you buy it at that price. (If it doesn't, you may not want to buy it.)

>> The owner will be happy to accept this price for the long-term stability it brings him. (If he isn't happy, it's no deal.)

WARNING

You want to negotiate hard here, but be fair. If you're dealing with a distressed seller who urgently needs to secure a deal, he may be willing to sell in the future at the current market rate, but be wary of agreeing on a price that's too low. If you've driven too hard a bargain, there's nothing much (other than the threat of legal action, which will cost you money) to stop him from defaulting on the deal and selling to someone else at the end of the agreement. *Remember:* Always be fair and ethical. You're looking for a win–win, not an I win–you lose!

The consideration

The *consideration* (payment you give to the owner in exchange for the option to purchase the property later) is perhaps the hardest part of the negotiation to understand.

Technically speaking, this payment can be as little as £1 or $1, which is enough to make the agreement legally binding. But you may struggle to get anyone beyond extremely distressed sellers to agree to such a small amount. In most circumstances, a £1 consideration may not be realistic and, as with any part of the contract, it's open to negotiation.

The consideration is the fee you pay for the *option* to purchase the property. It's not always a down payment that gets taken off the purchase price later on, although if you can negotiate that, all the better. This means you want to keep the consideration as low as possible to minimize your risk. For example, if you paid a whopping £20,000 for the option, and you later decide not to buy the property, the owner gets to keep your money, effectively for giving you exclusivity during that time period.

Don't forget the simple option contract. *Option contracts* (without the "lease" part!) are also a form of real estate investing and are often used by developers to secure land sites for a period of time while they try to gain planning permission for it. If and when they're successful, they'll complete the purchase of the land and build their plans out.

However, because it can be hard to get owners to come around to the idea of lease options, you'll probably have to offer more than £1. If it's a booming market, for example, you may need to pay a higher consideration and/or a higher purchase price to secure the deal. If that's the case, you'll need to think carefully about what sort of capital growth you expect from the property and factor that into your calculations.

Returning to the example of the house that's currently worth $200,000, where you've agreed to buy it for $215,000 in ten years' time. You could perhaps afford to pay the owner a $5,000 consideration because, in reality, you're expecting the property to be worth $230,000 in future. Even after the consideration and purchase, you're still in the money.

Ultimately, it's a case of negotiating the lowest consideration payment that you can afford and that the owner will agree to. In some cases, this may well be as little as $1, if the owner is just looking to have his mortgage paid and secure a buyer for the future.

Other safeguards

There are some risks associated with lease options, with perhaps the biggest being that the owner will default on his mortgage or try to sell the property without your knowledge. You'll want to take appropriate legal steps to protect yourself against these risks.

For example, you can have it written into your contract that the owner has to provide you with a copy of his mortgage statement every quarter, giving you the reassurance that your rent is going toward paying down the mortgage. You can also stipulate that the rent you pay must go toward paying the mortgage — definitely worth considering if the owner is in a lot of other debt. Alternatively, if you're really concerned, you could stipulate that you'll pay the mortgage company directly.

There's another legal document worth considering, too, and that is a *restriction on title.* Essentially, this means your agreement with the owner is included on the registered title deeds for the property. So, if the owner tries to sell the property without your knowledge, you'll be identified as a *charge* (in other words, an interested party), and you'll be notified accordingly. This gives you some level of protection against the owner selling out from under you.

Always work with a specialist real estate lawyer, who can advise you on the right documents, clauses, and wording to suit your needs and protect your interests.

Identifying Five International Locations Where This Strategy Would Work

In theory, lease options would work in any geographic location. So long as you can source the right kind of property that's right for your strategy, and you have a willing owner onboard with the idea, you can pretty much deploy this approach in any market.

I say "pretty much." Always talk to a local expert about the specific legalities of your chosen market, and work with a trustworthy local attorney to ensure your lease-option agreement is thorough and above board.

Because lease options are often considered a decent option for distressed sellers, it makes sense that this strategy would be successful in locations that are going through a period of economic recovery, rather than locations that are booming sellers' markets.

A few spots around the world come to mind:

>> **Spain:** When the market was booming, before the 2008 financial crash, a lot of investors piled in and bought at prices that were far too steep. As a result, some may still find themselves in negative equity although the market has

been recovering slowly there, which is good from a longer-term capital-growth perspective.

» **Berlin:** Berlin has a fairly stable property curve, which means you may come across sellers who are stuck in a rut and unable to offload their property.

» **Amsterdam:** Amsterdam is a top city for foreign investors, and one with high rental demand, which makes life great for you as an investor.

» **Cities like Grimsby, Leeds and Belfast, in the United Kingdom:** Previous industrial centers like these often have property prices lagging behind the rest of the United Kingdom, which may create an opportunity for lease-option investors.

» **San Antonio:** Cities like San Antonio, Texas, have, at the time of writing, witnessed a serious stagnation in the housing market.

Chapter **13**

Delving into Houses in Multiple Occupation

When I was just 24, I turned my home into a *house in multiple occupation* (HMO), renting out spare rooms to young professionals like myself. This HMO was my first step into real estate investment and was the springboard to a successful property portfolio that now includes many more HMOs. Plus, it was the start of some beautiful friendships! So, it's fair to say that I'm a big fan of HMOs.

And I'm not alone. Thanks to increasing pressure on our housing markets, HMOs are becoming more and more popular with both real estate investors and tenants. That's because, instead of renting out a whole property to one person or family, you can rent out individual rooms to individual tenants. Your tenants benefit from easy access to affordable housing, and you benefit from increased rental yield. It's a win–win.

REMEMBER

Because you're renting to more tenants, HMOs can deliver a great return on investment, usually significantly more than a traditional buy-to-rent. In fact, in high-demand areas, you can potentially double your rental income.

However, there are lots of factors to consider before you take the plunge, and, as with any investment strategy, careful thought and research is needed. In this chapter, I set out what you need to be aware of before you get started with HMOs and share my own experience of running numerous successful HMOs.

Note that *HMO* is a specifically British term, and because it's a strategy that's growing enormously in the United Kingdom right now, the content in this chapter — particularly the legal stuff — is geared toward the UK market. However, the concept of renting individual rooms in the same can and is applied all over the world. Turn to the end of the chapter to find five international locations where this strategy would work well.

Introducing HMOs

In very simple terms, an HMO is a residential property where rooms are rented out to multiple separate tenants (usually young professionals). So, what was a three-bedroom house with two reception rooms could potentially be converted into a five-bedroom HMO, rented to five separate tenants.

WARNING

The legal definition of what constitutes an HMO can vary from jurisdiction to jurisdiction, so it's important to be really clear whether your property qualifies as an HMO. If it does, then you may be subject to special licensing and regulations (see "Staying on the Right Side of the Law" later in the chapter).

Where I live, in England, the government planning department defines an HMO as a property with

>> At least three tenants living there

>> Tenants forming more than one household (a *household* being a single person or members of the same family living together, including married and co-habiting couples)

>> Shared kitchen and bathroom facilities

So, back when I was a fresh-faced 24-year-old and began renting out my spare bedroom, my house wasn't classed as an HMO because there were only two people living there (myself and my roommate). But when I converted the garage to make a third rental bedroom and rented the second spare bedroom (having well and truly caught the property bug), that's when it certainly became an HMO.

REMEMBER

An HMO doesn't have to be a house; it can be a shared apartment. The main defining criteria is that the amenities (kitchen and bathroom) are shared by multiple separate tenants. A property that's been converted into three apartments, each with its own private, self-contained amenities, is not an HMO.

TECHNICAL STUFF

In England, there's an additional planning permission definition to understand, and that's *large HMOs*, which fall within the "sui generis" planning use class. These are

>> Rented to more than six people (not of the same household)

>> With shared kitchen and bathroom facilities

Large HMOs have required mandatory licensing by local authorities for some time (even if you have just five people living in the property not six!), although the rules are constantly changing and as of October 1, 2018, local UK authorities are requiring licensing for regular "small" HMOs, as well. You can find more on licensing later in this chapter — it's a very important part of running HMOs to understand and adhere to. Always check with your local government as to what the current licensing requirements and planning rules are because they often change (especially as the emerging market of HMOs is becoming more mainstream). These changes also often differ between planning regulations and licensing regulations, so it's important to ensure you're up on both areas and ensure both sets of regulations are adhered to.

Breaking Down the HMO Financial Model

The best way to explain the HMO financial model is with a quick example.

Say I buy a three-bedroom house and rent it out to one household as a straightforward single rental. Depending on what part of the country the house is in, I might earn £1,000 a month in rental income. Not bad, and plenty to cover the mortgage.

However, as a budding real estate investor, I'm looking for more than "not bad." So, I turn the large study and dining room into two extra bedrooms and rent out each of the now five bedrooms individually (either to single persons or couples), and I can expect to earn around £450 from each room. That's a monthly rental income of around £2,250. In this way, compared to a regular buy-to-rent property, HMOs ordinarily deliver a much higher yield.

WARNING

Be aware, though, that the costs with HMOs also tend to be higher than regular buy-to-rents. More tenants means higher utility bills, insurance, maintenance costs, and management fees (if you use a managing agent). Then there's the higher chance of *void periods* (where one or more of the rooms are vacant) and the extra time and cost involved in finding all these tenants.

TIP

In my experience, I've found that HMO costs typically add up to around 10 percent to 15 percent of the gross income each year. This is a good rule of thumb when working out your HMO finances, but keep in mind that with a managing agent this could be even higher. For me, even taking into account these higher costs, an HMO is still financially more attractive than a standard single rental. My company fully manages our own HMOs in house — I employ people to take care of my properties, rather than pay a third-party managing agent — so we keep the costs as low as possible.

Now that you understand the basic financial model, you've probably garnered a good idea of the typical pros and cons of HMOs. On the sunny side:

>> **You usually earn more than you would with a standard rental.**

>> **HMOs are a fairly low-risk investment.** That's because, even if one of your rooms is empty for a while, you'll probably still be earning enough to cover the bills and mortgage. In a standard rental, no tenant means no income at all. That's why I actually consider HMOs a *lower* risk than single rentals in many cases.

And the not-so-sunny side:

>> **Your costs are higher.** Water, electric, gas, maintenance costs . . . everything will be higher when you have multiple tenants living in a shared property.

>> **HMOs take up more of your time.** If you're managing the HMO yourself (which you probably will be doing, at least in the early days), you're responsible for finding, settling in, and managing all the tenants. Nowadays, I pay an in-house managing agent to handle this for me. This frees up more of my time, but it does mean my costs are higher (see "Scaling up Your HMO Portfolio" later in the chapter for more).

>> **HMOs mean more red tape.** Licensing of HMOs and the specific planning rules for HMOs mean your knowledge needs to be greater than with some more straightforward rental properties.

Sourcing HMO Properties

When it comes to sourcing HMOs, there are three main options to consider:

>> Turning your own property into an HMO

>> Buying a property to turn into an HMO

>> Buying an existing, up-and-running HMO

The last option is great in that the property has already been converted for multiple tenants and (hopefully) already has tenants in place. However, a functioning HMO may command a premium price, and is likely to be out of reach for an HMO newbie. By far the most common approaches are to turn your own property into an HMO or to buy a property and turn it into an HMO. Both of these two options *add value*, which is so important in real estate investing (see Chapter 9). Let's look at both of these options in a little more detail.

Converting your existing home into an HMO

This is how I got started, and it's a great, low-barrier entry to HMOs.

REMEMBER

If you're considering turning your home into an HMO, you must inform your mortgage provider; depending on your mortgage and the size of HMO, you may need to change your mortgage. You also need to find out from your local housing authority whether you need a special license and planning permission. You'll then have some work to do to make sure your property meets various legal requirements, like fire safety (again, more on the legal side coming up later).

But it's not just legal stuff you need to take care of. There are also lots of practical things to think about if you're going to make your property work for more people:

>> **Do you need to convert a small bedroom into an extra bathroom?** Lots of people sharing one bathroom can be a strain. Plus, it'll turn off quality tenants.

>> **If you have more than one reception room (separate living and dining rooms, for instance), do you want to turn them both into bedrooms or leave one as shared living space?** Many tenants like access to a communal living space.

>> **Is there potential to convert the loft or basement into an additional bedroom?** You'd obviously need to weigh the cost and planning implications of this work versus the additional income you'd make.

>> **Do your appliances need upgrading to cope with the extra wear and tear?** For example, how long do you think a dishwasher will last in a house of five hungry millennials?

>> **In terms of décor and fixtures/fittings, what do you need to do to ensure the property is suitable for and attractive to your target audience?** I talk more about target audience later in this chapter.

REMEMBER

As a live-in landlord, you'll be expected to make sure that repairs and replacements are done quickly and to a high standard. Unless, of course, you enjoy frosty stares and awkward silences over the breakfast cereal. . . .

Buying a property to turn into an HMO

If you're purchasing a property to convert into an HMO, you'll need to secure funding. This is usually done through a mortgage (see Chapter 6 for traditional finance options and Chapter 8 for some interesting, creative routes to financing property).

WARNING

Depending on the planned size of your HMO, finding a mortgage may be more challenging than a typical buy-to-rent property, and you may have to pay higher fees and interest rates. Generally, the bigger the HMO, the more challenging and costly it gets to find a suitable mortgage; a commercial mortgage may be your best bet. To get the right deal for you, it's vital you talk to a mortgage broker with relevant HMO experience.

Other things to consider at this stage include the following:

>> Depending on the size of the property and planned number of tenants, you may need planning permission and a license (see "Staying on the Right Side of the Law" coming up).

>> Find out which rules and regulations would apply to your property before you commit to buying it to avoid nasty surprises and unexpected costs/delays.

>> Sorting out licensing, planning, and any renovation work takes time, so factor this additional setup time into your calculations on what you can afford. Until the tenants are in place, you're the one footing the bills — and the mortgage!

TIP

It's worth buying the biggest property that you can reasonably afford. For example, a six-bedroom house will make you more in rental income than a four-bedroom house — for not much more in terms of effort, time ,and costs. Extra bedrooms mean better economies of scale and a higher income-to-costs ratio, all money in your pocket!

Deciding Who You Want to Rent To

Before you buy a property or start converting your property into an HMO, you need to think about what type of tenant you want to attract, because this will affect a lot of your decisions along the way. The main tenant profiles HMO investors target are

>> Professionals (usually young professionals who are struggling to get on the property ladder)

>> Students

>> Low-income-housing tenants

Each type of tenant has advantages and disadvantages. Professional tenants are seen as being more reliable payers, but they tend to be fussier about the quality of their accommodation (expecting a nice kitchen, high-speed Internet, en-suite bathrooms, and attractive bathrooms, for starters), so you may need to spend more on setting up the property and keeping it looking good.

Students tend to create a bit more wear and tear (or maybe that was just me and my friends?) and move on each year, but on the plus side, they're usually less fussy about the quality of amenities.

Finally, many investors shy away from low-income-housing tenants, but they can be a savvy choice. For example, in my area, the low-income-housing provider will typically rent the property for five years at a time and cover all the utility bills, void periods, and rent arrears during that period.

TIP

As a first-time HMO investor, much of your decision will probably come down to the type of people you want to deal with (or even live with). Personally, I've seen the best results and had the best experiences renting to professionals, and that's the audience I focus on in this chapter.

If you want to target students and low-income-housing tenants, turn to Chapter 14 for more information.

Finding the Best Location for Your HMO

Whenever you're buying a property to turn it into an HMO, you need to make a decision on the best location for your HMO. Largely, this will come down to your target market. You'll only attract student tenants when you're close to a university, for instance.

Likewise, an HMO that's targeted to professionals will need to be in a busy town or city, where there's plenty of work. They'll also expect a location that is either within walking distance of the city center or somewhere with good transport links.

Other key considerations for location include

>> **Supply and demand:** Sites like SpareRoom (www.spareroom.com) and Roomi (www.roomiapp.com) are really helpful for assessing this, because you can see how many rooms are available to rent in an area and how many tenants are looking for rooms.

>> **Local population:** You need to do your homework on factors like local population (age, education, and so on), average earnings, largest source of work in the local area, and whether the population is growing. Sites like Mouseprice (www.mouseprice.com) are helpful for this, along with local council demographic data. In the United States, census data from www.census.gov is a good starting point.

>> **Potential yield:** Rent prices vary from place to place, so do the math on how much it costs to buy property in a given area versus the typical room rent rates. Head to sites like SpareRoom (www.spareroom.com) and Zoopla (www.zoopla.co.uk) to research this.

Research is obviously important at this stage, but so is local knowledge. When setting up your first HMO, stick within an area and demographic that you know pretty well. That's what I did when I was starting out, and it worked well for me.

Staying on the Right Side of the Law

HMOs tend to be more tightly controlled than standard single rentals, so there's slightly more to understand in terms of management regulations, planning permission, and official licensing.

The guidance in this section is not intended as a replacement for expert legal or financial advice, and you'll obviously need to do some homework on the specific HMO rules and regulations set out by your local government. As with any real estate strategy, it's important to understand exactly what you're getting into before you get started.

Complying with HMO management regulations

In England, HMO management regulations — Management of Houses in Multiple Occupation (England) regulations — apply to all HMOs, whether they need to be officially licensed or not. (More on HMO licensing coming up in "Dealing with mandatory HMO licensing.")

REMEMBER

These regulations set out the legal requirements for anyone running an HMO and are largely designed to ensure the property is safe and habitable. This includes

>> Providing rubbish disposal facilities

>> Making sure the property is structurally sound and free of hazards

>> Maintaining and keeping common areas (entrances, stairways, hallways, etc.) clean

>> Repairing fixtures, fittings, and appliances in common areas in a proper, timely way

>> Repairing fixtures and fittings in the bedrooms in a proper, timely way

>> Making sure there's a safe means of escape in the event of a fire and that smoke alarms and fire safety equipment are installed and maintained

>> Providing essential services like electricity, gas, water, and drainage without unreasonable disruption

>> Supplying an annual gas safety certificate to the council (when gas is being used)

>> Making sure that electrical installations are safe and that an electrical safety report is done every five years (to be given to the council on request)

>> Displaying the landlord's (or managing agent's) name, address, and telephone number in the property

WARNING

Heavy fines can be imposed on anyone found to be breaching these management regulations.

Read more about health and safety for HMOs in the section "Looking at the key health and safety considerations for HMOs."

Sorting out planning requirements

In theory, planning permission for smaller HMOs is currently not required in most areas, but, in practice, whether you need formal planning permission depends entirely on your local council.

REMEMBER

A number of councils in England and Wales have chosen to invoke something called *Article 4*, which means formal planning permission is required to turn a regular residential home into an HMO. One of your first tasks is to find out whether Article 4 applies in your area.

Article 4 is designed to limit the number of HMOs in an area by removing permitted development (being able to change the use of a property without needing formal planning permission). There are many reasons why councils may want to limit the number of HMOs in their jurisdiction, but it's often due to common problems associated with certain HMOs, like increased noise complaints, or landlords offering poor-quality, unsafe accommodation, or too many HMOs in a concentrated area (like around a university).

REMEMBER

If your local council has invoked Article 4, it doesn't mean you won't be able to turn a property into an HMO, but it does mean you'll have to get formal planning permission so the council can have its say. Contact your local authority to get the ball rolling, and always ensure planning permission is in place before you start renting the property as an HMO.

Dealing with mandatory HMO licensing

It's important to note that management regulations, planning permission, and licensing are all separate things. Every HMO must comply with the management regulations, but not every HMO will require planning permission or mandatory HMO licensing.

A recent change (as of October 1, 2018) in the UK means that mandatory licensing now applies when a property is rented to five or more tenants who form more than one household and who share kitchen and bathroom amenities.

REMEMBER

Generally, HMOs that are rented to four or fewer tenants don't need a license, but always check with your local council to see whether you need to obtain an HMO license for your property.

TIP

If your local council has a dedicated HMO Enforcement Officer, he should be your first port of call for advice. Failing that, contact your council's Housing Office. If you're in the United States, the Department of Housing and Urban Development (HUD) may offer guidance and support.

Understanding how HMO licensing works

To secure an HMO license, you'll need to apply to your local council (or, if you're using one, your managing agent can apply for you).

The council will usually send someone to inspect the property and look at the following:

>> **Whether the property is suitable for the number of proposed tenants, in terms of size and facilities.**

>> **Whether the HMO manager (that's you or your managing agent) is considered fit to run an HMO.** Typically, this means you don't have a criminal record and haven't been found guilty of breaching landlord duties in the past.

>> **Whether the property poses any health or safety hazards.** If any unacceptable risks are identified, you'll have to fix the issues before you can be given a license.

Depending on your council, other conditions may be added to your license. For example, your council may specify that certain improvements are needed before you can get your license, or it may set out certain rules for managing your HMO (such as managing the behavior of tenants).

An HMO license is valid for a maximum of five years, after which you'll need to renew it, and you'll need a separate license for each HMO you operate. You'll need to pay for each HMO license and display a copy of the license at the HMO.

WARNING

If your HMO does require a license and you rent out rooms without obtaining the proper license, you can face an unlimited fine. You may also be prevented from running HMOs in the future.

Complying with HMO licensing regulations

To get (and keep) an HMO license, you'll need to comply with HMO licensing regulations. For the most part, these regulations tie in with the management regulations set out earlier in the chapter (health and safety, fire safety, gas and electrical safety, and so on). So if you're diligently following the management regulations anyway, you shouldn't run into trouble with these rules.

However, in addition to good management principles, HMO licensing regulations also cover occupancy limits. This means your license will be for a certain number of occupants and if you're found to be breaching this limit, you can face very stiff fines and have your license revoked.

REMEMBER

It's really important to apply for the correct occupancy limit in the first place. If you later decide to increase the occupancy, you'll need to apply to change your license.

TIP

Talk to your local council's HMO Enforcement Officer or Housing Officer to get advice on licensing regulations.

Looking at the key health and safety considerations for HMOs

Whether you're subject to mandatory licensing or not, HMO management regulations mean that you have to ensure that your property is free of major hazards that can impact the health and safety of your tenants or visitors to the property.

Largely, this means following your common sense and making sure the property is structurally sound and not a danger to people. However, there are also specific rules to follow around gas and electric safety and fire safety.

Gas and electric safety

As an HMO manager, you'll need to have an annual gas safety check done on any gas appliances and related flues provided in the property (boilers, water heaters, gas fires, and so on). A copy of your Gas Safety Check Certificate needs to be sent to the council every year.

You'll also need to have all fixed electrical installations (wiring, sockets, lighting, and so on) inspected every five years or sooner (this is the currently testing interval in the United Kingdom), so that you can get an Electrical Installation Condition Report. This doesn't need to be sent to the council, like the gas certificate, but you should keep it safe — if the council requests a copy, you'll need to produce it quickly.

You should display copies of both the gas and electric certificates in the HMO property.

REMEMBER

Gas and electric inspections must be done by registered professionals — so either a Gas Safe engineer or a qualified electrician from the Registered Competent Person Electrical Register.

Fire safety

Fire safety rules for HMOs are more stringent than single rentals because the risk of fire or harm is generally higher in HMOs. This increased risk is because

>> Electrical circuits have to cope with higher loads due to more tenants.

>> More tenants are using the same escape routes.

>> There are (usually) more internal locks, which can impact escape.

>> Occupiers often have duplicate appliances, meaning there are more ignition sources in the property.

>> Unlike a regular household, in an HMO there isn't usually one "responsible" person who goes around each night checking everything is off (although, if you're a live-in landlord, you can do this).

REMEMBER

All this means that fire is one of the key hazards that inspectors look at in HMOs. Different councils will have different requirements (no big surprise by this point in the chapter!), and much will depend on the size of your HMO, the property itself, and how many people you have living there. Generally speaking, though, the following fire safety measures are required:

>> A mains-wired, interlinked fire alarm system (so if one alarm goes off, they all go off) with alarms placed in all the bedrooms, communal areas, and hallways. Larger HMOs require a higher-spec fire alarm.

>> Locks on all exit doors — including bedrooms and front and back doors — that can be opened without a key (thumb turn locks are ideal).

>> Fire doors with self-closing mechanisms in the bedrooms and any communal areas.

>> Escape routes kept clear and free of any obstruction.

>> A fire blanket in the kitchen.

>> Fire extinguishers in the hallways (not always mandatory but advised).

In larger HMOs, emergency lighting may be required.

Managing Your HMO

You've found the ideal HMO property, you've sorted planning and licensing, and you understand what's expected of you in terms of management regulations. Now you're ready to start attracting tenants and managing your HMO on an ongoing basis. This is the really rewarding part of the HMO journey: giving people quality accommodation and receiving a great return on your investment!

REMEMBER

If you choose to work with a managing agent, she'll be able to take care of the everyday running of your HMO. And she'll be able to advise you on the best approaches for your property, local area, and target audience.

However, when you're just starting out with HMOs, you may prefer to manage the property yourself, like I did. Then, after you've found your feet and perhaps expanded your portfolio (see "Scaling Up Your HMO Portfolio," later in this chapter), you may want to bring in a managing agent or in-house ember of staff to take over. For the purposes of this section, I assume you'll be managing the property yourself for now.

Sorting tenancy agreements

You'll need to have a contract or tenancy agreement with each tenant in the HMO. Ordinarily, contracts are for 12 months at a time (after which, you'll need to reissue the contract), but six-month contracts are also common. I opt for as long a contract as possible to save on administration costs and to minimize tenant turnover as much as possible.

TIP

Although plenty of contract templates are available online, I recommend talking to a lawyer with HMO or multitenant experience to get the best contract advice for your circumstances. For example, if you're going to be a live-in landlord, you may want to add a clause that gives you greater freedom to end someone's tenancy early — say, if living with him proves to be impossible!

REMEMBER

In general, HMO contracts will cover

>> The term of the agreement, usually 6 to 12 months

>> Whether there's a fixed period during which neither party can end the arrangement

>> How much notice either party has to give in order to end the agreement

>> How much the rent is and when this is payable (usually monthly — specify which day of the month it's due)

>> How much deposit is required and which deposit protection scheme (see the sidebar "Protecting your tenants' deposits") it will be placed into

>> Whether bills are included in the rent (see the sidebar "Should utility bills be included in the rent?")

>> What happens if tenants don't pay their rent on time

>> Tenant responsibilities, such as the following:

- Keeping their room clean and in good condition

- Not damaging the property, furniture, and fixtures and fittings

- Letting the landlord know when repairs are needed

- Not causing a nuisance (such as loud noise) for other tenants and neighbors

>> Landlord responsibilities, such as the following:

- Giving appropriate notice (usually 24 hours) before entering the property (obviously not applicable if you're a live-in landlord)

- Conducting repairs in a proper and timely manner

- Keeping communal areas clean and in a good state of repair

- Providing facilities such as water, electricity, and drainage, without unreasonable disruption

- Providing trash disposal facilities

- Ensuring that smoke alarms and fire safety equipment are installed and maintained, and that there's a safe means of escape

- Ensuring proper safety checks, like the annual gas safety check and electrical installation check

PROTECTING YOUR TENANTS' DEPOSITS

In the UK, tenancy deposit rules apply to any assured shorthold tenancy (AST) where a deposit is taken. The idea is to safeguard tenants' deposits and provide a faster, cheaper way of resolving any deposit disputes further down the line or when a tenant checks out.

Under the rules, the deposit must be placed in a statutory, government-backed tenancy deposit scheme, such as the Deposit Protection Service, MyDeposits, or the Tenancy Deposit Scheme, within 30 days of receiving it and written details of the scheme provided to the tenant within the same timeframe.

Remember: The rules for tenants' security deposits vary around the world. For example, in New York, for rental properties with six or more units, landlords must place tenants' deposits in an interest-earning account. Always check what rules apply to your property in your jurisdiction.

Returning to the UK rules, the key question is, does your HMO count as an AST? If you're a non-resident landlord, then, yes, your contract will probably fall under an AST agreement, which means you must protect tenants' deposits in a government-backed scheme. If you're a live-in landlord, you'll generally have more freedom over what kind of contract you can issue. Always get professional legal advice on which contract best suits your needs and ensure you comply. If I were you, I'd always protect a tenant's deposit whether you're legally required to or not. This gives your tenants confidence and both of you a third-party mediation service if there are any disputes.

Finding and vetting tenants

Earlier in the chapter, we looked at the key tenant groups for HMOs: professionals, students, or low-income-housing clients.

REMEMBER

Whichever audience you decide to target, never, ever mix tenant groups. If you start marketing your property to professionals, they won't be happy if you bring in a couple of students further down the line — and a house full of students won't exactly appreciate an old man (a 30-something professional) crimping their style.

Attracting the right tenants

So, how can you attract quality tenants to your property? The key word is *quality*. The success of your HMO, in part, relies on being able to attract and keep great tenants — people who are tidy, considerate, and reliable.

REMEMBER

Without doubt, the best way to make sure you're attracting high-quality tenants is to keep your rents competitive in relation to the local market (overcharging will always drive people away) and provide quality accommodation that people actively want to live in.

Having decided on a competitive rent and ensured your property is desirable for your target audience, you can then set about advertising for tenants.

TIP

My two favorite methods for finding tenants are

>> **Advertising online:** In both the United States and United Kingdom, SpareRoom (www.spareroom.com) is one of the leading websites for professionals wanting to rent a room. You can advertise for free on the site, or upgrade to a paid "bold" or featured ad for greater visibility. In your ad, include as much detail as possible on both the room and communal facilities (is there a garden or yard, for instance?), along with multiple, high-quality, high-resolution photographs. Prospective tenants will also want to know about the local area, particularly transport links.

>> **Enlisting the help of existing tenants:** When you've attracted your first tenants and worked with them for a while, you'll have built up a strong reputation as a landlord — and this means that more and more future tenants will come your way via word of mouth and personal recommendations. So, when you have a vacancy, enlist the help of current tenants to spread the word in their social circles (both in real life and on social media). There's one big incentive for them to help you: They get to live with people they already know and get along with (which, in turn, makes life easier for you as the landlord). Maybe offer them a small referral fee for their efforts as well — it will be cheaper than advertising and shows them how grateful you are for their help.

SHOULD UTILITY BILLS BE INCLUDED IN THE RENT?

One question that always comes up for first-time HMO landlords is whether to include bills in the rent or have the tenants take care of the bills themselves.

There are pros and cons to both approaches. On the plus side, professional tenants tend to prefer the simplicity of an all-inclusive price (and not having to sort out bill sharing with other tenants whom they may not know that well), so including bills will undoubtedly make your property more attractive.

The downside is that when tenants aren't responsible for paying the utility bills, they can play pretty fast and loose with their energy usage. And this can mean big bills for you! To help mitigate this risk, it's worth investing time and money in making sure your property is as energy efficient as possible.

Double- or triple-glazing windows, adding energy-saving lighting, fitting motion sensors to all the communal lighting (so they turn off after a short interval), and installing good insulation and draft-proofing on doors are all sensible measures to take. You may also want to consider installing smart thermostats that let you control the heating remotely from an app on your phone. And, last but not least, you should always shop around to find the cheapest utilities and review this on a regular basis to ensure you keep getting the best deal.

All things considered, particularly when dealing with professional tenants, I prefer to cover the bills myself and absorb them into the cost of the rent. This includes

- Heating
- Electricity
- Water
- Council tax
- Internet
- TV
- Cleaning

Carrying out due diligence on prospective tenants

You should carry out thorough reference checks on every tenant before entering into an agreement with them. You can do this easily online using a tenant screening service like the one provided by Experian (www.experian.com).

To help you vet prospective tenants, ask them to complete an application form setting out the following details:

>> Name and date of birth

>> National insurance or social security number

>> Current and previous address

>> Contact details for current and previous landlord or rental agent

>> Current income, employer's name and address, and how long they've worked there

>> Details for their previous employer (if they've been with the current employer for less than, say, two years)

>> Contact information for at least two personal references

TIP

I recommend having the reference check carried out by a professional screening service, like Experian, because they'll be able to conduct a proper credit check, which will pick up any bad credit or unpaid debts. However, if you wanted to conduct a simple background check yourself, you could:

>> Ask the tenant's previous landlord for a reference.

>> Call the tenant's employer to check that he's employed where he says he is.

>> Speak to the personal referees to get a feel for what the tenant is like as an individual.

REMEMBER

As an essential safeguard, always make sure you secure the appropriate payments and signed tenancy documents in advance before you hand over the keys. A sensible deposit is equivalent to one month's (or even six weeks') rent plus one month's advance rent. Where applicable, this deposit will need to be protected by a government-backed deposit protection scheme. (See the sidebar "Protecting Your Tenants' Deposits" for more on this.)

Managing your tenants and the property

The goal is to treat your tenants as customers and provide an excellent level of customer service, just as you would in any other area of business.

REMEMBER

Not only does this make for a more pleasant working relationship (especially important if you're living in the property side-by-side with your tenants), but it also means your tenants are much more likely to recommend your property to people she knows. This makes it much easier to attract tenants in the future.

Dealing with common tenant problems

Even the most diligent, customer-service-focused landlord will experience the occasional problem with tenants. This may include making a nuisance for other residents or neighbors, or not paying the rent on time.

In my experience, problem tenants are mercifully rare, especially if you're dealing with professional tenants. But if problems do crop up, be prepared to take action quickly. It can be tempting to let problems slide and hope they'll sort themselves out, but that's a mistake. One bad apple in an HMO can drive away other excellent tenants.

So, how can you tackle problem tenants?

>> **Try to talk through the problem in an open, frank and constructive way to reach an amicable agreement.** Often, just making it clear that, if the problem continues, you won't renew the tenancy or give him a good reference for future properties is enough to get someone to get his act together.

>> **If that doesn't work, it's time to weigh up whether you want that person to continue living in the property.** If you want him out, you'll need to issue him with a formal notice — in the United Kingdom, that means either a Section 21 notice (if you want him to leave at the end of his tenancy agreement) or a Section 8 notice (if you want to end the tenancy early on the basis that the tenant has broken the terms of the tenancy agreement). Always check the relevant eviction procedures in your location and instruct a specialist attorney or eviction specialist because the notices need to be drafted perfectly or they may not stand up in court (if it comes to that).

Trying to drive out a tenant through underhand (some would say passive-aggressive) means, like shutting off the water supply and generally making life difficult for him, is illegal. When you want to evict a tenant, always address the problem head on and take proper legal action.

Keeping the property in good order

If you want to attract and keep quality tenants, it stands to reason that you'll need to keep your property in good condition and deal with any maintenance issues quickly and effectively.

Because of the higher number of tenants, HMOs tend to need more maintenance than single rentals. This means it's more important than ever to keep on top of maintenance and check the property regularly.

If you're a live-in landlord, it's obviously easy to spot when something needs fixing. But what if you're managing an HMO that you don't live in?

>> Encourage tenants to contact you with any maintenance issues as soon as they crop up.

>> Make sure tenants all have your contact details (or those of your managing agent) and that the details are displayed somewhere prominent in the house.

>> Be proactive and inspect the property yourself regularly — monthly is a good idea, or every three months at a minimum (remember to provide at least 24 hours' notice that you'll be entering the property).

>> Cultivate good relationships with your dream team (see Chapter 3), so that they can help you fix issues quickly. Having a great plumber on speed-dial will save you a lot of hassle!

TIP

In addition to keeping on top of maintenance, you'll also need to make sure that common areas, like kitchens, bathrooms, and hallways, are kept clean and tidy. I highly recommend employing a cleaner to take care of this for you (you can build the cost of this into the rent). As an added bonus, having a cleaner will also make your property more appealing to young professionals. Plus, you have a regular member of your staff visiting the property to keep an eye on it.

Scaling Up Your HMO Portfolio

Your HMO investment is going well, so what next? You'll probably want to expand your portfolio to take on more properties and more tenants!

REMEMBER

With more properties and more tenants comes more work. Finding and vetting tenants, conducting viewings and inspections, handling all the licensing requirements, and managing the maintenance can easily add up to a full-time job. So, you'll probably want to get professional support to help you scale up and continue to provide a great level of service.

This is where a good managing agent (whether external or in-house, either full-time or part-time) is worth his weight in gold. So, if you haven't already engaged an agent to manage some or all of your HMO workload, now is a great time to consider it. Yes, you'll have to sacrifice some profit to cover the agent's fees or salary, but you'll have more freedom and more time to look at expanding your business, and you should still get a good return on your investment — even taking into account the fees.

TIP

Look for a person with experience managing HMOs if possible, rather than some-one who's only ever dealt with single lets. You want someone with an eye for detail and who's great with people. She should be an excellent problem solver and must have the ethic to do things correctly.

Identifying Five International Locations Where This Strategy Would Work

Although this chapter is largely geared toward the specifics of running HMOs in the United Kingdom, the strategy of renting out your property on a room-by-room basis, rather than as a single let, can apply anywhere in the world.

REMEMBER

It would work well in any market with a high influx of young people (students and professionals) and would be particularly effective in cities with high property prices. In other words, if young people can't afford to buy a home, or even rent a whole house or apartment themselves, then a multitenant property is a great option.

Here are just a few international locations where I think this strategy would work well (other than the UK's major cities), all with staggeringly high rental prices for single rentals:

>> San Francisco

>> Dublin

>> Frankfurt

>> Hong Kong

>> Melbourne

Chapter **14**

Renting to Students and Low-Income-Housing Tenants

In Chapter 13, I cover renting a property on a room-by-room basis to individual tenants. That chapter is focused on renting to professionals, but two other key demographics are attracted to multitenant properties: students and low-income-housing tenants. In this chapter, I explore the nuances of renting to these two groups.

REMEMBER

Clearly, students and low-income-housing tenants are two different demographics, so this chapter isn't about catering to both groups in the same property. It's never a good idea to mix different types of tenants in the same house.

The reason I'm covering these two different tenant profiles in the same chapter is because they both come with similar risks and they're broadly similar in terms of requirements (affordable, low-maintenance accommodation, for instance).

Many landlords shy away from renting to students and low-income-housing tenants, but as you see in this chapter, with careful preparation and management, these demographics can provide very healthy returns for real estate investors.

Knowing What's Involved in Renting to Students and Low-Income-Housing Tenants

Renting to students and low-income-housing tenants is a very specific strategy, with considerations and requirements that are unique to these tenant groups. So, how do you know if this is the right strategy for you? In this section, I walk you through the basics of catering to students and low-income-housing tenants.

Understanding why you may want to rent to multiple tenants in one property

First things first, this chapter is largely focused on offering a multitenant product — a house or large apartment that's shared by multiple individuals rather than a single household. Depending on where you are in the world, this type of property may or may not count as a house in multiple occupation (HMO).

TIP

If you haven't yet read Chapter 13, which is all about HMOs, I urge you to circle back to that chapter before delving into the nuances of students and low-income-housing tenants. Even if you're outside of the United Kingdom and your property doesn't count as an HMO, the basics of setting up and running a multitenant property will still apply. Before you get started, you need to build your knowledge of multitenant properties.

REMEMBER

But why multiple tenants? Because students and low-income-housing tenants are generally looking for more affordable properties at the lower end of the price spectrum, a single rental (a property that's rented to one household or one tenant only) is unlikely to deliver a very attract yield. Put simply, by renting to multiple tenants in the same property, you can maximize your rental income. You can find more on the multitenant financial model in Chapter 13.

Identifying your tenants' needs

For any tenant group, it's important to understand the unique needs of your target audience. So, what are some of the key considerations for targeting students and low-income-housing tenants?

>> **You'll usually have to offer the property fully furnished.** These groups are unlikely to have very much (or any, in the case of students) furniture of their own.

» **You'll need to carefully research pricing in your chosen location.** Affordability tends to be a major priority for these audiences.

» **You'll need to consider that the market determines pricing for these categories, not so much the product.** With other strategies, you can usually earn a higher rent by offering a higher-quality accommodation, but that's unlikely to work for these types of tenants, unless you're targeting wealthy (perhaps overseas) students.

» **You'll need to consider *when* you'll get paid.** If your tenant is actually the local housing authority (which, in turn, appoints and pays for tenants), it may, depending on the authority, pay in arrears rather than in advance.

» **You'll need to choose the right location carefully for both types of tenants.** Students need to be very close to campus. Low-income housing tends to be in urban city centers where the local authority can house people quickly and easily. Either way, you'll need to do your homework on local supply and demand.

» **You'll need to account for the fact that students usually want the property during the school year only (9 months instead of 12).** To avoid missing out on three months' rent, many landlords have their student tenants sign a 12-month agreement, regardless of how many months they'll be in the property for.

» **You'll also need to time the preparation and marketing of your property carefully if you're renting to students.** If you don't have tenants in place before the start of the academic year, you may end up with an empty property and no new student intake for another year.

I cover these considerations in more detail throughout the chapter.

TIP

If you've decided to rent to students, don't discount the many, many students who travel abroad to study. Targeting foreign students is a great sub-strategy because you can often charge a higher rent for a better-quality product. That's because students who can afford to travel overseas to study are generally pretty affluent, and their parents — who will naturally be worried because their children are so far away — are often happy to pay for higher-end properties. It can also be a good way to overcome the typical misgivings landlords have about renting to groups of students, because you'll generally have just one or two students in the property (smaller properties can become more viable due to the higher rents possible with overseas students). Student housing is always location specific, though, so be sure to check that this is the case in your preferred area(s).

Looking at the Pros and Cons of Renting to These Tenant Groups

When you understand the pros and cons of renting to these tenant groups, you can plan for them accordingly. So, let's take a look at why you may want to rent to students and low-income-housing tenants — and the common downsides that you need to be aware of.

Addressing the negative connotations and downsides

It's fair to say that both students and low-income-housing tenants get a bad rap — sometimes justified, sometimes not.

I bet you've already thought of a few major clichés about these groups: Students will party constantly, make too much noise, and trash your property. Low-income-housing tenants are unreliable, they won't pay their rent on time, and they'll trash your property.

That's why so many landlords are wary of dealing with these groups. Yet, in my experience, most of these concerns come from investors with no experience actually dealing with students or low-income-housing tenants. In other words, lack of knowledge can breed fear. When you know what you're dealing with, you can plan accordingly and reduce these risks.

REMEMBER

So, with that in mind, let's rip off the bandage and lay bare the common challenges associated with renting to students and low-income-housing tenants:

>> Low-income-housing often has a higher turnover rate, which makes more work for you in terms of finding and settling in new tenants.

>> With student properties, depending on the location, there may be a lot of competition with other properties, so you need to price carefully and make sure you're meeting your target audience's needs if you want them to choose your property.

>> Because you're managing the property more intensively (by renting to multiple tenants, rather than a single household), there'll be more wear and tear on the property. This means you'll have to do more maintenance on the property, and you'll need to budget accordingly for this.

>> It can be harder to manage these tenants groups (noise complaints, tenant behavior, and so on), so you'll need to be a strong communicator.

>> Particularly with students who are used to living at home, they may not be great at keeping the property clean and tidy, so very regular inspections may be required. Personally, I'd inspect every month, perhaps even twice a month if the need arises.

>> Tenants may have trouble paying their rent on time, particularly with low-income-housing tenants (whereas students can often fall back on the Bank of Mom and Dad).

>> It can be very hard to vet tenants with little employment or rental history. For students, you can overcome this by having a parent as a guarantor. For low-income-housing tenants, you can seek personal references or rent directly to the housing authority (in which case, the housing authority will be responsible for paying the rent).

>> Students usually only want the property for 9 months, but you can require them to sign a 12-month lease.

REMEMBER

In most cases, there are simple steps you can take to plan for the downsides and reduce your risk. For example, if you're worried about students making a lot of noise and trashing your property, you can mitigate against this by having a low-maintenance property that's easy to touch up. Paint the walls with white vinyl silk paint that can be easily wiped down; even if you have to give the place a fresh coat of paint between tenants, that doesn't cost much in terms of time or budget. You can also have antisocial behavior rules written into your contract and display noise notices in the property. With careful planning and management, almost all the concerns are easy to overcome (turn to "Physically Preparing Your Property for Use" and "Managing Your Property Effectively," later in the chapter).

Ultimately, though, only you can tell whether these negatives are a deal breaker for you as an investor. Personally, I think it's a case of assessing the risk versus the reward.

Looking at the positives

REMEMBER

There are plenty of reasons why investors actively want to rent to students and low-income-housing tenants:

>> This is a pretty high-income strategy, providing you're renting to multiple tenants in the same property, rather than a single household.

>> Generally speaking, there's enormous demand for affordable accommodation among both students and low-income-housing tenants. Obviously, this varies from town to town, and some areas are more affluent than others, so you'll need to choose your location carefully.

- » In the United Kingdom, students don't pay council (property) tax. So if you're covering the bills (included with the rent), you've got one less cost to factor in.

- » With students, you can often get a guarantor, usually a parent, to co-sign the lease, giving you some added protection if they run into money troubles after spending all their student loan money on beer and pizza!

- » Another pro for students is that they know lots and lots of other students, which is great for word-of-mouth marketing of your properties. So, if someone moves out midway through the year, your tenants can fill the vacancy for you. (And depending on the type of tenancy agreement you choose, they may be responsible for covering the rent for a vacant room — more on contracts coming up later.)

- » Both demographics are generally happier with a lower-spec property, which keeps your costs down. I'm not talking about offering crappy accommodation here; I'm just saying that you don't need to go all out on stainless-steel appliances and crown molding for these target groups.

As you can see, there are plenty of upsides to working with these tenant groups, providing you go into it with your eyes wide open, having prepared the property (and yourself) accordingly.

Sourcing the Right Kinds of Property for Students and Low-Income-Housing Tenants

I cover the basics of sourcing multitenant properties in Chapter 13, so be sure to read that if you haven't already. However, above and beyond the general principles in Chapter 13, there are specific considerations for sourcing suitable properties for students and low-income-housing tenants.

Finding the right location for students

Location is a critical factor for both students and low-income-housing tenants, although both have slightly different needs.

REMEMBER

The right neighborhood for attracting students is one that's obviously close to the university's campus. However, that's not the only consideration here. Students tenants will also favor a property that

>> **Is in or close to a vibrant part of town, with plenty of amenities and entertainment on offer:** Proximity to bars, shops, and at least one pizza place will appeal to most students!

>> **Has good access to public transport:** Lots of students don't have cars. So, a good local network of buses, trains, and taxis will be important.

>> **Is in an affordable, yet safe, area:** As a parent, I can safely say that no one wants to drop her child off at university for the first time and leave him in a neglected, crime-ridden neighborhood. So, you really need to find a decent enough area with property prices that translate into a rent that's profitable for you, but affordable for your target audience.

TIP

If you want to be very specific and target affluent foreign students, research which universities have the highest number of overseas students in your chosen country. You'll probably have more wiggle room in terms of monthly rent for foreign students, which may open up a wider choice of neighborhoods.

Identifying the right location for low-income-housing tenants

This group has the same needs in terms of affordability and general safety of the neighborhood, but proximity to local amenities and entertainment is likely to be less of an issue.

TIP

If you're targeting low-income-housing tenants, it's a good idea to look at economic factors affecting the local market for low-income-housing tenants. For example, has the local government had its housing budget slashed? If so, that may make it harder for you to rent through the local housing authority. (That said, there may still be plenty of people receiving housing benefits who are forced to find accommodation through the private rental market.) You may also want to look at the local employment market — rising unemployment can mean more tenants looking for cheaper accommodation (for example, renting a room instead of a whole property).

Looking at the property itself

In terms of the size of the property, for low-income-housing tenants, a larger property with multiple bedrooms (at least four or five bedrooms, and perhaps even more than that) is likely to create a much better yield and make it financially worth your while, bearing in mind the increased management and maintenance. This generally limits your choice to large houses only and rules out most apartments.

The student market is a little different. Many students rent in smaller groups of three or four, so you can easily rent out a three-bedroom house or apartment for a good return. In fact, a very large property, filled with other students that they don't know, may put some students off.

Likewise, a foreign student may want a more upmarket but smaller property to himself (a nice one-bedroom apartment, for instance). A doctoral student may also be open to a single-tenant property at a higher price point. So, essentially, when you're renting to students, you have a wider range of properties to choose from.

REMEMBER

Whatever size property you choose, there are some basic considerations that apply to both tenant groups:

>> The property should be clean, tidy, well presented, and easy to maintain, without your having to spend a lot of money to get it to that point.

>> Something that already has neutral décor will appeal to the widest possible range of tenants and is easy to spruce up with a coat of paint if needed.

>> In addition to having a communal kitchen, it's a bonus if the property has another common area to hang out in (such as a lounge or den). This is particularly important for students.

>> Think about the property's immediate neighbors. If you're renting to a bunch of students on what is otherwise a quiet, family-oriented street, you may be setting yourself up for a lot of complaints from the neighbors. The absolutely ideal property will have plenty of similar tenants in the immediate vicinity or be a busy town or city-center location.

After you've found the right property, you'll no doubt need to do some work (although hopefully not too much) to prepare it for your target audience. You can find more on that topic in the section "Physically Preparing Your Property for Use," later in this chapter

Marketing Your Property and Finding Tenants

How you go about finding tenants will differ depending on whether you're aiming the property at students or low-income-housing tenants. So, in this section, I explore the two groups separately. But first, before you can start marketing the property, you need to decide how much you're going to charge.

Making sure the rent is competitive

As with any real estate strategy, you have to be sure that your returns make it all worth your while. For students and low-income-housing tenants, given that you'll probably have to work harder to manage and maintain the property, it's even more important to make sure your financial model is sound and factors in all your regular costs, including the following:

» Utility bills, property taxes, and insurance

» General upkeep of the property

» Lightly redecorating the property where needed at the end of each tenancy

REMEMBER

In addition to carefully working out your ongoing costs, you need to spend time researching the local market to understand how much you can reasonably expect to charge each month. Pricing competitively is especially important with this strategy. You can't charge more than the going market rate because your property has chrome fittings and a nice bathroom, when, in general, those things matter less to students and low-income-housing tenants.

Enticing students to your property

Renting to students involves certain time pressures, because thousands of students are trying to find accommodation in the months leading up to the start of the academic year. If you miss this window, and all the good tenants have already found accommodation, your property may end up empty.

REMEMBER

In this competitive, time-pressured environment, it's crucial that you can attract quality tenants quickly. That means offering a well-priced, well-presented property through the right channels.

Here are some of the best channels for finding student tenants:

» **Advertising online:** Websites such as Student.com (www.student.com), Student Accommodation UK (www.accommodationforstudents.com), and craigslist (www.craigslist.org) are great starting points. You can also advertise through online student forums and Facebook groups that are dedicated to your chosen area. When advertising your property, be sure to give plenty of detail on the property and local amenities, and include lots of quality photos.

» **Encouraging word-of-mouth marketing:** This is a critical channel for finding student tenants because students are surrounded by other students. After you have some student tenants in place, and you've demonstrated your chops as a great student landlord, your existing tenants will be able to help you fill vacancies with ease.

>> **Reaching out to the local university:** Many universities supply a list of approved landlords to new students, and you want to make sure you're on their list as a professional, ethical operator. Lots of universities also run accommodation fairs, connecting students with available properties, so check out whether your chosen university does this.

>> **Advertising through local rental agents:** Some agents have good links with the local university already and are well placed to target students for you. There's obviously a cost involved in working with agents, although it will free up more of your time for other profit-enhancing activities. You need to weigh whether this is right for you depending on your commitments, your goals, and, frankly, your preference for how you want to spend your time.

TIP

When students are happy in their accommodation, they may want to stay put for another year, and perhaps even until they graduate. So, after you've found good tenants, look after them! You'll build a great reputation and have no trouble finding future tenants.

However, if for some reason you do find yourself with an empty student property and little interest from students (because they've already found accommodation elsewhere), you'll need to have a backup plan in mind. You could, for example, rent the property out to low-income-housing tenants for this academic year and then return to students. Or, if it's a slightly higher-spec property, you may be able to attract young professionals (see Chapter 13).

Attracting low-income-housing tenants

Broadly speaking, there are two ways of finding tenants in the low-income-housing category:

>> **Working with the local housing authority:** The local housing authority may rent the property from you directly and then place tenants in the property.

>> **Finding tenants yourself (or hiring a rental agent to do it for you) through the regular private rental market:** These tenants are generally low-income tenants who would otherwise struggle to afford accommodation, so the government subsidizes them with housing benefit.

TIP

The first option is the ideal scenario because your tenant is the local housing authority. Renting to either a local housing provider or the local government authority is a smart solution because it often lowers your risk as a landlord. For example, in my local area, I know a local low-income-housing provider that may rent the property directly from the landlord for up to five years at a time. And during that tenancy period, it's the local housing provider who covers all the utility bills, void periods, and rent arrears.

Get to know the local low-income-housing providers or the folks at the local housing department to see if they may be willing to rent your property on a longer-term basis. And even if that's not an option, they may be able to refer tenants to you or pay you directly for the tenants on a month-by-month basis.

If you need to source tenants yourself directly, the same basic principles apply as in Chapter 13 — you can advertise online through portals like SpareRoom (www.spareroom.com) and encourage existing tenants to help you spread the word among their social circles.

REMEMBER

When advertising your property online, make it clear that it's open to those on housing benefits. Many landlords stipulate that they won't accept tenants on welfare. By stating that you're willing to accept tenants who receive a housing benefit, welfare, or, recently renamed in the United Kingdom, universal credit, you're differentiating your offering from other properties that are available.

Vetting tenants

As with any rental property, it's really important to reduce your risks by carefully vetting the people you're renting to. For low-income-housing tenants, you can follow the vetting steps outlined in Chapter 13 as much as possible.

With students, vetting is slightly trickier, because they're unlikely to have much credit or rental history to support their applications. That's why I always recommend having guarantors (typically, their parents) co-sign rental agreements, to give you some recourse if they fall behind on their rent. You can also seek personal references from tutors or employers (if they've had jobs).

Drafting the Tenancy Agreement

When you're dealing with students and low-income-housing tenants, your tenancy agreement needs to cover all the expected clauses around rent payments, landlord responsibilities, and tenant responsibilities. But in addition to these standard clauses, you may also want to include some terms that are unique to these tenants groups — just to give you some added protections and your tenants some extra clarity.

Choosing the right agreement

What sort of agreement should you go for? The short answer is: It depends on who exactly you're renting to.

REMEMBER

For low-income-housing tenants, assuming you're renting to the tenants directly, you'll want to individually contract with each tenant in the property, rather than rent the whole place out as a house share. Having a separate agreement with each individual tenant gives both you and your tenants maximum protection. Turn back to Chapter 13 for a list of the standard contractual terms that you'll probably want to include in your individual tenancy agreements.

With students, you can do the same thing and contract individually with each student in the house. However, with this particular demographic, many landlords find it beneficial to have all the tenants sign a joint tenancy agreement (with parents acting as guarantors, of course). Either way, the basic contract terms set out in Chapter 13 still apply.

TIP

A joint tenancy agreement is essentially like a regular house share among friends. All the tenants share equal responsibility for the property and the rent, which delivers some key advantages for you and the students you're renting to:

>> **If one student drops out partway through the year, the others are responsible for covering that student's portion of the rent, giving them a big incentive to fill the room for you.** Naturally, this must be clearly stated in the contract, but it's also a good idea to ensure your tenants fully understand that's what they're signing up for.

>> **If someone vacate a room, the remaining students have more control over who moves in because they have collective responsibility for the tenancy.** Most students would much prefer to bring in someone they already know to take over an empty room, rather than have the landlord simply bring in any old stranger. Whenever someone new moves into the property, you'll need to draw up a replacement joint tenancy agreement and have all tenants sign it.

Financially, with a joint tenancy, you're essentially still charging on a room-by-room basis, and can still take individual payments from each tenant (which ensures your financial model is still worth your while and is easier for the tenants to manage). It's just that, in terms of the contract, the rent is all combined together into one collective responsibility.

REMEMBER

I always recommend having students sign a 12-month contract so that they pay for the whole year, even though they may vacate the property before the 12 months are up (they'll likely leave at the end of term to go back to their hometowns). An added advantage of this, besides your not missing out on three months' rent, is that it encourages students to continue their tenancy on to the next academic year, providing they're happy in the property. That way, they don't have to pack up all their stuff for three months and then move again.

Adding in additional clauses for these tenant groups

In addition to the standard clauses listed in Chapter 13, you may want to consider some additional clauses to help manage tenant behavior and reduce your risks.

For example, useful additions might include

>> **A noise policy that sets out what's unacceptable in terms of noise:** It's a good idea to have a "noise limit" or "quiet hours" written into the contract, such as no loud music or noise after 10 p.m.

>> **A tenant behavior clause emphasizing the need to respect others in and around the property:** That includes the neighbors.

>> **A rule that only tenants may stay in the property overnight.**

Sorting out the security deposit

You may be renting to people on a budget, but it's extremely important to get am upfront security deposit from each tenant. After all, these tenant groups have a bit of a reputation for causing damage — not as such in a deliberate way, more through inexperience or neglect. The security deposit is usually equivalent to one month's or six weeks' rent, but the maximum deposit you can charge may be stipulated by your local laws.

TIP

There are now a number of deposit insurance schemes cropping up that negate the need to take an actual cash deposit. These can be great because they reduce the entry cost for your tenants and, thus, give you a potentially wider audience to target. Just makes sure the insurance covers you effectively — read the provider's terms and conditions thoroughly.

To avoid potential disputes further down the line, you should protect your tenant's deposit in an approved deposit protection scheme. This is now the law in the United Kingdom; check your jurisdiction to see what the law requires. You can find more on this subject in Chapter 13.

Physically Preparing Your Property for Use

Just as with any property that you're renting out to tenants, you want to ensure you're offering a clean, well-thought-through space that people really want to live in. Even though these tenants may prioritize affordability, and you won't need as high a spec as you would for professionals, students and low-income-housing tenants still want a comfortable, pleasant place to live.

REMEMBER

The property should feel like a home and be as bright, spacious, and inviting as possible. A dark, cramped, and depressing property is only going to feel like a moneymaking machine for the landlord, and because of this, it'll never attract the best-quality tenants or encourage them to stay and look after the place.

So, when you're preparing a bright, comfortable, and pleasant space for students and low-income-housing tenants, what sorts of things do you need to consider? I walk you through the details in this section.

Kitting out the property for your target audience

Earlier, I mention that you'll typically be offering fully furnished accommodation to these tenant groups. That means

>> Chairs and sofas in any communal space.

>> A table and chairs in the dining room (if there is one) or kitchen (if there's space).

>> Appliances in the kitchen, including refrigerator, oven, microwave, toaster, and possibly other small appliances. You may want (or be legally required) to include multiple appliances if it's a very large property with lots of tenants.

>> Basic cooking utensils, cookware (saucepans and so on), cutlery, and crockery.

>> A bed, dresser, and night tables in each bedroom.

>> Rug, light fittings, and curtains or blinds in each room.

TIP

In addition to these standard furnishings, there are other ways to make your multitenant property more desirable and comfortable for students and low-income-housing tenants. For example:

» Students always appreciate desks in their bedrooms, giving them quiet, private places to work.

» If space and budget allow, consider installing a small wash sink in each bedroom to take the load off the main bathroom(s).

» You may also want to include a small fridge in each bedroom.

» Wherever possible, have extra sockets fitted in the bedrooms to allow for all the extra gadgets and chargers that most tenants (especially students) use on a daily basis. This prevents tenants from overloading the electrical outlets with extension cords. Plus, it makes their lives easier.

» Consider installing a mechanical or digital keycode lock on the front door and bedroom doors instead of a regular key lock. This is something I do on my properties because a short entry code is easy to remember, and keys are easy to lose! You really don't want to be getting calls in the middle of the night because someone has lost his keys (again).

» Make sure that things like the fuse box, Wi-Fi router, and any other items that all tenants may need to access are housed in a communal space, not in someone's bedroom.

» If tenants are paying their own bills (I talk more about whether to include bills in your rent in Chapter 13), you may want to consider installing pay-as-you-go meters for electricity and gas.

REMEMBER

Always take a full inventory of furniture and other items in the property, and note what condition they're in at the start of the tenancy. This inventory should be signed by you and your tenants. A good third-party inventory & check-in agent can be worth his weight in gold here, especially if there is a dispute about damage later down the line. Not only will he do the legwork for you (assessing the condition of the property and furniture items present when the tenant moves in), but he'll also effectively act as a third-party witness because his detailed report (usually with photos) is hard to disagree with.

Preparing for plenty of wear and tear on the property

Because you'll be managing your property more intensely, with multiple tenants instead of one tenant or household, it stands to reason that the property will endure more wear and tear. This is par for the course and not really anything to worry about. But, as the scouts say, "Be prepared!"

TIP

Just a few simple steps will help to drastically minimize the amount of work you have to do, keep the property in good order, and keep your ongoing costs down. So, make life easier on yourself and tenant–proof your property in the following ways:

>> **Install built-in furniture.** Built-in furniture may cost a little more to install at first, but it'll be more hard-wearing and outlast any alternative. Instead of buying those ultra-cheap dressers from IKEA (how long do you really think they'll last in a high-use property like this?), have a simple, sturdy built-in wardrobe and shelves installed in each bedroom.

Likewise, you can build a solid bed frame into the corner of each bedroom, instead of paying for cheap freestanding beds that won't be able to take much, ahem, "action." You can build large drawers underneath for more storage as well.

>> **Opt for hardwearing and low-maintenance flooring throughout the property that's able to cope with lots of foot traffic.** Laminate flooring will always be better than carpet in this scenario. You can always add thick, inexpensive, and hardwearing rugs to make the place seem more cozy.

>> **Install long-lasting (and energy-efficient) LED lightbulbs, if you haven't already, and then install movement sensors in all communal areas to save energy and avoid tenants leaving the lights on by mistake.**

>> **Choose soft furnishings (sofas and chairs) in dark colors.** A cream sofa with four students? No thanks! In addition, covers that can be easily removed and cleaned are always a good choice.

>> **Fit metal, office-style blinds instead of curtains or fabric blinds in each room.** Yes, they're not the most attractive things ever, but it's amazing how dirty regular curtains and blinds get. This alternative is modern and easier to maintain.

>> **Paint the walls in simple, washable, white vinyl silk paint, which is super easy to wipe down and clean.** It's also cheap to buy and easy to slap on, for when you need to touch up the walls or do a full repainting job. There is nothing worse than having to repaint a whole room when it's just one wall that needs repainting so keep the paint the same type and color.

Ultimately, do whatever you can to make your property as low maintenance as possible, for both you and the people who live there.

Making sure the property is safe for your tenants

As a landlord, you're responsible for ensuring your accommodation is safe and secure for tenants. And in a multitenant property, you may be subject to more stringent health and safety rules, depending on where you are in the world and how many people you have living in the property.

WARNING

Always do your homework on which management and health and safety regulations apply to your property. Your local environmental health or housing department is a good starting point for this.

TIP

Whether or not your property qualifies as an HMO, I'd recommend following the principles outlined in the HMO management regulations (see Chapter 13). By and large, these are great common-sense principles that any landlord should abide by.

Depending on the size of your property and number of tenants, health and safety requirements may be as simple as fitting fire alarms and firefighting equipment (which, again, is good common sense for any landlord), or they may extend to fitting fire doors and emergency lighting. Turn back to Chapter 13 for more on health and safety in multitenant properties.

For security purposes, I've already mentioned that a keycode lock on the front door may be a better choice than a standard key lock. In addition to this:

>> Tenants will expect a lock on each bedroom.

>> Window locks are a must throughout the property.

>> Any additional exterior doors (such as a door to the back garden) should be fitted with deadbolt locks.

>> Consider fitting exterior security motion-sensor lights, as well.

REMEMBER

Always tell your insurance company that you're renting to students or low-income-housing tenants, and stipulate how many tenants you have in the property. If you don't, your insurance may not be valid. In addition, make it clear to tenants (in their contract!) that they also need to take out their own separate insurance to cover their personal possessions.

Managing Your Property Effectively

When your rental property is up and running, you'll probably find it's a little more work to keep it running smoothly, compared to a standard single rental. That's because you'll need to keep a close eye on the property itself (purely because it'll be experiencing more wear and tear), and you may need to manage tenant behavior more closely.

Checking in on the property more regularly

Because the property is being used more intensively, you should be really diligent with your regular inspections. When a property is rented to a single tenant or household, you can get away with giving the place the once-over every three months or so. But that's not the case with a multitenant property.

I recommend monthly checks to ensure you can keep a proper eye on the property and nip any maintenance or cleanliness issues in the bud before they become a bigger, more costly issue to fix. If you do experience problems with tenants not looking after the property, you could potentially introduce more regular inspections until the problem is resolved.

But looking after your property isn't just about physically inspecting it — it's also about communicating successfully with your tenants so they're absolutely clear on what is and isn't acceptable.

Always display notices in communal areas of the property (ideally a hallway or kitchen) that remind tenants of their responsibilities to keep the property clean, tidy, and free of rubbish. You should also make sure they know how to report any maintenance issues or repair needs to you, so that problems aren't left to get worse and worse.

You may also like to send a monthly email newsletter to your tenants, which is an opportunity to remind them of their responsibilities, highlight any maintenance issues, and update them on any repair works in the pipeline. Email communication like this is great for keeping a paper trail of warnings and requests.

Managing tenants' behavior

Generally speaking, two of the most common concerns with students and low-income-housing tenants are noise and antisocial behavior. Overcoming both challenges is a matter of communicating really well with your tenants.

Always make it clear to your tenants in writing — through the contract, notices in the property, and other written communications — what constitutes acceptable and unacceptable behavior. Keeping a written paper trail of emails and notices will help you provide evidence in the future if you need to evict a tenant.

Most of the time, though, it won't come to that. If a tenant is causing trouble in the property — perhaps by creating a nuisance for other tenants or being too noisy — a warning is usually enough to bring that person back in line. Making it clear that you'll evict him from the property if you have to, and that you won't give a reference for any future tenancy, usually does the trick.

However, if things don't improve and you need to go down the route of removing a tenant from the property, act swiftly. You don't want other good tenants to leave the property because they can't bear living with the problem tenant. Turn back to Chapter 13 for more on dealing with problem tenants.

You may want to appoint one of the tenants to be the "responsible person" or "house rep" in the house. They can help to manage the property, keep on top of maintenance and cleanliness issues, and help to keep tenants in line. As an incentive, they can get a discount on their rent.

Looking at Five International Locations Where This Strategy Would Work

If you're going down the low-income-housing route, it's very difficult for me to pinpoint particular countries or towns that you should pay attention to. That's because, even within one town, there are huge differences in specific neighborhoods and locations. London, for instance, has both insanely affluent areas and very deprived neighborhoods where people are genuinely struggling to make ends meet.

For that reason, when you're just starting out with renting to low-income-housing tenants, I would always advocate starting with an area you know fairly well — an area where you already have a good grasp of the local nuances, supply and demand, and market pricing. You may even have contacts with your local housing authority, which may come in very handy.

When renting to students, it's easier to pinpoint general areas to explore in more detail. The following cities are particularly desirable among students for their excellent universities and high quality of living:

>> Tokyo

>> Toronto

>> Melbourne

>> Edinburgh

>> Boston

» Putting the "service" into serviced accommodation

» Finding the right property

» Running your serviced accommodation business like a boss

Chapter **15**

Providing Serviced Accommodation

What sort of accommodation do you look for when you're going on a vacation or business trip? Ten years ago, your default choices were a hotel, motel, or perhaps a cute bed-and-breakfast. Now, though, you have a much wider selection. You might, for example, spring for an aparthotel for your next business trip, or book a funky downtown apartment for your anniversary weekend in New York. If you did, you'd be among the growing number of guests who favor serviced accommodation.

REMEMBER

The serviced accommodation model has grown enormously in recent years and is seriously disrupting traditional views of hospitality, largely thanks to the unstoppable rise of Airbnb (www.airbnb.com). Nowadays, many guests want more than a sterile, cookie-cutter hotel room; they want a comfortable, stylish, home-away-from-home feel, in a more private, self-contained space.

This growth and demand makes serviced accommodation an exciting, attractive model for real estate investors. But it's not a business to dive into without doing your homework; because this is such a fast-growing industry, regulation is still evolving rapidly and is subject to change.

In this chapter, I look at the ins and outs of the serviced accommodation model and offer practical tips for running a successful serviced accommodation business, while staying on the right side of the law. But first, I start with a thorough definition of serviced accommodation.

Defining Serviced Accommodation

Serviced accommodation is a fully furnished, usually self-contained accommodation that is rented on a short-term basis and comes with housekeeping and other amenities and services. It blends the service element of a hotel with the space, privacy, comfort, and independence of a home.

Instead of renting the property on a 6- or 12-month lease, as you might with a regular rental model, with serviced accommodation you rent out your property for much shorter periods of time — often by the night, although weekly and monthly models also work well for certain guests and/or locations. This higher turnover of guests can make for a highly profitable business (more on the financial model coming up later).

For me, there are two winning concepts that have made serviced accommodation so popular in such a short space of time: One is "home away from home" and the other is "living like a local." What do you picture when you think of these concepts?

Perhaps you're picturing a unique apartment in an artsy, up-and-coming part of town, far away from hordes of tourists. Or maybe you see yourself lounging around in your pajamas at 11 a.m., safe in the knowledge that there's no morning housekeeping coming to disturb you. Perhaps you picture making a cup of coffee or opening a beer in your self-contained kitchen instead of braving the depressing hotel bar. All these images sum up why guests love serviced accommodation.

What type of accommodation does it cover?

Strictly speaking, *serviced accommodation* is an umbrella term because it can be applied to lots of different types of accommodation.

REMEMBER

Types of serviced accommodation typically include

>> **Individual serviced properties, like self-contained apartments or houses:** Depending on the local market, these may be rented to business people or tourists (if you're interested more specifically in the tourist market option, turn to Chapter 16 to find out about vacation rentals).

>> **Aparthotels, which are dedicated buildings containing multiple self-contained, serviced apartments:** These are more like hotels in that they often have a 24-hour front desk and perhaps have other hotel-like amenities on-site, such as a gym.

>> **Corporate housing that's rented by corporate clients looking for a more comfortable, cost-effective place to house visiting employees:** This is more comparable to a regular rental model, except instead of renting on a 12-month basis, you may rent the property for a month at a time.

These types of accommodation aren't new, as such. Most booking platforms, such as Booking.com (www.booking.com), have offered apartments alongside regular hotel rooms for many years. The rise of Airbnb and increasing demand for more independent travel have turned serviced accommodation into an industry in its own right in recent years.

REMEMBER

As you can tell, serviced accommodation is usually entirely self-contained, with a private kitchen, bathroom, and living area — just like a regular home. However, given that Airbnb also allows guests to rent rooms as well as a whole property, serviced accommodation can in theory stretch to renting out short-term accommodation on a room-by-room basis, with certain amenities being shared by guests.

In this chapter, however, I largely focus on the more common types of serviced accommodation (namely, individual serviced properties that are rented to tourists and business travelers, plus aparthotels).

What about the "serviced" part?

Anyone can understand the idea of renting out an apartment via Airbnb or Booking.com. But it's the "serviced" part where things get slightly murky. What kind of services are you expected to provide? How can you blend the dedicated-service nature of a hotel with the independence of an apartment?

There's no one-size-fits-all answer to that question. You can pretty much offer any kind of services you like in order to differentiate yourself from the competition — from giving local tips on where to eat, to booking chauffeur-driven cars. Turn to the section "Deciding What Level of Service to Offer," later in this chapter, for a more in-depth look at service options.

In general, though, serviced accommodation is defined by being private and self-contained, offering travelers the chance to feel like they're staying in a real home, rather than a bland hotel room. That means travelers generally expect to have included as a minimum:

>> **Taxes, utility bills, and charges, so there are no nasty hidden extras** (like having to pay for hotel Wi-Fi) upon check-in.

>> **Private cooking facilities:** Whether that means a full-size kitchen or a simple kitchenette, the idea is that guests have the space and equipment they need to prepare drinks and basic meals.

>> **A private bathroom.**

>> **A living area with a TV and space for dining.**

>> **Independent entry to the property, either through their own key that they collect upon check-in or a keypad entry system.**

Depending on price range and the type of property, nice-to-haves may include:

>> **Dishwasher and washing machine in the kitchen, or a laundry room in the building**

>> **Access to services such as a gym, pool, and meeting rooms**

>> **A concierge service or friendly host who provides personalized local recommendations and help with booking local events, outings, restaurants, and travel**

>> **A 24-hour front desk or a phone number to call if they need help with anything**

What guests don't expect from serviced accommodation is

>> **Food:** Because serviced accommodation comes with private cooking facilities, guests don't expect to be fed , not even at breakfast time. That said, many hosts leave some sort of food for their guests, such as tea bags, good coffee, snacks, or even a bottle of wine.

>> **Daily housekeeping:** A daily intrusion from housekeeping would kind of ruin the private, home-away-from-home feel. Therefore, cleaning and linen changes typically take place either at the end of the stay or on a weekly basis if guests are staying longer than a week. Some operators offer extra turn-downs at the client's request (sometimes for an extra fee).

Who stays in serviced accommodation?

You might have noticed I'm using the word *guests* rather than *tenants* throughout this chapter, which highlights how serviced accommodation is more of a hospitality business than a residential real estate strategy.

So, with your thoughts tuned to guests rather than tenants, what kinds of guests can you expect to welcome to a serviced accommodation property?

>> **Professionals looking for a more relaxing, homey place to stay while they're away on business:** When you're on the road a lot, hotels (and hotel food) can get old pretty fast.

>> **Families on a budget who like having the option to cook for themselves rather than eat out every night, and who appreciate the extra space that an apartment or house offers:** Anyone who's ever shared a cramped hotel room with their kids — or, for that matter, any teenager who's been forced to share a hotel room with her parents — will immediately see the appeal of this!

>> **Independently minded couples and solo travelers who are looking for a more personal, individual travel experience.**

>> **Group and parties (bachelorette parties, groups of friends, and so on) for whom serviced accommodation presents a cost-effective option, with a much more convivial atmosphere than multiple, separate hotel rooms:** This kind of guest has unique challenges and operators often tend to try avoiding them for obvious reasons like potential damage to their property.

Looking at the Pros and Cons of Serviced Accommodation

Serviced accommodation offer lots of advantages for real estate entrepreneurs compared to regular rental strategies, but it's not all rosy. There are plenty of pitfalls to be aware of if your serviced accommodation business is to be a success.

Taking a glimpse at the positives

Let's dive into what I see as the biggest advantages of serviced accommodation.

Enormous guest demand

At the time of writing, Airbnb alone has facilitated more than 400 million guest arrivals, which clearly shows the incredible popularity of self-contained accommodation.

REMEMBER

Here are just a few of the things guests love about serviced accommodation:

>> **That home-away-from-home feeling.**

>> **Much more space:** In fact, the average one-bedroom serviced apartment is twice as large as a standard hotel room.

>> **Unique accommodation that's bursting with personality:** Savvy hosts make sure their properties are stylish enough to stand out on a crowded booking platform like Airbnb. (You can find more on preparing your property later in the chapter.)

>> **The convenience of being able to cook for yourself, or enjoy a cost-effective breakfast at "home."**

>> **Better value compared to staying in a hotel, particularly for groups and families.**

>> **Total privacy and freedom for guests to come and go as they please.**

>> **Local knowledge and recommendations from friendly hosts (a real plus for guests who can't afford a fancy hotel with concierge service).**

Flexible, scalable business model

One of the things I love about serviced accommodation is how flexible it is. Want to rent out a granny annex in your garden? That'll work. Want to dip your toe in with one single serviced apartment? Brilliant. Want to progress to half a dozen apartments around town? Ka-ching! Have the experience, capital, and team to run a full-on aparthotel? As we say in the UK, quids in!

TIP

There's a serviced accommodation model that works for pretty much any kind of real estate entrepreneur, which means you can start small and easily scale up as your expertise and experience grows.

High income

Perhaps the biggest advantage, though, is the high returns. Because you're typically charging by the night or week, your income is significantly higher than if you were renting the same property out as a standard rental on a one-year lease.

REMEMBER

In other words, if you have two identical apartments in the same building and you rent one out for 12 months and the other by the night — or even on a weekly basis — you've got the potential to earn much more on the second property than you would on a yearly lease on the first.

WARNING

However, a higher turnover of guests means not only are you using the property more intensively, which, in turn, means you can expect higher costs, but you're also probably more likely to have a lower occupancy level (more periods of lost rent). So, you'll have higher servicing and maintenance costs *and* potentially higher void periods. Having said all that, if well run, the rewards of higher overall income are clearly there for the taking.

Table 15-1 demonstrates the potential for much higher income from a serviced accommodation model (renting per night or per week) compared to an average residential rental property use, even when all extra costs and lower occupancy rates are considered. The list of costs is not exhaustive, of course, but this demonstrates the basic financial concept. Also, I've assumed you're running each model yourself (no agency or full-time management costs).

TABLE 15-1 **Comparing Serviced Accommodation to Standard Rentals**

	Nightly Model	Weekly Model	"Standard" 12-Month Lease
Average income	$110 per night	$400 per week	$950 per month
Occupancy level	80%	85%	95%
Gross average income per month	*$2,677*	*$1,473*	*$903*
Costs to deduct per month			
Cleaner/housekeeper	$300	$40	$0
Laundry	$150	$20	$0
Replacement products (toilet paper, shampoo, and so on)	$150	$20	$0
Commission taken from website where you list the property (range from 10% to 20%)	$268	$147	$0
Utility bills/costs of running the property	$300	$250	$200
Total costs	*$1,168*	*$477*	*$200*
Total gross profit per month (income minus costs)	**$1,509**	**$996**	**$703**

TIP

Serviced accommodation tends to be very price sensitive, particularly if you're targeting tourists who'll only be staying a night or two and who are generally driven by price and reviews. So, when considering the financial model for your serviced accommodation business, look carefully at pricing for similar properties in your location and among your target market. You can find more on pricing in the section "Getting the Right Business Processes and Systems in Place," later in this chapter.

Assessing the downsides

A serviced accommodation property may make a lot more money than a standard residential rental property, but it's also much more of a headache to run. I'd go so far as to say serviced accommodation isn't for the fainthearted. But when you know the risks and downsides, you're better placed to plan for them.

With that in mind, let's take a look at the less attractive side of serviced accommodation.

Higher risk of void periods

With a higher turnover of guests comes a higher chance that one or more of your properties will, at times, stand empty. For example, if you have ten apartments that you rent out by the night, chances are, you'll have a night or two every week where each of those apartments could be vacant. What's more, depending on your location, occupancy rates can vary drastically throughout the year.

TIP

Blending guest types and pricing models can be a good way to minimize void periods. For example, if you're offering a one-bedroom apartment for rent on a nightly basis to tourists, you can also offer special rates for weekly and monthly rentals — thereby attracting longer-staying guests. Similarly, the average aparthotel on any given night may have a mixture of business and pleasure travelers checked in. If you can attract a variety of customers to your property, for both short and longer stays, you reduce your chances of the property sitting empty.

Alternatively, you can offer other incentives to get people through the door. Here's a great example from my local town of Reading. It's a large town, with many big employers, which means it attracts a lot of business travelers. As such, there are lots of smart hotels and aparthotels that are frequently fully booked from Monday through Thursday, charging as much as £150 (about $192) per night. But on Fridays, all those business travelers head home, leaving hotels and aparthotels struggling to get people through the door. As such, my wife and I have gotten some insane deals on luxury places for the weekend, often with a meal or other incentive included, for a nightly rate of £80 (about $102). For us, it's a cheap date night away from the kids, and for the business, it's a way to make a little money on what would otherwise be an empty room with zero income.

Evolving regulation

It's fair to say that regulation took a while to catch up to the serviced accommodation model. But that's changing. Many jurisdictions are significantly tightening up on serviced accommodation rules, so you need to be prepared to keep abreast of changing laws in this fast-moving sector.

Immerse yourself in the industry by attending industry events and getting accredited by relevant industry organizations such as the Association of Serviced Apartment Providers (ASAP; https://theasap.org.uk). When you're immersed in the industry, you'll be much better placed to sense when changes are coming. You can find more on regulations and planning later in the chapter.

Considerably more work

Probably the biggest disadvantage, though, is just how much work is involved in serviced accommodation. Although there are varying levels of service (see "Deciding What Level of Service to Offer," coming up next), you'll undoubtedly have to put in more work than you would with a standard residential rental property. Sure, it's less work than a hotel, but it's still a lot of work, and until you have a team in place to run it for you, it's far from a hands-off passive-income model.

Not many rental agents or managing agents specialize in serviced accommodation, so be prepared to be quite hands-on and put your own sweat and time into making your serviced accommodation business a success. *Business* is a key word there. Running serviced accommodation is more like running a full-time business than many other more "passive" real estate income strategies.

Some of the practical everyday things that serviced accommodation newbies often overlook include the following:

>> **Online reviews can make or break a property, so quality accommodation and thoughtful service are a must.** If you don't like dealing with people, serviced accommodation really isn't for you.

>> **You need to provide, and maintain, everything that makes a property a home, from the furniture to the plates and cups.** Read more about this in "Preparing Your Property for Serviced Accommodation Use."

>> **Who's going to be there to check in guests and hand over the keys (or will you have a keypad entry)?** Who's going to clean the property and change the linens and towels after each guest checks out? Who'll be doing all that laundry?

TIP

With these considerations in mind, you'll need a good dream team of people to help you run the business, especially if you're going to run multiple apartments. In addition to the regular dream teamers I mention in Chapter 3, you may choose to have a hybrid housekeeper/property manager to be there to check guests in and clean the property after they leave — or, if you have a lot of properties, you'll have to allocate these roles to different people. And if you're running an aparthotel, you'll need round-the-clock front desk staff.

Because customer service is so important, the people you work with must be detail oriented and extremely diligent. You need people who care and are service driven if you're going to excel at serviced accommodation.

Deciding What Level of Service to Offer

Later in this chapter, I talk more about physically preparing your property for serviced accommodation use, and what items and equipment you need to include in the property. For now, let's look at what you might be expected to deliver in terms of service.

Covering the basics

For a straightforward apartment rented out via online booking platforms, your service offering can be as simple as

>> Checking guests in and handing over the keys (this doesn't have to be done in person if you have a key safe or lockbox outside the property or a keypad entry system)

>> Leaving some flyers for local attractions on the table

>> Checking out guests (or again, arranging for them to leave the keys or secure the property themselves)

>> Cleaning the apartment and changing the bed linens and towels after the guests have left

With this basic approach, there's minimal need for anyone to be available to look after guests, or for you to go above and beyond to make your guests' stay memorable. You're purely providing attractive, comfortable accommodation. That's it. But is that really the best way to make your property stand out on a busy booking platform? You're far better off spending a little time and effort to impress your guests so that they want to come back in the future and write a positive online review singing your property's praises.

In the following sections, I fill you in on a few ways hosts provide more personal service.

Wowing guests with personal touches

One way to differentiate yourself from the competition is to provide a downright awesome service, from first contact to checkout. Your serviced accommodation may be more home-away-from-home than A-lister-luxury, but you can still wow your guests with luxurious touches.

TIP

Look for ways to make your guests' stay more convenient or memorable. These may include

>> **Sending a personalized email after booking to thank guests for their reservations:** Tell them how much you're looking forward to welcoming them, and give them any helpful information they may need on getting to the property and making the most of their stay.

>> **Providing a celebratory bottle (or half-bottle) of wine or fresh flowers upon arrival, especially if you know your guests are there for a special occasion:** We once stayed in an Airbnb apartment for my birthday, and the host gave us a delicious chocolate cake!

>> **Providing thoughtful food and drink items:** These might include a selection of tea bags, quality coffee, sugar, honey, milk or cream, and bottled water.

>> **Offering help with booking travel and making local reservations:** This is especially if the guests are coping with a language barrier.

>> **Providing a personalized guide to the local area:** This may be a three-ring binder that you leave on the kitchen counter or coffee table. It can include your house rules, who to contact in case of emergency, neighborhood attractions, bars and restaurants you recommend, insider tips, a few pointers on the local language, and the location of the nearest 24-hour pharmacy.

>> **Luxury toiletries or even your own branded shampoos and soaps, like those you'd find in a nice hotel.**

>> **Laundry facilities, or a laundry service, especially if guests are going to be staying longer than a week.**

>> **Free airport transfers, if feasible.**

REMEMBER

You can always tweak things as you go along, so listen to guest feedback and alter your service offering based on what you learn.

However luxurious or high-end your service extras, the most important thing is to provide the things that are most helpful, convenient, and desirable for your target audience. In other words, you need to decide on your primary audience in order to differentiate yourself for that market.

Tailoring your offering to your target audience

Different audiences have different needs. For example, leisure travelers will want recommendations on must-see attractions, while business travelers may want to know where they can have a quiet business dinner. Both may want to know how to navigate the local public transport network.

Know your market and understand what your guests are looking for. This means you need to do your homework on how to deliver the best experience for the type of people you want to attract. To research this, I recommend

>> Studying reviews of similar properties to see what guests like most and least about the property and service

>> Checking out what the competition is doing by staying in local competitors' properties and looking for things you can do better

>> Encouraging guests' feedback and following up after their stays to find out what they most appreciated and what you can do better in the future

Sourcing Serviced Accommodation Properties

When you understand your target audience, you're able to start sourcing the right kind of property for their needs. As with any type of real estate strategy or business, never source without knowing your target audience.

Unless you're sourcing or building a dedicated aparthotel, your serviced accommodation property is going to be a pretty standard property (an apartment or house), just used in a different way. Therefore, you can source properties through all the usual means: browsing online, looking in the local estate agent's window, or even sourcing properties yourself by targeting local homeowners.

In other words, how you go about sourcing suitable properties for serviced accommodation is much like sourcing for any other rental strategy, and you'll find plenty of helpful tips throughout this book.

However, there are some specific considerations to keep in mind as you assess properties for serviced accommodation use.

Looking at the quality and size of the property

Assuming you're not aiming at low-budget travelers (not a great income-earner), think of serviced accommodation as a high-end rental strategy, attracting high-quality guests, just on a short-term basis. That means you're looking for a fairly high-end property.

REMEMBER

Your guests will expect hotel-like quality from your property — something that looks stylish, inviting, and well finished. So, seek out properties that have a high specification of fixtures and fittings, or properties that have the potential to be developed into high-spec rentals (circle back to Chapter 9 for more on developing properties).

Size of rooms is another important factor. In general, you're looking for rooms that are as spacious as possible, are well designed, and make thoughtful use of the space. A separate lounge area is usually expected, although this may depend on your target audience. For example, if your property is in a very expensive city and you're targeting tourists staying for a couple of nights only, you can perhaps get away with a small studio apartment. The corporate market tends to prefer more spacious properties.

Keep in mind that, even if you find a fantastic, high-quality property, you'll still need to do some work to prepare it for use as serviced accommodation. You can find more on that coming up.

TIP

It's always good to have a plan B, so if you ultimately find that the serviced accommodation business doesn't work for you or that it's just too labor intensive, as long as you have a well-chosen property in a strong location, you should have no trouble renting it out as a regular residential long-term rental that's aimed at high-end professional tenants.

Choosing the right location for your guests

Just as with the size and quality of the property, the right location for your serviced accommodation offering will hinge on who you're aiming at.

REMEMBER

Location is perhaps more critical and sensitive for serviced accommodation than it is for the other real estate strategies in this book (with the exception of vacation rentals, covered in Chapter 16). So you'll need to carefully assess the location of each potential property and ask yourself questions such as the following:

>> Are there tourist attractions and/large employers nearby, guaranteeing a ready supply of visitors to the area?

>> Are there good public transport links so guests can get around easily?

>> Is there a decent choice of bars, restaurants, and convenience stores within easy reach?

>> Is the property in a safe neighborhood?

>> Is it going to be noisy for guests? Most guests want the convenience of a central location, but they don't want to stay above a noisy bar or right next to a tram line with trams clinking along the rails all night (another Airbnb experience of mine).

If you want to invest in serviced accommodation in overseas locations, I give some ideas on global Airbnb hot spots at the very end of this chapter.

WARNING

What type of property you buy and where you buy it may be influenced by local rules and regulations. For example, there's no point buying a property in a jurisdiction that's looking to clamp down on short-term rentals. Turn to "Navigating Planning and Regulations" later in this chapter for more on this subject.

TIP

If buying the right kind of property in your chosen location is out of the question (perhaps because the market is too strong and prices are sky-high), you might consider renting a property and — with the landlord's permission — subletting the property as a serviced accommodation business. This is known as "rent-to-rent," and you can read more about this exciting strategy in Chapter 11.

WARNING

As with any real estate model, you need to make sure you're not in breach of your mortgage terms. If you don't, you run the risk of not being able to use the property in the way you intend or, worse, losing the property. So, whether you're buying a property for use as serviced accommodation, or renting out an existing property as serviced accommodation, you need to inform your mortgage provider of your plans. This may mean you need to work with an experienced, independent broker to find the right mortgage for your needs.

If you already own the property, you may be able to try running the property as serviced accommodation for a short period of time and still be within the bounds of your mortgage (so you don't need to change your mortgage until you're sure this is the right business for you). Your broker will be able to advise you on what's possible within the terms of your mortgage.

Preparing Your Property for Serviced Accommodation Use

After you've sourced the right property for your target audience, you need to physically prepare the property for use as serviced accommodation. Again, this means really knowing your target audience and the sorts of thing they'll expect from the property.

Planning for the practicalities of welcoming guests

If you're not going to greet your guests and hand over the keys in person (or employ someone to do this for you), you need some physical mechanism of allowing guests entry to the property.

One good way of doing this is to have a keypad entry system, where guests can open the front door with a code that you give them just before check-in. This method is secure and convenient for guests, because it means they can arrive at a time that suits them without worrying about being there to meet the host at a certain time.

TIP

However, for an apartment, a keypad entry system may not be possible (unless you own the whole building and can have a separate code entry system on the main door to the building). In this case, many hosts choose to have a small keysafe or lockbox outside the building's front door; guests open the safe or box with a code you give them, and inside are the keys to the building and apartment. Again, guests often love the convenience of this approach.

Getting the decor and overall look of the property right

You need to make sure the property is attractive and stylish so it makes a great impression — visually on online booking platforms, and in person when your guests arrive.

Again, the overall look of the property should be designed in line with the type of people you're likely to attract. For example, an Airbnb in traditional Oxford may be decorated with old-world charm (think dark colors and lots of mahogany), while the same type of property in funky East London may be decorated more like an artist's loft (think hammocks, hanging plants, and bright colors).

REMEMBER

Whatever style you go for, quality, relevance, style, and personality are paramount. You're not going for the same kind of functional, hardwearing decor, fixtures, and fittings as you would with a standard residential rental model, where your tenants will put their own stamp on the property. You're looking to stand out and attract high-quality guests through a more luxurious finish and personal touches.

So, where in a regular rental property, you may have plain white walls and laminate flooring, in serviced accommodation, you may have a nice feature wall with eye-catching wallpaper, plus artwork, high-end floor tiles, attractive rugs, and soft furnishings.

Equipping the property with everything your guests need

When equipping the property, think about your target guest and ask yourself, what does that type of guest need to make his stay as convenient, comfortable, and pleasant as possible?

REMEMBER

This generally means ensuring the property has

>> **Free Wi-Fi:** You should include the password in the three-ring binder of information you leave for your guests.

>> **All furnishings you'd generally expect in a home:** This includes beds, dressers, sofas, dining tables and chairs, and a TV.

>> **A well-equipped kitchen:** In addition to the standard appliances (refrigerator, stove, microwave, and dishwasher, if possible), you should provide crockery, cutlery, a tea kettle, a toaster, and a coffee machine.

>> **Basic cleaning products:** This includes dishrags, sponges, dishwashing detergent, and laundry detergent, as well as toiletries.

>> **Basic food items:** This may include spices, coffee, tea, snacks, and so on.

>> **Bed linens, towels, and slippers.**

>> **Thoughtful touches, like an umbrella, maps, and personal recommendations on local restaurants, bars, and attractions.**

>> **For business travelers, a dedicated space to work.**

You may want to install a security system for the property, including external security cameras. You'll also need to make sure the property is safe for guests and free of hazards. You can find more on that coming up in the next section.

Always take an inventory of items in the property and check the property against this itinerary at regular intervals. Also, remember to tell your insurance provider that you're using the property as serviced accommodation and make sure that you have the right kind of insurance for this use. You made be advised that you need public liability insurance as well. Always take professional advice on the right level of coverage for your business.

Navigating Planning and Regulatory Restrictions

One thing that serviced accommodation newbies often overlook is the kinds of restrictions placed on this type of property use, and the fact that planning consent may be needed to run a residential property as serviced accommodation. You don't want to make the same mistake.

Justifiably, local governments want to control what goes on with housing in their areas, including what types of buildings are built and how local buildings are used. That's why we have zoning and planning laws around the world, to make sure the local area benefits the local community.

Not everyone is a fan of the serviced accommodation model because it means more people coming into an area, increased traffic (vehicle or foot), more wear-and-tear on local amenities, higher potential for complaints from neighbors, and fewer quality properties left available for local residents to rent. For this reason, many jurisdictions have sought to limit the number of serviced accommodation properties in their areas. You'll, therefore, need to check whether any such restrictions apply in your chosen area.

For example, in London, you're not allowed to rent your whole residential property for more than 90 days without planning permission. To clarify and help enforce the planning rules, in 2017, Airbnb introduced a 90-day limit on renting "entire homes" in Greater London. With this "90-day rule" in place, people can still rent out their properties without planning permission for up to 90 days a year. Assuming you want to rent out the property for more than 90 days, in Greater London at least, you'll need formal planning permission to change the property from residential use to serviced accommodation use.

You may or may not need formal planning or zoning consent to use your property as serviced accommodation, and this will vary from location to location and according to how many nights of the year you're renting the property, along with the type of service you offer.

Always take specific local advice from a real estate lawyer, a good planning consultant, and the local housing department to clarify which regulations apply to your serviced accommodation business. You absolutely need to be working *with* regulations, not against, and never be tempted to cut corners or try to flout the law.

In addition to planning laws, you may also have to comply with certain management regulations and/or health and safety laws. If you think about it, there are many risks involved in having people stay in your property. If someone leans on the shower curtain and it falls down, for example, and they fall out of the shower and hurt themselves, you could be held liable. That's why proper insurance is essential, as is making sure your property is safe for your proposed use.

Depending on your jurisdiction, this may mean you need to install firefighting equipment, fire alarms, fire doors, and emergency signage in the property. If you circle back to Chapter 13, the list of management regulations and health and safety requirements will give you a good idea of what might be required, but always seek advice that's specific to your property, use, and local area.

Getting the Right Business Processes and Systems in Place

You'll need to invest time and money in various processes and software tools to ensure the smooth running of your business — and the complexity and range of these processes and systems will depend on how many properties you're running and the level of service you're offering.

Perhaps the most critical business processes for serviced accommodation are

>> Handling reservations across different platforms

>> Carefully pricing your offering and adjusting pricing throughout the year to suit the market

>> Promoting your properties effectively

Wherever possible, look to automate as many of these processes as you can, for example by using a centralized bookings tool and sending automated welcome and follow-up emails to your guests. You can find more on investing in systems and technology to grow your real estate business in Chapter 3.

Managing reservations

Many serviced accommodation operators advertise their properties on more than one booking platform at the same time (for example, Airbnb and Booking.com), so that they get maximum exposure — and you'll want to do the same. You'll also, ideally, have your own website where guests can book direct (thereby saving you commission that you'd otherwise have to pay the booking website). All this means you'll have bookings coming in from multiple sources, which can be challenging to coordinate.

TIP

Invest in your own booking management system that aggregates reservations from the various different sources and manages your multiple listings and bookings through one centralized system. I use Eviivo's (www.eviivo.com) Booking Engine for this, but there are lots of similar tools out there, so do your research and find the one that you think will suit you the best. Using one of these systems can substantially increase your occupancy rates by getting you on many, many more booking portals than you may be able to do manually. Many list you on more than 40 different portals for maximum exposure — imagine trying to manage all those listings and bookings, especially at peak times!

As part of the reservation process, you'll also need to think carefully about your payment terms and cancellation policy. For a regular apartment, payment is usually taken upfront via the booking platform, and you'll have a choice of cancellation policies. For example, there may be a certain timeframe where guests can cancel and get a full refund, where they can cancel and get a 50 percent refund, and a point at which no refund will be given. Personally, I recommend having a strict cancellation policy for maximum protection.

For an aparthotel, however, some guests may expect to pay upon check-in or checkout, as they would in a normal hotel, which may leave you more open to last-minute cancellations. In this case, you can offer various booking options, such as a special discounted rate for advance prepayment (with no cancellation option), or a small deposit upfront, or a more expensive rate that allows for cancellation up to 24 hours before arrival.

REMEMBER

Keeping on top of payment policies for the various booking platforms is essential for healthy cash flow. If you run out of cash, even if you're fully booked for the next month, you'll struggle to stay in business. This means you not only need to be aware of when exactly the platform takes payment from guests, but also when they transfer that money to you. One portal may pay you upon each booking, for example, while another may roll all bookings into a weekly or monthly payment run.

WARNING

Make sure guests are made aware of the property's terms and conditions (such as any noise policy, arrival and departure times, cancellation policy, payment terms, and so on) at the time of booking. The major booking platforms allow you to stipulate terms and conditions as part of the property description. And if guests are booking directly through your own website, it's a good idea to have a check box that guests click to confirm they've read and understood your terms and conditions.

Optimizing your pricing

I've mentioned that serviced accommodation is a very price-sensitive business. In a very busy market, you can price high. If there are slow seasons in your area, you'll need to price lower. You may experience crazy demand from Friday through Sunday, but struggle to get people through the door at other times — or vice versa.

What's more, pricing will also vary depending on whether you're charging by the night, by the week, or by the month. It's a good idea to offer different prices for different lengths of stay, which encourages a mixture of shorter- and longer-term guests.

REMEMBER

All this means you're not just setting a price and sticking to it. You need to be continually tweaking your prices — and this is known as *dynamic pricing*. If you've ever hailed an Uber at peak "surge pricing" times, you've experienced dynamic pricing. It's designed to allow businesses to price their wares according to market changes, the season, the day of the week, local supply and demand, local events, and so on. To put it bluntly, if you aren't doing dynamic pricing, you're not optimizing your income.

All the major booking platforms allow for dynamic pricing, and provide tools to help you price dynamically without tying yourself in mathematical knots!

TIP

Create and regularly update an events calendar that's specific to your local area and lists the big local events that attract lots of visitors. For example, are there certain conventions that happen every year, or is a big one-off exhibition coming up next year? Is there an annual music festival? Is your city going to be European Capital of Culture in two years' time? At these peak demand times, you'll be able to charge more than usual, perhaps two or three times as much.

Marketing your property

You need to cast your net far and wide and ensure your property is listed on all the major booking platforms, particularly Airbnb and Booking.com, although there are also lots of smaller, more localized platforms like Wimdu (www.wimdu.com)

and Wunderflats (`www.wunderflats.com`). *Remember:* Many centralized management booking systems (discussed earlier in this chapter) will list across multiple platforms for you, which saves you time signing up for them one by one and managing all those different portals yourself.

TIP

Invest in professional-quality photos to ensure your property really stands out online. Include a well-written, detailed description of the property that's bursting with warm personality, and really emphasize the level of service that guests can expect. Don't forget to revisit your online listings at regular intervals to make sure everything is displaying properly and to update details (as you tweak your service offering, for example).

REMEMBER

In the early days, the major booking platforms will obviously form the main thrust of your marketing activities. However, as you build up your reputation over time, you can reduce your costs (for example, not pay commission to a booking agent) by encouraging guests to book directly through your own website in the future. This can really improve your margins.

To encourage more direct bookings, you can

>> Give guests a business card, postcard, or flyer that directs them to your website for future bookings.

>> Offer guests a discount for booking directly next time.

>> Collect your guests' contact details (with their permission, of course) to re-market to them for return stays, perhaps including special offers in a weekly or monthly newsletter to give them a reason to sign up to your email marketing list.

>> Follow up with guests after their stay to ask for feedback. You can then use great reviews in your advertising and on your website.

>> Spread the word among your network via social media.

>> Invest in online paid advertisements and search engine optimization (SEO) to get your website noticed.

>> Approach big employers in the local area to see if they'd recommend you as an accommodation provider for visiting executives.

>> Connect with other local businesses who can point potential guests in your direction. For example, a wedding planner can recommend you as a great option for wedding guests who have traveled from afar, or the local convention center may be willing to list you as a recommended accommodation provider.

Managing Your Serviced Accommodation Business on an Ongoing Basis

After you've gotten your property set up, you've put your business processes and systems in place, and you've settled into the routine of welcoming guests and delivering an awesome experience, things should be running smoothly. However, there are certain things you need to keep in mind if you want to continue delivering a fantastic service.

REMEMBER

This ongoing care and attention includes

>> **Maintaining quality accommodation:** You'll need to do a regular deep clean and spruce up the property once a year with a fresh coat of paint. Take this opportunity to update the decor and furnishings as required, and replace anything that's tired or broken as and when needed. Kitchen items, in particular, are prone to breakage.

>> **Encouraging guests to leave online reviews:** You can ask for feedback via questionnaires, too. Then us the best reviews in your marketing activities, and take the time to reply to reviews and thank guests for their feedback.

>> **Continually engaging in market research to keep up with what your competitors are doing and keep abreast of the market:** It's a nice excuse to check yourself into a lovely local Airbnb every now and then — hey, you gotta do your homework!

>> **Tweaking your pricing, business systems, processes, and service offerings as you gain more experience and as your market evolves:** Think of this as a nonstop process of learning so that you can continually optimize your business.

REMEMBER

That last point is an important one for me. Because serviced accommodation is built around short-term rentals, you have a constant feedback loop going. That means you should be constantly tweaking and improving what you do based on what your guests like and don't like, in order to maximize your income and attract great guests for many years to come.

Identifying Five International Locations Where This Strategy Would Work

Like most of the strategies in this book, serviced accommodation can be done successfully around the world. However, different locations will be suited to different models — some cities will be more appropriate for corporate-style aparthotels, while other locations are better suited to the tourist-focused Airbnb model. That means it's tricky to make concrete one-size-fits-all recommendations here.

But as an example, let's take a standard, city-center Airbnb apartment that's aimed at tourists. To identify some of the best international locations for this model, simply look at the most profitable and in-demand Airbnb cities in the world — cities where occupancy rates are high and so are the nightly rates.

Based on these criteria, some of the hottest Airbnb cities in the world include

>> Vancouver

>> San Diego

>> Paris

>> Sydney

>> Tokyo

» **Managing your costs, void periods, and seasonality challenges**

» **Marketing and managing your property with ease**

Chapter **16**

Providing Vacation Rentals, at Home and Abroad

O wning vacation rentals is a strategy that appeals to many investors, largely because of the strong rental yield, but also for the lifestyle aspects. After all, renting out vacation properties in sunny Florida and dealing with happy vacationing families may seem a whole lot more appealing than renting to students in Fort Worth. And it's even more appealing if your ultimate long-term goal is to retire to one of your properties.

Perhaps most excitingly, there's a specific vacation rental strategy to suit any passion — from family-friendly ski chalets in Austria, to luxury seaside villas in Spain, to quirky artist retreats in Sweden, to romantic stone cottages in Wales, to surfer beach huts in Hawaii. Whatever your individual interests, there's a good chance you can turn it into a viable vacation rental business.

REMEMBER

As with any real estate investment, you really need to do your research, and spend time learning the local market and building your local dream team (see Chapter 3) before you put your money on the line. What's more, choosing the right location and carefully managing your cash flow are even more critical with holiday rentals than they are with other rental strategies, so these areas deserve your close attention.

In this chapter, I walk you through the basics of providing successful holiday rentals, from finding the right location to managing your finances and the property on an ongoing basis.

Knowing the Difference Between Vacation Rentals and Serviced Accommodation

If you've already read about serviced accommodation rentals in Chapter 15, you may be asking yourself what the difference is between vacation rentals and serviced accommodation?

This chapter is a natural sequel to the chapter on serviced accommodation, and there's no doubt that there are a lot of similarities between the two. For example, the financial model is similar in that you're renting out your property on a nightly, weekly, or perhaps monthly basis. So, in that sense, both serviced accommodation and vacation rentals are shorter-term, higher-earning rental strategies compared to longer-term rentals, like a standard 12-month lease. Plus, service requirements and delivering a thoughtful, comfortable, and memorable experience for your guests are the same. You'll also find that a lot of the marketing and ongoing management tasks are very similar.

TIP

So, if you haven't yet read Chapter 15, I encourage you to circle back and read about putting the "service" into serviced accommodation. In fact, at various points in this chapter, I'll direct you back to Chapter 15 to avoid repetition.

But what about the differences? For one thing, serviced accommodation is very often centered around cities and towns. Think of the location of the average aparthotel or Airbnb apartment, and you're probably picturing a bustling city center that attracts lots of visitors, whether they be tourists or business travelers.

Meanwhile, the average vacation rental is focused squarely on tourists who are on, well, *vacation*. This means that location is an even bigger concern for vacation rentals than it is for serviced accommodation. You can find plenty more information on location later in this chapter.

REMEMBER

Another difference is that seasonality is a much bigger deal for vacation rentals than it is for serviced accommodation. An Airbnb apartment in Barcelona may attract year-round visitors, but a villa on a Greek island? No so much. Again, I go into more detail on seasonality challenges later in the chapter.

The property itself may also be fundamentally different, or be set up in a slightly different way, depending on the type of vacationer you're aiming at. With serviced accommodation, you may provide a desk so that business travelers can work, but with vacation rentals, you need the property to be much more geared to leisure. Think hot tub instead.

THE TAX ADVANTAGES OF VACATION RENTALS

Depending on where you are in the world, there can be several tax advantages to investing in vacation rentals compared to standard, longer-term residential rentals. Here I give some examples of tax breaks in the United States and United Kingdom, but be aware that the specifics vary from country to country and depend on how many days of the year your property is rented. As with any of the real estate strategies in this book, always talk to an expert tax advisor to discuss your individual tax position because the tax rules and regulations are always moving.

In the United States, investors who operate short-term rentals such as holiday rentals are able to deduct "ordinary and necessary" business expenses — although to qualify for maximum tax deductions, your property must be classed as a full-time rental business. That means you only use the property for personal vacations for fewer than 14 days a year (or 10 percent or less of total rentable days).

Potential deductible expenses for a U.S. taxpayer with a full-time rental business include major improvements to the property, the cost of appliances and furniture, mortgage interest costs, property taxes, and fees for online booking platforms like Airbnb.

Likewise, in the United Kingdom, holiday rentals can be treated like a business for tax purposes, which makes them a more attractive tax prospect than regular buy-to-rent investments. Deductible expenses in the United Kingdom include mortgage interest costs, council tax, utility bills, repair costs, and capital expenses like furniture. However, for your vacation rental to qualify as a business for U.K. tax purposes, you have to meet some pretty strict criteria.

For example, at the time of writing, the property has to be available for rent as a holiday rental for at least 210 days a year, and actually rented for at least 105 of those days. With this in mind, it's even more important than ever to buy in the right location to ensure you can rent the property for as many days a year as possible.

As a general rule, wherever you are in the world, it's important to manage your tax position proactively. An expert tax advisor or accountant will be able to advise you on all the things you can and can't deduct from your income. And at the end of the day, the more costs you can reasonably deduct from your income, the less tax you pay.

Choosing the Right Location for You

I know it sounds obvious, but your vacation rental must be in an actual vacation destination. A beautiful cottage by the sea isn't necessarily a fantastic vacation rental if there's no local infrastructure geared up for vacationers. Most people don't want to drive five hours from the nearest airport, bump down dirt roads for miles, or stay far away from any sort of attractions, shops, or restaurants.

REMEMBER

The most successful, high-earning holiday rentals are located in popular, established holiday hot spots. Whether it's a skiing holiday, a walking holiday, or a good old-fashioned beach holiday, your best chance of maximizing bookings and income is to focus on a region that's ideal for your target audience's vacation needs. This section shows you how.

Deciding which country is best

First thing's first, do you want to invest in vacation rentals in your home country or abroad? The answer to that will depend on your goals, your passion, and what's realistically accessible to you as an investor. Return to Chapter 2 and you'll find lots of practical advice for weighing investing at home versus investing abroad.

In an ideal world, a holiday rental should be an interesting and enjoyable business to run. But, like any business, that's only really the case when you're following your passion. So, when you're weighing whether you want to invest at home or abroad, ask yourself what locations you love and what sort of vacations you're most passionate about yourself.

Are you, for example, nuts about diving in the Red Sea? Surfing in Cornwall? Hiking in Vermont? Golfing in Portugal? Enjoying the gastronomic wonders of Italy? When you have an idea of general location, whether it's at home or abroad, you can start to drill down to specific vacation areas and do more detailed research (more on that coming up next).

REMEMBER

If you're investing in a market that's unfamiliar, don't rush in. No matter how passionate you are about that country, take your time to get to know the region and build a network of knowledgeable local experts who can help you make the very best investment decisions for your goals. You can find more on creating a local dream team and finding international help in Chapter 3.

Finally, if you want to invest internationally, but you don't have a preference or passion for a particular country, head to the end of this chapter. There you'll find some inspirational suggestions for top vacation spots around the world.

Drilling down to the right location

Having narrowed down your choice of country (which may or may not be your home country), you can then start to focus on specific regions that work for the type of vacation experience you're offering.

REMEMBER

In practice, this isn't just about finding the right geographic location; it's also about assessing whether you can get the right kind of property in that location, and whether the local area is right for your target audience.

To give an example from the United Kingdom, let's say you're positioning your vacation rental as a romantic retreat for couples. In this case, the bustling Brighton seafront, in East Sussex, isn't the best place for it. (Not to impugn Brighton, which is a fantastically vibrant seaside destination, but it's heaving with visitors on weekends and attracts rowdy groups of bachelor parties. Think Atlantic City, without the casinos.) On the other hand Rye, also in East Sussex, is a picturesque little town complete with cobblestone streets, antique shops, and charming pubs — perfect for a quiet, romantic getaway.

TIP

You need to have your location, your property, and the local vibe all working hand in hand to deliver the experience you're aiming for. Here are some additional considerations for drilling down to a specific location:

>> **Your vacation rental should be easy to reach, whether it's by road, bus, rail, plane, or boat.** Good local road infrastructure is a must, and having some options for public transport (including a local taxi service for those lazy, wine-fueled vacation dinners) is also desirable.

>> **With the exception of struggling writers who need an isolated retreat to finish their epic debut novels, most people on vacation want to be close to local amenities.** They don't want to trek miles to buy a loaf of bread or have a beer, so your property should be close to some shops, bars, and restaurants.

>> **Your location should offer plenty of attractions that suit your target audience, and they should be within easy reach.** That may be golf courses, country walks, the beach, or theme parks, depending on who you're targeting.

Doing your due diligence on the vacation market in your target area

Having hit upon what you think is the ideal spot for your vacation rental, you then need to do your homework to confirm that your assumptions are correct.

TIP

This research may include

>> **Looking up annual visitor numbers for the area in general, and assessing how visitor numbers rise and fall across the seasons (more on seasonality coming up next in the chapter):** The local tourist information board is a good starting point for this sort of research.

>> **Looking up visitor numbers for specific local attractions, like theme parks, national parks, and the like, to get a feel for what's particularly popular in that area:** At the very least, this will help you when you come to market your property, because proximity to the most popular attractions will be a big selling point.

>> **Spending time in the area to get a feel for what it's like to vacation there:** This may include staying in or viewing other local holiday rentals to understand the typical service offering and clientele.

>> **Talking to local managing agents who manage other vacation rentals for investors:** They'll be able to fill you in on typical rental yields for the area, void periods, seasonal peaks and troughs, and so on. You may choose to hire one of these managing agents to look after your property for you, or you may prefer to manage it yourself, but there's no harm in having the initial discussion. You can find out more about managing your property later in this chapter.

Planning for Costs, Cash Flow, and Variations in Occupancy

The financial model of vacation rentals is undoubtedly similar to serviced accommodation in that you earn more by renting out the property on a short-term basis (see Chapter 15 for a financial comparison of short- and long-term rentals), but vacation rentals can experience greater fluctuations in income across the year, depending on the type of vacation rental and its location.

REMEMBER

This fluctuation across the year means it's more important than ever to manage your costs and cash flow carefully, and to plan for the impact that different seasons may have on your finances.

Let's start with a look at cash flow and costs, before moving on to some practical ways to overcome seasonality challenges and boost your rental income in "off" seasons.

Thinking of cash flow and costs from an annual perspective

Every property experiences *void periods*, where the property stands empty for a while. Even on a long-term rental, you may have a gap between one tenant moving out and the next one moving in, meaning you as the landlord are covering the mortgage and costs out of your own pocket for that period. However, when the new tenants are in, providing they're happy in the property, you have very little risk of void periods until the end of their tenancy. That's not the case with vacation rentals.

Higher turnover of guests, higher chance of void periods

With a vacation rental, you may have void periods across the entire year, either due to a slowdown in bookings (perhaps because of the economy no one wants to go to Spain this year and people prefer to "staycation" at home), regular short-term gaps between bookings, or just plain old seasonal dips in visitors to the area.

Unless your vacation property is truly rentable all year (more on seasonality and void periods coming up next), you'll be making the bulk of your money in the busier tourist months, and earning either a lot less or next to nothing in the slow off-season months. In other words, you'll be making hay while the sun shines . . . or the snow falls, if you're running a ski chalet.

REMEMBER

So, unlike a regular property, where you may manage your finances on a month-by-month basis, with a vacation rental, you really need to look at your numbers from an annual perspective, carefully analyze your income peaks and troughs across the year, and plan for how you'll service your costs across the entire year.

For example, if your property makes its money in the late spring, summer, and autumn months, and you earn very little income between November and April, and you're paying a mortgage on that property, you need to be earning enough in the summer months to cover your mortgage and other costs throughout the lean winter months.

Lucky, then, that holiday rentals generally deliver much higher rental income than standard residential properties. Therefore, with careful planning, you can comfortably accommodate natural void periods, cover your costs, and run a successful business.

Managing your finances carefully

Here are my top tips for managing your cash flow and costs like a pro:

>> **Work out how many weeks of the year your property is likely to be rented, according to local visitor patterns, local occupancy rates, and the general seasonality of the area.** Don't forget to factor in any weeks of the year where you and your family may want to use the property, which means you won't be earning an income. (In general, it's obviously better to use the property when paying guests don't want to, such as the winter months in a hotter location or warmer months in a ski location!)

>> **Research the rental prices of similar properties in the area to work out the gross income you can expect to earn.** Don't forget to account for price rises and dips according to demand (local properties may charge their highest rental prices in the school holiday weeks, or Thanksgiving weekend, or Christmas, for example). You can find more on dynamic pricing coming up in the section "Marketing Your Vacation Rental," later in this chapter.

>> **Make a list of all the annual costs of running the property, including any mortgage payments, mortgage interest, utility bills, general maintenance (allow for 1 percent to 2 percent of the property's value), insurance, booking commissions, cleaning, professional fees, and so on.** You may also have some one-off fees when you're just getting started, like professional photography for your online listings.

>> **Now that you know your full costs, work out how many weeks of the year you need to rent out the property to cover these costs.** This number should be less than the actual number of weeks that you realistically expect to rent the property; otherwise, you'll be making no money. For example, you may need 20 weeks of occupancy to cover your costs, but your expected rental schedule is in fact 30 weeks.

TIP

If you need to boost the number of weeks in a year that you can rent the property, I give some practical ideas for making your property attractive in off seasons in the section "Overcoming seasonality challenges," later in this chapter.

>> **Work out a detailed cash flow projection, setting out your expected income and expenses across the year, so that you can carefully plan your incoming and outgoing money and track actual figures against your projections.** I strongly recommend working with a great bookkeeper and accountant to keep your finances in order.

Understanding seasonality and void periods

It should be clear by now that seasonality is a big consideration with vacation rentals. Most of the other real estate strategies should experience steady occupancy throughout the year (if you're doing your job as a landlord right, anyway), but with this strategy, you may be at the mercy of the seasons and visitor flow.

REMEMBER

Seasonal demand for your property will depend on where your property is, what kind of property you have, and what kind of vacation experience you're offering. For example, a family villa in a hot climate, by the beach, will most likely experience its highest demand in the school summer holidays, and will see little or no demand when September hits. But a cute country cottage, with long walks and cozy pubs nearby may attract romantic outdoorsy types long into the winter months, particularly for key winter holidays like Christmas, New Year's, and Valentine's Day.

That's not to say that one type of property or vacation rental strategy is better than another. That big family villa may absolutely rake in the cash during the summer months and comfortably sit idle for the winter, while the cute cottage may experience lower, but more steady rental prices across the year.

What's important is to find the right vacation model that suits your goals and your passion, and then carefully plan for the seasonality of that model. And don't forget: There are plenty of things you can do to increase the appeal of your property across the seasons.

Overcoming seasonality challenges

The absolute best way to attract year-round visitors is to buy in a location that doesn't really have drastic seasonal variations in weather. Florida and the Canary Islands, for example, are popular year-round destinations, and they may make better locations for a family villa business than, say, Turkey or Greece.

That may not work for you, however, depending on your goals and passion. And that's fine. Most vacation rentals have to deal with some sort of seasonal differences and challenges, so you won't be alone.

TIP

Here are my favorite ways to overcome such challenges and attract visitors to your property across the different seasons:

>> **Explore alternative vacation propositions for off-peak times.** For example, a ski chalet in Switzerland will naturally be at its busiest between early December and the end of April. However, the property can have a second life in the summer months by being marketed at hikers and climbers. (Switzerland is a paradise for walkers, as well as skiers.) Consider whether your property can meet different uses in the summer and winter months.

>> **Prepare your property to be as enticing as possible in all seasons, such as having a working fireplace in the lounge and luxurious blankets on the deck chairs for that cozy winter feel.** You can find more on preparing your property for use across the seasons later in this chapter.

>> **Consider clever ways to market your property in the off-season, including special packages or discounts.** You can, for example, create a magical Christmas package that includes a luxury food basket, champagne, a beautifully decorated property, and a personal visit from Santa for the kids.

>> **Partner with local tour operators and clubs to offer attractive experiences and excursions that will entice guests at off-peak times.** For instance, you could offer mountain bike tours in partnership with the local bike club, foraging and cooking lessons with local culinary experts, or a day of horseback riding in the forest courtesy of the local stable.

>> **Look at the local event calendar and actively market your property to that event's target audience.** For example, maybe your area has a big cross-country running event, a music festival, or an annual motorcycle meet. The audiences for all those events are likely to be different, but you can target them all at those particular times of the year.

Sourcing the Ideal Property for Vacation Rentals

The process of sourcing property for vacation rentals is much like sourcing property for any other use, in that you'll be searching online and via local agents. However, there are some specific things to consider when you're looking at vacation properties.

I've already stressed the importance of finding the right location for your vacation rental, so in this section I'll assume you've already drilled down to a specific target area. Now, you just need to find the right property.

The first consideration is, naturally, what type of property will suit your target audience? A tiny, two-room lakeside log cabin, for instance, despite all its rustic charm, simply won't work for most families; if families are who you're aiming at, you'll want something bigger. Meanwhile, a larger property — say, a five-bedroom villa — will work well for large families and groups of friends, but the high rental price will mean the property is out of budget for smaller families and couples. Before you start sourcing the right property, think about who you're aiming your product at (based on who vacations in that area and your particular passion).

TIP

Take your cues from the competition, here, so view (online and in real life) as many similar vacation properties in your target area as possible. This will give you a strong idea of the type of property that appeals to your audience.

REMEMBER

Look for the following when you're sourcing property for vacation rentals:

» **A high-quality finish:** Vacation rentals are typically high-end (think: luxury). Look for a property that's already presented this way or one that has the potential to be developed with this goal in mind (more on developing properties in Chapter 9).

» **Enough space:** You want a property with spacious rooms that are in proportion with each other. For example, if you have a huge, double-height living room but a small, narrow kitchen, that will limit your property's appeal.

» **A spacious, attractive hallway/entrance:** First impressions count. Plus, it's practical for families and larger groups where you have multiple people dumping their coats, beach bags, shoes, and so on the second they walk through the door at the end of each day.

» **A fireplace or hot tub:** People are romantics at heart, so it's no surprise that fireplaces and hot tubs (which are popular in both summer and winter) count among the most popular features for guests.

Unless you're buying an existing vacation rental, you may not find a property with these desirable features already installed, but you should at least ensure your property has the space and potential to add these features yourself.

» **Private outdoor space:** In our everyday lives, most of us spend too much time indoors, so when we're on vacation, we want to be outdoors as much as possible. That means private outdoor space is a major bonus, whether it's a deck, balcony, terrace, pool area, or low-maintenance yet attractive garden. Even in colder months, having the space to enjoy a nice glass of wine and beautiful views is what makes those vacation moments so special.

» **Designated, off-street parking:** This is another key external feature that guests rank highly.

» **Peaceful surroundings and quiet, considerate neighbors:** Few people want to stay next to a rowdy bar or smell the pigs from the neighboring pig farm!

WARNING

If you're purchasing the property with a mortgage, keep in mind that, depending on where you are in the world, if your vacation property is classified as a business, you'll probably need a special, perhaps commercial, mortgage. Work with an expert, independent mortgage broker to identify the right mortgage option for you, or you may want to consider some more creative financing options, like the ones I set out in Chapter 8.

Preparing Your Property for Use

When you've found the right property, you'll probably have to do some preparation work to make it suitable for your target audience, to entice people to your property, and to ensure your guests have an awesome vacation. This is a really exciting stage, but there's a lot to think about. This section runs through the key things you should consider.

Providing the "wow factor" through service

I talk a lot about service in Chapter 15, so if you skipped over that in your eagerness to get to vacation rentals, maybe pause here and give that chapter a read before you start to consider the level of service you want to offer.

REMEMBER

In general, though, this part is about preparing your property so that it delivers those thoughtful little touches that delight guests, inspire five-star reviews, and encourage recommendations and repeat bookings. This may include offering:

>> Luxury toiletries, a bottle of wine, a homemade load of bread or cake, or a basket filled with local delicacies

>> All the information your guests need to get the most out of their stay in the area, such as maps, flyers for popular attractions, information on local walks and wildlife, and your personal recommendations on where to go for the best food and drinks

>> Entertainment-themed touches, like board games and a deck of cards, just in case the weather doesn't play ball

TIP

Your service offering provides an excellent way to add personality to your property and distinguish yourself from your competition. Another way to do this is to be more open about who — or rather, what — is welcome in your property. Dog-friendly properties are increasingly popular among travelers, so consider whether you're willing to welcome pets and, if so, include pet-friendly touches like toys, dog bowls, maybe an outside wash-down area, and a doggy towel for when Fido comes back wet from the beach.

Including all the practical things your guests need

Your property should include all the everyday practical items that make a vacation home comfortable, livable, and practical. This will be similar to the considerations set out in Chapter 15, and includes

>> **Those 21st-century must-haves — reliable, fast Internet and a good-size TV:** These days, even grownups can't go without social media on vacation for too long.

>> **All the furniture, such as beds, sofa, dining table, and chairs:** Don't be tempted to buy cheap and cheerful furniture — it'll only cost you more in the long run. Instead, invest in quality furniture that'll really last and continue to look good for years. Oh, and if the beds aren't comfortable, you can be sure your guests will mention it in their reviews.

>> **Ample storage space for clothes and luggage:** Your guests will probably be staying for more than a couple of nights, so keep that in mind. Wherever possible, have built-in cupboards, closets, and shelving installed — it'll save you money in the long run.

>> **Bed linens and towels for the bathrooms and kitchen:** Again, invest in good quality, 100 percent cotton here, because it'll need to take regular washing at high temperatures. Personally, I've always found it really lets a vacation property down when the bed linens and towels feel cheap and nasty. Guests expect better than they can get at home when they're paying for it, so a good night's sleep is high on their expectation list!

>> **A fully equipped kitchen complete with all the appliances, plates, cups, and so on that your guests will need:** Whereas in a serviced apartment, the kitchen may be a basic kitchenette, a vacation rental really needs a proper, full-size kitchen, complete with dishwasher, washing machine, and dryer. Your guests will likely be staying for a week or two, so the ability to cook a decent meal (especially if they're staying over an important holiday like Thanksgiving) and do some laundry is vital.

>> **Simple food items:** You should provide tea, coffee, sugar, milk or creamer, spices, and cooking oil so that your guests don't have to hit the grocery store the second they arrive.

These costs should be taxable, depending on the tax position in your country. Head back to the sidebar "The tax advantages of vacation rentals" for more on this.

Making sure your property is bursting with personality

Online booking platforms like Booking.com make it easier to advertise your property, but they also mean your property will be competing with many, many other properties for potential bookings. Your property really needs to stand out in photos if you're going to maximize your bookings!

REMEMBER

This means the decor and overall look of your property should go way beyond providing a functional, practical space. Instead, you should decorate and present the property in a way that's full of style and personality. Whether you're invoking the old-world charm of a hunting lodge or that latte-loving L.A.-living vibe, present your property in a unique, quirky way that really speaks to your target audience.

Making the property as season-proof as possible

With seasonality being a key issue for vacation rentals, you need to think carefully about how you can prepare the property in a way that makes it attractive and comfortable all year, rather than for a few precious months.

Here are two sure-fire ways to do this:

>> **Providing adequate cooling and heating, as per the local climate:** If your guests are too hot in the summer (especially at night, and especially if they have children), they'll pull no punches in their online reviews. Similarly, if the property is cold and drafty in the winter, they'll be quick to warn other guests of this.

>> **Adding cozy, desirable extra touches like a fireplace, thick blankets and rugs, and slippers:** If you're aiming to attract guests in the winter months, picture your property as the snug winter retreat of a Danish movie star and you can't go wrong.

TIP

You may want to consider investing in eco-friendly window glazing and insulation. Not only will this create a more comfortable environment for guests, whatever the season, but it'll also lower your heating and cooling bills.

Paying attention to the exterior

I've already mentioned the universal appeal of hot tubs, so there's no doubt that outdoor space means more bookings. Even when a stunning beach or national park is right on your property's doorstep, never overlook your guests' desire to chill out "at home" for a day or in the evenings. Your job is to make sure they can.

REMEMBER

As with the interior of your property, you should look for ways to add personality-filled, thoughtful touches to your outside space, such as the following:

>> **If you have a pool, include some loungers and pool toys.** Who can resist a giant inflatable flamingo on vacation? Certainly not my wife and kids! (I'm far too serious for such things myself. Ahem.)

- **Other furniture that encourages people to chill out and smell the roses:** This may include everything from rocking chairs to hammocks.

- **An outdoor dining table and chairs:** Even if you're only able to provide a small breakfast table on a balcony, your guests will appreciate it.

- **A fire pit (and ready-chopped wood):** Not only does this give your guests an Instagram-worthy place to gather and toast marshmallows in the evening, but when they share their pics on social media, you're getting free advertising!

- **Fun games to appeal to young kids and the young at heart:** This may include a mini outdoor bowling lane, a giant chess board, a swing set, or even a tree house.

- **Outdoor dining and cooking options:** Offer a barbecue or, for maximum wow factor, an outdoor pizza oven.

Making sure the property is safe and complies with local laws

I know it's not as exciting as making your property cozy and comfortable, but your property also needs to be safe and free of hazards.

REMEMBER

The health and safety guidelines for landlords in Chapter 13 provide a good rule of thumb for any kind of rental property, but you should seek expert advice on the specific requirements for your type of property and proposed use in your country. In general, though, you'll probably be expected to ensure that

- Gas and electrical safety checks are carried out regularly.

- Appliances are properly maintained and faulty ones are replaced promptly.

- Fire safety equipment such as smoke detectors, fire blankets, and fire extinguishers are installed.

- Carbon monoxide alarms are fitted in every room that features a wood-burning stove or gas fireplace

Your vacation property may also be subject to planning or zoning restrictions, and these restrictions may even limit how many days or weeks a year the property can be rented out as a vacation rental. Circle back to Chapter 15 for more on planning and zoning considerations, and always seek expert local advice for your property and region. There can be some specific restrictions for vacation rentals that are always changing, so read up before you cough up!

You may need special insurance for your vacation rental, such as public liability insurance. Talk to an insurance broker with experience in vacation rentals to discuss the right level of coverage for your business.

Marketing Your Vacation Rental

At its simplest, good marketing for a vacation rental is about getting on the right online booking sites, encouraging direct bookings whenever possible, and ensuring you have professional-quality images and descriptive copy for your property. In this section, I look at these key areas one by one.

Advertising your property on the right online platforms

You can advertise your property through local agencies that specialize in the type of vacation market you're aiming at — and this may be a useful part of your marketing strategy. However, these days, online listing sites are far and away the top choice for holiday rental investors to advertise their properties. That's because these sites provide a simple way to get your property in front of an audience of millions.

The top listing platforms for vacation properties include

>> Airbnb (www.airbnb.com)

>> Booking.com (www.booking.com)

>> FlipKey (www.flipkey.com)

>> HomeAway (www.homeaway.com)

>> VRBO (www.vrbo.com)

Getting started on these booking sites couldn't be easier. You simply set up an account, add photos and a description of your property (more on that coming up later), set your pricing structure, and confirm any specific terms and conditions, such your chosen refund and cancellation policy.

With most online booking platforms, you don't have to pay an upfront fee to advertise your property; instead, the site takes a commission on each booking (typically, between 3 percent and 15 percent of the total booking price). This is a good incentive to actively seek your own bookings direct from guests (see the next section).

Having your own website

In addition to advertising on the main booking platforms (see the preceding section), it's always a good idea to create your own professionally designed website to help you attract direct bookings and save on commission.

Just like the booking platforms already mentioned, your own website should include lots of fantastic images of your property, plus a thorough description, a mechanism for guests to make a reservation, and contact details in case potential guests have any questions before they book. Reviews and testimonials are nice to have as well.

REMEMBER

Having a website isn't quite enough, though. You need to be actively driving people to visit that website and book directly with you. For ideas on encouraging direct bookings through your own website, head back to Chapter 15.

Investing in professional pictures and awesome descriptions

Whether you're advertising your property on online booking platforms or your own website, pictures are worth a thousand words . . . and so are words, for that matter. If you're showing poor-quality images and lazy, error-riddled descriptive copy, what does that say about your commitment to service and quality?

Capturing images that are worthy of a lifestyle magazine

Photos are typically the first thing potential guests see when they look at your listing, so you should invest in a professional photographer and high-quality images of your property. Great images can make a dramatic difference in the number of bookings you get.

REMEMBER

You'll want to include photos of every room and the outdoor space, but it's also critical to ensure your property's personality shines through. So, don't forget to capture images of quirky decor, the garden hammock, the wood-burning stove, your thoughtful welcome gift, or the stunning sunsets on offer from the back terrace. Your *header image* (the first one guests see before clicking through to your property) should really capture what makes your property unique.

TIP

If you're offering different experiences for different seasons (summer boating on the lake versus a romantic winter getaway) make sure your images reflect the diversity that your property offers. You can't fake snow on the surrounding hills if your pictures are being taken in May, but you can "fake" a snug winter scene indoors, complete with candles, a roaring fire, faux fur throws, and a Christmas tree!

Acing the description of your property

The opening statement of your property description should sum up, in one snappy sentence, what it is about your property that makes for a super-special vacation. This should include something unique about the property ("Enjoy the best sunsets around from your private hot tub at this romantic lakeside cottage . . .") and nearby desirable attractions (". . . situated just a few minutes from the entrance to Pine Forest Reserve").

Having nailed the opening statement, you need to entice guests with a thorough description of the property. Be sure your property description answers all the following questions:

>> How many rooms are there and how many people does the property sleep comfortably?

>> What practical features are included? Wi-Fi? Parking? Weekly housekeeping?

>> How close is the property to major local attractions, as well as shops, bars, and restaurants?

>> What's public transport like in the area and how easy is it to get to the property by car, train, and so on?

>> What are the interesting little details that will make your guests' stay memorable? Don't forget to mention that secret treehouse for the kids, the cozy fireplace, the quirky architecture, the amazing views, or the charming pizza oven.

>> Is the property appealing for year-round use? If so, what experience can guests expect in the winter months?

>> How do you offer a unique and memorable vacation experience, such as arranging tours and excursions (like mountain biking or horseback riding) through local partners?

TIP

Review your description with the cold, dispassionate eye of an editor (shout out to my *For Dummies* editor!), and be on the lookout for errors and idiosyncrasies that will clearly mark your copy as amateurish. Ideally, get a professional to help you with this, but if you're checking it yourself:

>> Do a thorough proofread and double-check (in fact, triple-check) for any typos or grammatical errors.

>> Tighten up long, rambling sentences and paragraphs. Use lists, which are much easier on the eye, when describing the property's features.

>> Don't overuse exclamation point! If you really can't resist an exclamation point (I know, it's difficult), restrict yourself to one, well-used exclamation point in

the whole description. Absolutely no more than that or you'll look like a crazy person!!! See what I mean?!?! No, seriously!!!!!

>> Don't use capital letters unless it's at the start of a sentence or proper noun. This is a professional property description, not some crazy celebrity's Twitter rant.

Cultivating great reviews

Reviews are a critical part of the decision-making process for potential guests (along with price, photos, and service offering), so it's vital you encourage guests to review your property after their stay.

The online booking platforms will take care of this for you (indeed, reviews are mandatory on Airbnb), but wherever guests have booked directly through your website, you should be diligent about following up, asking for a review, thanking guests for their feedback, and publishing the best reviews on your website.

REMEMBER

Guest reviews are a goldmine of information on how to improve your property and service offering. Try not to take negative feedback personally; instead, see it as an opportunity to improve the experience for the next guest. Always respond to any negative reviews online and address any problems to ensure the customer ends up delighted. Often, a bad review online can be a great opportunity to show other potential guests how well you deal with problems and turn them around into a positive for all concerned.

Managing Your Vacation Rental

The process of successfully managing your vacation rental is very similar to managing serviced accommodation — for example, investing in a centralized booking system that aggregates bookings from multiple booking sites — so I urge you to revisit that chapter before you read on.

Here, I focus on how the ongoing management of vacation rentals may differ from serviced accommodation.

Working with a managing agent

With a vacation rental, there's a very strong chance that your property will be located somewhere other than where you live — it can be a few hours away, located on the other side of the country, or even in a completely different country on a different continent.

REMEMBER

This makes everyday management of the property and your guests, not to mention periodic maintenance, far trickier than running an Airbnb apartment in your hometown. For this reason, you'll likely want to work with a managing agent or compile your own dream team of people who can manage the property for you in your absence (see Chapter 3). You need people who can take care of guest changeovers, clean the property, and handle regular maintenance needs.

If you want to consider working with a managing agent, shop around before you sign on the dotted line. Price (how much commission they charge) will no doubt be a factor in your considerations, but so should quality of service. Instead of just going with the cheapest provider, work with the most reputable one you can find. After all, it's your reputation on the line, as well. Shoddy cleaning, the property not being ready on time, or a broken oven will result in poor reviews from customers.

TIP

Wherever possible, seek personal recommendations from other investors in the area. And when you're comparing potential managing agents, be on the lookout for hidden costs, such as charging for each guest changeover — those costs can eat into your margins. Make sure you're comparing apples with apples, when you compare agents.

Pricing dynamically throughout the year

Compared to a serviced accommodation model, pricing for vacation rentals may be much more fluid. You may experience much wider swings in demand across the year than, say, a serviced apartment in London, which means it's more important than ever to price your property dynamically, according to the season, local events, and demand.

You can find more on dynamic pricing in Chapter 15, but rest assured that all the major booking platforms have snazzy tools that take the headache out of pricing.

TIP

On top of dynamic pricing, conduct at least an annual review of your pricing model, comparing your prices to those of your local competition and taking account of any changes in the area. For instance, a new high-speed rail line that suddenly connects your sleepy seaside village with a major city will add significant value.

Identifying Five International Locations Where This Strategy Would Work

If you don't have a particular location in mind for your holiday rental business, allow me to inspire you with a few tantalizing international locations. The following holiday hot spots offer year-round beauty and interest, and experience strong levels of demand:

>> Kissimmee, Florida

>> Marbella, Spain

>> The Lake District, United Kingdom

>> Nice, France

>> Lake Garda, Italy

REMEMBER

Whenever you live in a different country from your holiday rental property, you'll need practical, on-the-ground help if you want to avoid jumping on a plane every five minutes to check in guests or deal with maintenance issues. Always work with local experts and agents who come highly recommended from people you trust. Don't forget: Your local dream team (see Chapter 3) can guide you on bigger-picture issues, like the nuances of the local market or the peculiarities of rules and regulations in that country.

5

The Part of Tens

Get into the mind-set for success and incorporate success-building habits into your everyday routine.

Discover additional real estate strategies that you may want to build into your portfolio.

Chapter **17**

Ten (Or So) Practical Ways to Get into the Mind-Set for Success

Are you looking to get into the right frame of mind for entrepreneurial success? In this chapter, I set out some simple techniques, quick exercises, and easy-to-access resources that will help you supercharge the mind-set approaches covered in Chapter 5.

REMEMBER

When it comes to adopting good habits, repetition is key. So, when you find a technique that works especially well for you, try to build it into your everyday routine. The tips set out in this chapter are designed to help you do just that.

Tapping Into Education Resources

Your goal is to become an information sponge, so join online forums and social media groups that are related to your chosen strategy. Sign up for relevant newsletters (and, you know, actually *read* them) and gobble up books written by successful entrepreneurs (not just property investors).

TIP

An online course is a great way to develop practical knowledge in a specific field — and all from the comfort of your own home. You can find lots of affordable real estate–related courses at `www.udemy.com`, including the following:

>> "The Property Cycle: How to Identify the Best Time to Invest" (`www.udemy.com/share/100knm`)

>> "How to Build a Real Estate Cash Buyers List" (`www.udemy.com/share/100438`), a useful course for anyone keen to explore selling property leads or property development

>> A range of courses about analyzing property investments

>> A whole host of courses on other real estate topics, such as property management, Airbnb hosting, and shooting real estate videos

Using Productivity Apps and Tools

When it comes to making the most of your time (especially when you're juggling property investing alongside a day job), technology is your friend. Use it wisely and you'll never miss another important task again.

TIP

Here are some of the productivity-enhancing tools that I use on a weekly or even daily basis:

>> **Dropbox** (`www.dropbox.com`)**:** I use Dropbox for storing files, which means I can access all of my documents and work anywhere, anytime. iCloud (`www.icloud.com`), OneDrive (`www.onedrive.com`), and Google Drive (`www.google.com/drive`) are other options to consider.

>> **Fiverr** (`www.fiverr.com`) **and Upwork** (`www.upwork.com`)**:** These outsourcing apps let me assign tasks to freelancers on the fly.

>> **Evernote** (`www.evernote.com`)**:** I use Evernote for taking notes during meetings, updating my goal list (see "Cementing Your Goals Using a Vision Board or Goal List" later in the chapter), and keeping my to-do list up to date. This way, all my notes and lists stay synced across my various devices, no matter where I am.

>> **Google Calendar** (`www.google.com/calendar`)**:** I use Google Calendar for managing my time, booking meetings, and setting reminders. My virtual personal assistant — a freelance assistant who works in a different location from me — is also able to access and update my calendars as and when necessary.

>> **Infusionsoft** (www.infusionsoft.com): Infusionsoft is customer relationship management (CRM) app. It allows me to keep up with marketing and sales communications and list management tasks while I'm on the move, ensuring I never forget to send my follow-up emails!

>> **Gmail** (www.gmail.com): Gmail is an online alternative to Microsoft Outlook or Apple Mail. It took a little while to change the way I monitored and managed my emails, but now that I've mastered the layout, it acts as a mini CRM, allowing me to "snooze" important emails for a later date (maybe a client follow-up) or set reminders and to-do lists. There are also various add-ons for bulk mailing, and other highly useful tools. You can bulk low-priority emails into a folder to show up only once a week and then set them as "Archived" all in one hit! It's a great inbox management tool, which has made me super-efficient at emails. Give it a try!

Learning to Be in the Here and Now

We're surrounded by distractions every minute of the day — from the busy morning routine of walking the dog or getting the kids off to school, to the information overload of constant emails and social media. I don't know about you, but I also have a busy internal voice that's continuously telling me what I have to do next, who I have to call, what time I have to be somewhere, and so on.

All these distractions leave little time to focus on what's happening right now, in this moment. And that can be very bad for our mental health. Enter mindfulness.

The mindfulness movement, being closely related to meditation (see Chapter 5), is all about bringing awareness to the present moment. It has become huge in recent years, and with good reason. Proven benefits of mindful practice include reduced stress, improved memory, and better focus, and it's even used to treat depression.

REMEMBER

Ideally, we would all practice mindfulness every minute of every day, but life has a habit of getting in the way. However, if you can take a few minutes out of each day to quietly focus on the here and now, you can reduce your stress levels, sharpen your focus, and boost your mood.

This may mean enjoying a few minutes of silence in the morning or a period of quiet reflection at the end of the day. For some people, saying a prayer is a good way to be more in the moment. Or you could try doing a bit of mindful breathing.

The following mindful breathing exercise can be done anywhere, anytime:

1. **Sit in a quiet place, either on the floor or on a chair, or lie down if it's more comfortable.**

2. **Begin to breathe deeply, pushing out your belly as you breathe in through your nose. As you breathe out through your mouth, let your belly fall back.**

3. **Pay attention to the sensation as the breath moves in and out of your body, and focus on that feeling as you continue to breathe in and out for a few minutes.**

   It's very hard to clear your mind of all thoughts completely, so don't worry if niggling thoughts keep bubbling to the surface. Just try to acknowledge each thought, without frustration, and then let it go, bringing your attention back to your breathing.

If you prefer a little more guidance, try Headspace (www.headspace.com)! Headspace is a brilliant meditation app that's suitable for total beginners. It gives you introductory courses and simple ten-minute guided meditations to follow. You can select meditations from a range of categories, such as boosting your confidence or enhancing your career, so you're bound to find a meditation that suits your needs.

Learning to be more present in the moment doesn't mean you never think about the future. Of course it's still important to have goals and know which direction you're headed (see "Cementing Your Goals Using a Vision Board or Goal List" later in the chapter). It's just that being more mindful will help you filter out distractions and become more focused and calm, improving your productivity and business performance.

I've found that a brief morning meditation is a wonderful way to spend more time being in the here and now. But why not try meditating before an important meeting, as a way to clarify your thoughts and get the most out of the meeting? This is a really useful exercise to help you get the most out of meetings with clients or colleagues, helping you focus better on the meeting itself and respond more positively to those around the table:

1. **Before the meeting, take a few minutes to sit quietly and check in with how you're feeling.**

   Are you still angry about something that happened earlier in the day? Are you anxious? Are you feeling tense because you have a mountain of emails to get through after the meeting? The last thing you want to do is bring those emotions with you into the meeting, so acknowledge them now, and then let them go.

2. **During the meeting, be mindful of how well you're listening to those who are speaking.**

   Don't pre-empt what they're about to say or, worse, try to finish their sentences for them. Don't start planning your response before someone has even finished speaking. Instead, just listen deeply and attentively to what's being said, without judgment.

3. **When it's your turn to respond, check back in with how you're feeling and where that response is coming from.**

   Speak from a place of clarity and calm, not anger, impatience or confusion.

Cementing Your Goals Using a Vision Board or Goal List

You have to know what you want in order to be able to achieve it, so setting and committing to your goals is an important part of success.

REMEMBER

When you commit to something on paper, it stops being a simple dream and becomes a firm goal. In that way, creating a vision board or goal list is a fantastic way to commit to your goals and focus your mind on what you really want.

A *vision board* is typically a collage of images that help you form mental pictures of your goals to help you continually reaffirm your goals visually. Or, if you're more of a verbal person than a visual person, it can be a simple written list of goals and affirmations (see more about affirmations later in this chapter). I've used both the written and visual methods in the past. Right now, I use a hybrid approach: a written list that I keep in my Evernote app, with some inspiring images embedded in the document.

REMEMBER

Whatever format you choose, the important thing is to get your goals down on paper (or on screen) and refer to it regularly as part of your routine. Remember to update your goal list regularly, as you achieve goals and identify new ones.

Your vision board or goal list is also a helpful prompt for visualization exercises, like the one I set out in the next section. If you regularly focus on and visualize your goals in this way, they'll become deeply ingrained in your subconscious mind, allowing the law of attraction to kick into action and start to move you toward your chosen goals.

TIP

There are some great examples of vision boards on the web! Search for *vision boards* on Pinterest or Google and see the types of boards others have created.

If, like me, you're not much of a touchy–feely, hippy type, you might be put off by the idea of a *vision board*. But don't be. It's actually an incredibly practical and powerful tool for settings goals. Call it your *goal list* if you prefer.

Trying Out a Visualization Exercise, Real Estate Style

I start each day by sitting quietly and looking at my goal list before closing my eyes and visualizing one of the goals on the list.

TIP

Here's how you can visualize one of your real estate goals:

1. **Sit in a peaceful, comfortable place.**

2. **Spend a few moments looking at your vision board or goal list and identify one specific real estate goal to focus on.**

   For the purpose of this exercise, let's say your chosen goal is to earn enough in rental income to be able to give up your day job.

3. **Close your eyes and form a clear mental image of yourself accomplishing that goal.**

   Tap into the emotions you'll feel when you achieve that goal. For example, how will it feel when you hand in your notice? How will it feel to wake up on your first morning as a full-time real estate investor? How will it feel to introduce yourself to new contacts as a real estate investor, not an accountant or hospital administrator or Uber driver?

4. **Smile as you visualize and feel the joy that will come from achieving your desired outcome.**

   Smiling is an important part of *believing* your visualization will come true.

5. **Imagine the sights, smells, tastes, and touch of your vision.**

   The more vivid your visualization, the more powerful it is.

6. **Sit in silence for a few minutes holding each picture in your mind.**

Incorporating Positive Affirmations into Your Day

We all have different things we want to achieve, so an affirmation that works for one person may not work for you. The key is to find affirmations that resonate with you, whether they're very specific statements that are related to your goals or general statements that inspire success and boost your mood.

You may like to borrow and adapt affirmations from people you admire, or mine self-help books, websites, and apps for examples (see "Downloading Helpful Mind-Set Apps" later in the chapter.) Or you can develop your own statements that inspire and motivate you.

TIP

Whatever affirmations you choose, the following tips will help cement them into your daily routine:

>> **Write down your affirmations on paper or electronically, or even record your own voice saying your affirmations in an affirmations app to help clarify what you want to say.** This may mean writing or recording a complete, specific statement like, "I am ready to become a published author this year." Or it may mean creating various prompts and cues for what to say, like, "Today I intend to . . ." or "I am . . ." for you to complete as you see fit.

TIP

ThinkUp (www.thinkup.me) features hundreds of positive affirmations that you can use and adapt. You can record your own affirmations and set notifications to help you get into a routine. Hearing your own voice back saying your chosen affirmations helps make it more personal and deepens the effects of the process.

>> **Repetition is key, so get into the habit of saying or listening to your affirmations at a certain time every day, whether that's as soon as you step out of bed, while you're in the shower, while you're looking in the mirror fixing your hair, or whatever.** If you also want to tap into them throughout the day or when you need a confidence boost, that's fine, too.

>> **Keep it fresh by adapting your affirmations to suit your present circumstances and your mood.** For example, if you're feeling low, try a general mood-boosting affirmation like "I am successful" or "I am full of energy." A powerful affirmation I once saw in a book simply said, "Today I intend to have a great day."

>> **Categorize your affirmations.** You may have health-related affirmations, business-related affirmations, or motivation- or confidence-boosting ones. By neatly categorizing your affirmations, you'll be able to tune into what you need at any particular moment.

Recognizing and Giving Thanks for Your Successes

I strongly recommend making gratitude a part of your daily routine, even when life isn't going the way you want — *especially* when life isn't going the way you want.

TIP

Here are three ways to inject a little gratitude into your day:

>> **Start the morning by saying, out loud, three things that you're grateful for, such as "I'm grateful for my family," "I'm grateful for the freedom that running my own business gives me," and "I'm grateful that I get to pick the kids up from school today."** Wherever possible, it's a good idea to mix this up and give thanks for different things every day.

>> **Say "thank you" throughout the day when things go well.** You can say thanks in your own mind — you don't have to say it out loud. This will open your awareness, ensuring that you start to notice more and more positive things happening around you.

>> **Keep a notebook by your bed and, before you go to sleep, write down three things that made your day great, whether it was a happy client, a new opportunity that came up, or even something your husband or wife did.** Looking back at older lists from time to time will inspire you and boost your gratitude even more.

One important aspect of saying thank you is giving back and helping others. Many of the top business leaders are some of the world's biggest philanthropists. However, giving back isn't just about donating money. Giving your time and expertise to help others is rewarding for you personally and helps to attract greater success and abundance back to you, too. Attracting success and abundance shouldn't be your motivation to help others — it's just one of the effects of the law of attraction. In addition to donating to a number of charitable organization, I enjoy giving my time and expertise to anyone who asks through www.propertyforum.com.

One of my longer-term goals is to be able to develop a number of real estate sites within a charitable foundation structure and then choose which charities to invest the profits into. I ask joint venture finance lenders (see Chapter 8) to invest their money at a nominal return (forgoing the majority of their interest to the charity) in return for helping me build profit to give back to the chosen charities. The joint venture lender's capital will be returned at the end and the profits distributed to the chosen charities of the foundation. It's a win/win project and one I'm already working toward. If you know anyone who'd be willing to be a part of lending for this project, get in touch and we can give back together!

TIP

Imagine what you could attract if you gave back on a regular basis, perhaps through a mentorship scheme or regularly giving your time or expertise to others.

Downloading Helpful Apps

Make technology work for you by downloading apps that help you incorporate mind-set and personal development techniques into your daily routine. In addition to the apps I mention earlier in the chapter, here are some of my favorite mind-set apps:

>> **The Secret Daily Teachings** (`www.thesecret.tv/products/the-secret-daily-teachings-mobile-app`)**:** This app is for anyone interested in harnessing the law of attraction. It includes daily quotes to inspire you and bring your attention back to your thoughts, feelings, and actions.

>> **Twitter** (`www.twitter.com`)**, Facebook** (`www.facebook.com`)**, and Instagram** (`www.instagram.com`)**:** Not only are these social media platforms a great source of information and property news, but I find they're also a great way to get daily inspiration. I follow people like Rhonda Byrne (author of *The Secret*), Oprah Winfrey, and other successful entrepreneurs, and I find their messages and quotes often inspire me and give me a boost.

>> **Sleepio** (`www.sleepio.com`)**:** Sleepio is a sleep improvement app that uses cognitive behavioral therapy techniques and lets you design a sleep improvement course that's right for you. Although sleep isn't typically included under the personal improvement category, I've found that focusing on my sleep routine has really enhanced my performance in business.

Chapter **18**

Ten (Or So) Other Real Estate Strategies to Consider

Throughout this book, I delve into multiple different strategies for earning income and capital growth through real estate investment. Developing a combination of these strategies will help you build a robust, diverse real estate portfolio. But the strategies you've read about so far aren't the only ways to make money through property and diversify your portfolio.

In this chapter, I briefly look at a range of other ways investors and entrepreneurs get into property investing or build property-related businesses.

REMEMBER

As with any strategy, education is a key part of success. So, if something in this chapter interests you, invest some time in learning more about the strategy or business model before you put your money (and your reputation) on the line. Turn to Chapter 17 for some tips on continually improving through education.

Delving into Buy-to-Rent (Single-Tenant) Properties

"I'm investing in real estate," you say to Beth from the gym. "That's interesting," she replies. "My uncle Dave does that." Chances are, Beth assumes you're buying a property and renting it out to tenants in a straightforward single rental (renting the whole property to one tenant or household). That's what most nonexperts think of when they hear the words *real estate investing,* which makes sense — single rentals are extremely common among first-time investors, or those who want a simple, fuss-free investment as a retirement nest egg.

REMEMBER

Single rentals are a good investment because they're very simple to understand, easy to set up, and, generally, straightforward to run. However, they're unlikely to deliver very impressive rental yields, certainly not market-beating returns. In my experience, renting out rooms in the property to separate tenants is a much better way to maximize your rental income (more on this in Chapters 13 and 14).

Most investors get started with a single-rental strategy, but this book is designed to help you progress beyond that, grow your portfolio faster, build wealth quicker, add more value, and overcome the common challenges of single-tenant rental investments (such as how to maximize your rental income in a highly competitive rental market).

If you want to really get into the nitty-gritty of being a successful buy-to-rent landlord, I highly recommend two books that will help you on that journey. The first is *Real Estate Investing For Dummies,* by Eric Tyson and Robert Griswold (Wiley), which is designed for U.S. readers. The second, for readers in the United Kingdom, is called *Renting Out Your Property For Dummies,* by Melanie Bien and Robert Griswold (Wiley).

Flipping Houses

In very simple terms, *flipping* a house means buying it and quickly selling it for a profit.

REMEMBER

To achieve that profit, you may do some minor cosmetic work to the property. But, generally, this strategy relies more on a rising market (or buying at a great discount) as opposed to adding any real value. The idea is to get in and get out as quickly as possible, so you don't want to be doing any expensive, time-consuming development work (see Chapter 9) on the property.

WARNING

Done well, this strategy can turn a tidy profit, and it can really help you grow your real estate business. However, there are some significant downsides to consider before you take the plunge:

>> **This strategy is only really successful in areas with extremely high demand for property, where demand outstrips supply.** Under these circumstances, the housing market moves quickly, and prices rise faster. If there isn't excessive demand, it can be extremely hard to sell quickly for a profit. (Unless you somehow managed to buy the property for a bargain price, in which case you can simply sell it for retail price and pocket the difference, this is how a good property sourcing agent can add value.)

>> **In a strong, fast-moving market, where demand outstrips supply, buying at a good price can be a real challenge for would-be flippers.** If you pay too much, and the market changes before you can sell the property, you could find yourself in financial hot water.

>> **In general, any strategy that relies on rising house prices is risky business.** In my opinion, you're far better off adding real value to the property in order to generate a profit, or earn steady, long-term income from the property.

>> **Too many investors overlook the costs involved in flipping houses.** It's not just about buying a house and making cosmetic improvements. You've got all the costs associated with acquiring the property (agent fees, legal fees, taxes, and so on), plus covering the mortgage and bills for the period that you own it. If you flip several properties a year, the acquisition costs alone can really add up.

All in all, while I wouldn't discount flipping as a valid strategy in certain market situations, there are lower-risk ways to earn money from property — ways that, unlike flipping houses, will work well under a variety of market conditions.

Running a Bed-and-Breakfast, Guesthouse, or Hotel

As a big fan of passive income (see Chapter 3), I have to say that the thought of running a bed-and-breakfast (B&B), guesthouse, or hotel sends shivers down my spine. I love hotels. I've stayed in some wonderful hotels around the world. But would I want to *run* one? No.

That's because this is an extremely intensive, hands-on business. Even if you're just running a small B&B by the seaside, you still have to be there every day to greet guests, give them a tasty breakfast, clean the rooms, change the sheets, deal with bookings and guest inquiries, and so on. The devil's in the detail, and if you're not a details person, you'll probably struggle to run a successful operation.

Sure, you can simply employ people to run your B&B, guesthouse, or hotel for you, but that's not an easy solution either. You still need to find and oversee awesome people who can handle all the little details on your behalf. And finding awesome people who can take care of things for you is very tricky in itself and comes with a cost.

REMEMBER

Broadly speaking, running a B&B, guesthouse, or hotel is never going to be a get-rich-quick scheme. But if it's something that ignites your passion, this strategy can work well alongside other, much more passive income strategies, like those outlined in Part 4.

TIP

Alternatively, if providing guests with a great experience appeals to you, but the intensity of running a B&B, guesthouse, or hotel doesn't, you may want to consider serviced accommodation (Chapter 15) or vacation rentals (Chapter 16) instead.

Owning or Running a Care Home

I don't know about your part of the world, but the costs of elder care in the United Kingdom are staggering. As I was writing this book, the average cost of housing in a residential care home is around £30,000 ($38,000) per year. And that's just the cost of living there — nursing care costs even more.

On the flip side, owning or running a nursing home or assisted living facility is clearly a strategy with high income potential. There's enormous demand for quality, safe accommodation for older people, and this demand is only going to increase.

WARNING

Those are some big plus points: rising demand and high income potential. However, there are plenty of other serious considerations around owning or running a care home:

>> **This strategy is extremely hands-on, and details matter.** In fact, details can mean the difference between life and death.

>> **The care industry is (rightly) highly regulated, so expect to cope with a lot of oversight from authorities.**

>> **People management is a critical skill in this business, not just in terms of the residents but the staff, too.** You need highly trained care staff with excellent people skills, and they need to be managed extremely well.

>> **Reputationally, this can be a high-risk strategy.** When things go wrong in the care industry, it often makes the headlines and provokes national outrage. I can think of several bad news stories about care homes in recent years that have become national talking points.

REMEMBER

This is a strategy with potentially very high returns, but passion and commitment to the details are key to making it work. Investing in long-term-care facilities is less about a real estate investment and more about providing a service (compassionate and high-quality care) to a vulnerable population.

Becoming a Real Estate Agent, Rental Agent, or Property Manager

The last couple of strategies are pretty high risk, so let's take a break and bathe in the warm, relaxing waters of a relatively low-risk business for a while, shall we?

If you're looking to build your knowledge and expertise in real estate, but you don't have the money to invest in property yourself, you can do a lot worse than becoming a real estate agent (selling homes), rental agent (marketing rental properties), or property manager (looking after properties on behalf of landlords).

REMEMBER

This strategy is a great way to learn the industry from the inside. You can develop contacts, earn income, and build a successful business for yourself. It's pretty accessible, too, requiring little in the way of startup money (if you're going into business for yourself). Later on, if you want to invest in properties, the knowledge and contacts you've gathered will be a huge help. But you may find it turns into a rewarding, lifelong career!

Becoming a real estate agent, rental agent, or property manager isn't for everyone, though. At the very least, you'll need to be

>> A great salesperson

>> A fantastic communicator and real people person

>> Highly driven and self-motivated

>> Very organized and able to juggle multiple projects and clients at once

If you tick all these boxes, you're passionate about real estate, and you're willing to learn, this could be the career move for you! Check out *Success as a Real Estate Agent For Dummies*, 3rd Edition, by Dirk Zeller (Wiley), to discover how to become a top-performing agent and build a successful real estate business.

Investing in Real Estate Investment Trusts

Do you want to achieve the generally steady returns of real estate investments, but you don't want the hassle of owning and actively managing property yourself? Then real estate investment trusts (REITs) can be a good solution.

Real estate investment trusts are investment products where property is the underlying asset. A REIT is a company or trust that owns and operates properties, such as office blocks, apartment blocks, retail properties, and other kinds of buildings that people or businesses rent.

TIP

REITs can be private or public, with public REITs being traded on the major stock exchanges, just like regular shares. Public REITs are subject to all the scrutiny and regulation of any publicly traded security, which tends to make them a safer bet than private REITs — so, unless you really know what you're doing, steer clear of investing in private REITs.

When investing in public REITs, you can choose and buy shares in specific REITs yourself or you can invest in a fund that specializes in REITs (many focus on a specific type of property, such as commercial offices). Investing in a REIT fund is great because it cuts out some of the hard work on researching suitable REITs; the fund managers choose the best investments on the investors' behalf (and, of course, they charge a management fee for the privilege).

But why choose REITs at all? Well, on the plus side:

» **You get a totally hands-off investment, without having to devote your time and energy to finding and managing properties yourself.** REITs are a great option for those who have money to invest, but not really the time (or inclination) to actively manage properties.

» **You usually get returns that are broadly comparable to buying stocks, with (generally speaking) less to worry about in terms of short-term volatility and a performance that mirrors that of the underlying asset (real estate).**

But on the down side, with any hands-off investment, returns are generally lower than they would be for an investment that you actively manage. In other words, investing in a REIT fund will usually deliver lower returns than buying a property and renting it out yourself.

Overall, I'd say REITs are a useful way to further diversify your real estate portfolio, but I recommend combining them with higher-earning, actively managed investments for better returns and a more well-rounded portfolio.

You can read a little more about REITs in *Real Estate Investing For Dummies,* by Eric Tyson and Robert Griswold (Wiley).

Offering Emergency Housing Accommodation

Emergency accommodation is similar to low-income housing (Chapter 14) in terms of the tenant profile, but the way it works is slightly different.

Emergency housing is short-term shelter accommodation for people who have no other options available to them, usually because they're homeless or in crisis. Emergency accommodation is arranged through the local authority housing department, which means, as a landlord, you rent the property to the local authority, and they find and place tenants in it.

There are, as you can expect, some big factors to consider before you turn one of your properties into emergency housing. For one thing, you can expect a high turnover of tenants — with some people perhaps staying for as little as one night — which means the property will be used very intensely. Circle back to Chapter 14 for more on the typical downsides of using a property intensely and how to overcome these challenges.

You can also expect to be welcoming some pretty challenging tenants, people who may be at the lowest point in their lives. You need to have a good understanding of their needs and be prepared for some potentially difficult tenant behavior.

That said, there's a clear need for this kind of accommodation, so the demand is there for a well-run business to be profitable while helping provide a valuable service to local authorities. Win/win again. Because you're being paid by the local authority, not the tenants themselves, you can usually charge a reasonable nightly rent for the extra work these tenants require and rest assured that you'll get paid on time and in full.

TIP

To really make this strategy work for you as an investor, you need to develop a very clear understanding of the local nuances in your target area, and build good links with the local housing authority.

Getting into Commercial Property

This book is focused firmly on residential accommodation. Why? Because people always need somewhere to live. Regardless of what the economy is doing, people always need a place to call home.

REMEMBER

Commercial property is much more subject to the ebbs and flows of the wider economy. If business taxes go up, you'll see more empty shops on Main Street. If the economy contracts, businesses go bust or downsize, leaving large empty warehouses and offices in their wake. You've likely seen this with your own eyes in your area at one point or another.

WARNING

The success of commercial real estate investments hinges on having good, stable business tenants in place. Without a tenant, it's just an empty building costing you money. "Duh, that's obvious," you say. But what's not immediately obvious is that it can take a long time to find good commercial tenants, which means your chances of *void periods* (where the property stands empty) are usually higher than they are with a residential property. And even if you do find a great tenant, will they be able to stay put if the economy changes? That's a couple of big "ifs" to consider.

So, clearly there are some key downsides to be aware of. But what about the upsides? There are some attractive advantages to investing in commercial property:

>> **Commercial leases tend to be much longer than residential leases (at least 5 years, often 10 years, or maybe even 20 years!).** If you can find a good tenant, that gives you some stability and potentially lowers your risk. The longer the lease, the more value this adds to the property.

>> **Depending on where you are in the world, you may receive more generous tax treatment on commercial investments than residential.** Your tax advisor or accountant will be able to tell you whether this is the case in your jurisdiction.

> » **Tenants are responsible for customizing and maintaining the property to suit their needs, which keeps your costs low (again, providing you can find, and keep, a good tenant).** Often they have a full repairing lease and have to hand the property back at the end of the lease term in the same condition at which they took it on. So, that means you often have no wear and tear to contend with like you do with residential investments.

All things considered, and unless your tenant is a big name like Microsoft or Coca-Cola, for example, commercial real estate investing is often considered higher risk than residential investments, but if you get it right, you can be in for relatively hands-off income for several years at a time. This strategy may be worth considering as part of a larger real estate portfolio or for larger investors if the right opportunity (with the right tenant) arises.

Trading in Freeholds

A *freehold* essentially means the outright, indefinite ownership of a building and the land that it sits on. If you buy an apartment with a lease of, say, 99 years, that's not a freehold (it's a *leasehold*) because you only "own" the apartment (for a term of 99 years), not the whole building, and not the land.

Take the example of a large block of 100 apartments. Each apartment is owned leasehold by individual owners, who pay what's usually known as *ground rent* to the individual or company who owns the freehold on the building. The freehold of that large apartment block can be traded, just like any of the apartments within the block can be sold.

WARNING

Trading in freeholds is best left to experienced investors, in my opinion. The legal technicalities are stringent, regulation in this area is evolving, and, unlike a regular house or apartment, it's difficult to add value and increase the amount earned through ground rent. What's more, these opportunities are difficult to source and sell, compared to a regular residential property. For this reason, I would only ever consider trading freeholds as part of a wider, diversified portfolio and never as a main source of income.

Index

A

accrediting organizations, 47

acquisition costs, 142

adding value, 19–20, 61, 66, 156, 208

adjustable-rate loans, 105–107

adjustable-rate mortgage, 72

Adobe Sign (website), 52

advertising
  for HMO tenants, 258
  online, 258, 273, 324
  to students, 273
  vacation rentals, 324

affirmations, 85–87, 339

Airbnb, 285, 301, 303, 324

Amsterdam, for lease options, 241

appraisals
  fees for, 110
  purpose of, 121
  research on, 133–134

appraisers, 123, 126–127

apps
  productivity, 334–335
  recommended, 341

architect, 43, 169–170

Article 4, 251–252

ASAP (Association of Serviced Apartment Providers) (website), 293

assets, comparing property to other, 8–9

Association of Serviced Apartment Providers (ASAP) (website), 293

Assured Shorthold Tenancy (AST), 218, 257

Australia
  for HMOs, 263
  for rent-to-rent, 222
  for serviced accommodations, 307
  for student/low-income properties, 283

B

bed-and-breakfast, 345–346

Belfast, for lease options, 241

Berlin, for lease options, 241

Bernstein, Gabrielle (author)
  The Universe Has Your Back, 90

Bien, Melanie (author)
  Renting Out Your Property For Dummies, 344

Booking.com (website), 286, 303, 324

bookkeeping software, 52

Boston, for student/low-income properties, 283

bricks-and-mortar valuation, 128, 129–130

bridge loans
  about, 113–115
  for property development, 167

brokers
  defined, 14
  as a real estate valuer, 123

budgeting
  considerations for, 26–28
  for property development, 171–174

Buffett, Warren (entrepreneur), 38

builders, for property development, 171

building contractors, 43

business, running portfolio as a
  about, 12–13, 37–38
  cash flow management, 55–57
  gathering a dream team, 42–49
  insurance, 57–59
  passive income, 38–41
  promoting, 53–55
  systems and technology, 49–53

business cards, importance of having for your business, 145

Business Networking For Dummies (Thomas), 81

business proposal, for selling your joint venture, 142–145

business-related benefits, of meditation, 96

buyers

attracting to your service, 194–195

as a real estate valuer, 123

sourcing properties for your, 196

buyer's market, 68–71

buy-to-rent, 344

buy-to-rent mortgages, 112–113

C

Canada

for serviced accommodations, 307

for student/low-income properties, 283

capital growth

defined, 237

earning, 229–230

care home, 346–347

cash buffer, 57

cash flow

managing, 55–57

planning for vacation rentals, 314–316

census data, 250

change of use, 208–209

Cheat Sheet (website), 4

CMS (content management system), 52

commercial investment valuation, 128, 130–132

commercial mortgages, 113

commercial property, 350–351

commission

for leads, 186

for retained buyer's agent, 194

communication, for property development, 175

condition of property

as a factor influencing value, 121

for rent-to-rent, 214

consideration payment

for lease options, 230–231

negotiating for lease options, 238–239

content management system (CMS), 52

contingency, 173–174

continuing education, 78–80, 333–334

controlling property, 149–150

convergent thinking, 96

Copenhagen, for rent-to-rent, 222

cost approach, for valuation, 128, 132

costs

acquisition, 142

ongoing, 211–213, 231

of outsourcing, 45–46

planning for vacation rentals, 314–316

for property development, 172–173

of property development, 167–168

country-specific risk factors, 29–30

Coursera (website), 79

craigslist (website), 54, 273

creative visualization, 88–91

credit cards, for property development, 167

credit check and reference procedures, 50

credit report fee, 110

credit reports, 111

CRM (customer relationship management) software, 52

crowdfunding, 75, 148, 149

CrowdProperty (website), 148

customer relationship management (CRM) software, 52

D

demand for property, as a factor influencing value, 122

Denmark, for rent-to-rent, 222

Department of Housing and Urban Development (HUD), 252

deposit, for HMOs, 257

deposit insurance, as a startup cost for rent-to-rent, 209

development appraisal, 142

development loans, 115–117, 165, 166–167

discount, 131

divergent thinking, 96

diversifying, with multiple revenue streams, 62–65

DocuSign (website), 52

domestic finance, International finance *vs.*, 118

down payments, 109

Dropbox (website), 334

Dubai, for property development, 177

Dublin, for HMOs, 263

due diligence
  for HMO tenants, 259–260
  for vacation rentals, 313–314

Dyer, Wayne (author), 90

dynamic pricing, 304, 328

E

Edinburgh, for student/low-income properties, 283

education, continuing, 78–80, 333–334

80/20 rule, 42

electric safety, for HMOs, 254

Electrical Installation Condition Report, 254

electronic signature system, 52

Elrod, Hal (author)
  The Miracle Morning, 90

email address, importance of having for your business, 145

emergency housing, 349–350

emotional benefits, of meditation, 96

equity releases
  as a financing option, 27
  for property development, 167

ethical rent-to-rent, 204

events, for networking, 81

Evernote (website), 334

Eviivo's (website), 303

exit options, for property development, 158, 160–161

"exit-led" investors, 144

Experian (website), 259

experts
  finding and vetting, 46–48
  getting advice from, 42–43

F

Facebook
  Groups, 80, 81
  website, 55, 341

feelings, focusing on, 93–94

fees, for loans, 110

financial model
  houses in multiple occupation (HMOs), 245–246
  for lease options, 228–231
  rent-to-rent, 209–213

financing. *See also* traditional finance
  about, 135
  applying overseas, 150–151
  controlling property, 149–150
  crowdfunding, 75, 148, 149
  effect on valuation methods of, 125–126
  joint ventures, 138–146
  nontraditional, 74–75
  options for, 27
  other people's money (OPM), 14, 136–137
  private lending, 146–148, 167
  property development, 165–169
  valuation, 13–14

fire safety, for HMOs, 254–255

Fiverr (website), 47, 334

fixed-rate loans, 105–107

fixed-rate mortgage, 72, 73

FlipKey (website), 324

flipping houses, 66, 68, 344–345

foreign exchange rate risks, 75–76

France
  for property information, 197
  for rent-to-rent, 222
  for serviced accommodations, 307
  for vacation rentals, 329

Frankfurt, for HMOs, 263

freeholds, 351

FreshBooks (website), 52

friends and family, as a financing option, 27

funding, tailoring, 72–75

Fundrise (website), 148

G

gas safety, for HMOs, 254

Gas Safety Check Certificate, 254

GDPR (General Data Protection Regulations), 82

Gelles, David (author)

Mindful Work, 97

general building contractors, 43

General Data Protection Regulations (GDPR), 82

Germany

for HMOs, 263

for lease options, 241

Gmail (website), 335

goal list, 337–338

goals

factoring into decision-making, 31

setting, 82–85, 337–338

Google Calendar (website), 334

Google Drive (website), 334

gratitude, 87–88, 340–341

Grimsby, for lease options, 241

Griswold, Robert (author)

Real Estate Investing For Dummies, 3rd Edition, 37, 344

Renting Out Your Property For Dummies, 344

gross income, 131

gross yield, 124

growth, relationship between leverage and, 102–103

guesthouse, 345–346

H

header image, on websites, 325

Headspace (website), 336

health and safety, HMOs, 253–255

high-earning strategies, 10–11

Hill, Napoleon (author)

Think and Grow Rich, 88

HMOs. *See* houses in multiple occupation (HMOs)

HMOs (houses in multiple occupation)

about, 243–245

as a crunch strategy, 69

financial model for, 245–246

legal issues, 250–255

locations for, 249–250, 263

managing, 255–262

scaling up your portfolio, 262–263

sourcing properties for, 246–248

who to rent to, 249

HomeAway (website), 324

Hong Kong, for HMOs, 263

hotel, 345–346

Hotpads (website), 54

houses in multiple occupation (HMOs)

about, 243–245

as a crunch strategy, 69

financial model for, 245–246

legal issues, 250–255

locations for, 249–250, 263

managing, 255–262

scaling up your portfolio, 262–263

sourcing properties for, 246–248

who to rent to, 249

"How to Build a Real Estate Cash Buyers List," 334

HUD (Department of Housing and Urban Development), 252

I

iCloud (website), 334

icons, explained, 3–4

improvements, needed for property development, 168–169

income

earning for rent-to-rent, 211–213

gross, 131

net, 131

passive, 12, 38–41

income approach, 128, 130–132

income/investment approach, for valuation, 128, 130–132

indemnity insurance, 58

independent financial advisor, 43

Infusionsoft (website), 52, 335

Instagram (website), 341
insurance, 57–59
insurance agent, 43
interest rates, 73–74
interest-only loans, 109–110
International finance, domestic finance *vs.*, 118
International strategies, 11–12
Internet resources
  Adobe Sign, 52
  Airbnb, 285, 324
  Association of Serviced Apartment
    Providers (ASAP), 293
  Booking.com, 286, 303, 324
  census data, 250
  Cheat Sheet, 4
  Coursera, 79
  craigslist, 54, 273
  CrowdProperty, 148
  DocuSign, 52
  Dropbox, 334
  Evernote, 334
  Eviivo's, 303
  Experian, 259
  Facebook, 55, 341
  Fiverr, 47, 334
  FlipKey, 324
  FreshBooks, 52
  Fundrise, 148
  Gmail, 335
  Google Calendar, 334
  Google Drive, 334
  having your own, 144, 325
  Headspace, 336
  HomeAway, 324
  Hotpads, 54
  iCloud, 334
  importance of having for your
    business, 144
  Infusionsoft, 52, 335
  Instagram, 341
  LinkedIn, 55
  OneDrive, 334
  Property Forum, 46, 54, 79, 191, 340

QuickBooks, 52
real estate education, 4
RealtyShares, 148
Rent Manager, 53
Rightmove, 185
Roomi, 250
Salesforce, 52
The Secret Daily Teachings, 341
Signable, 52
Sleepio, 341
SpareRoom, 54, 250, 258
Sprout Social, 52
Squarespace, 52
Student, 273
Student Accommodation, 273
ThinkUp, 339
Trustpilot, 48
TweetDeck, 52
Twitter, 341
Udemy, 79, 334
Upwork, 47, 334
VRBO, 324
Wimdu, 304–305
WordPress, 52
world property prices, 27
Wunderflats, 304–305
Xero, 52
Yelp, 48
Zillow, 54, 185
Zoopla, 250
investment mortgages, 112–113
investment value approach, 128, 130–132
investments, maximizing, 124
Ireland
  for HMOs, 263
  for lease options, 241
Italy, for vacation rentals, 329

J

Japan
  for serviced accommodations, 307
  for student/low-income properties, 283

Jobs, Steve (entrepreneur), 97
joint ventures, 138–146, 167

K

Kissimmee, FL, for vacation rentals, 329
knowledge
  as a market consideration, 34–35
  as a reason for investing abroad, 25

L

Lake Garda, Italy, for vacation rentals, 329
The Lake District, UK, for vacation rentals, 329
land loans, 115–117, 165
land tax, 238
landlord, 202–203, 216–217
language
  as a barrier, 150
  as a market consideration, 33
large HMOs, 245
law of attraction, 91–95
leads
  about, 180–181
  facilitating off-market deals, 185–186
  financial model, 186
  finding your niche, 184–185
  generating and selling, 183–192
  marketing, 190–192
  progressing from an investment property
    source to a retained buyer's agent, 181–183
  sourcing valuable properties, 186–190
lease options
  about, 223
  benefits for property owner, 232–233
  defined, 18
  financial model for, 228–231
  how they work, 224–228
  locations for, 240–241
  negotiating deal and contract, 236–240
  selling, 230
  sourcing opportunities for, 233–235
  strategies for, 227

leasing/rental element, of lease options, 224
Leeds, for lease options, 241
legal issues, for HMOs, 250–255
length
  of agreement, negotiating for lease options,
    237–238
  of lease, for rental agreement, 218–219
  of loans, 107
leverage
  defined, 101
  relationship between growth and, 102–103
liability insurance, 58
licensing HMOs, 252–253
LinkedIn
  Groups, 81
  website, 55
loan application fee, 110
loan guarantees, 115
loans
  adjustable-rate, 105–107
  bridge, 113–115, 167
  development, 115–117, 165, 166–167
  fixed-rate, 105–107
  interest-only, 109–110
  land, 115–117, 165
  length of, 107
  personal, 27, 167
  repayment, 109–110
  second-charge, 115
  term, 115–117
loan-to-value (LTV) mortgage, 72, 102, 108–109
locations
  as a factor influencing value, 122
  for HMOs, 249–250, 263
  for lease options, 240–241
  for property development, 162, 176–177
  for property information, 196–197
  for rent-to-rent, 214, 222
  for serviced accommodations, 297–298, 307
  student/low-income properties, 283
  for students, 270–271
  for vacation rentals, 312–314, 329

London, for rent-to-rent, 222

longer-term strategies, 17–20, 62–63

low-income/students housing tenants, renting to
about, 265
as a crunch strategy, 69–70
drafting tenancy agreements, 275–278
finding property for, 272–275
locations for, 283
managing property for, 281–283
marketing property for, 272–275
physically preparing property for, 278–281
pros and cons of, 268–270
sourcing property for, 270–272
what's involved in, 266–267

LTV (loan-to-value) mortgage, 72, 102, 108–109

LTV percentage, 104

M

macro-economic factors, 56

managing agent, for vacation rentals, 327–328

Marbella, Spain, for vacation rentals, 329

market comparison approach, for valuation, 128,
129–130

market fluctuations
about, 61–62
diversification, 62–65
foreign exchange rate risks, 75–76
mass market opposition, 71–72
strategies for boom markets, 65–68
strategies for credit crunches, 68–71
tailoring funding, 72–75

market value approach, 128, 129–130

marketing
property, 190–192
serviced accommodations, 304–305
for students/low-income properties, 272–275
vacation rentals, 324–327

markets
about, 23–24
assessing your risk profile, 28–31

budget considerations, 26–28
number to focus on, 35–36
property management, 31–32
reasons for investing abroad, 24–25
selecting, 33–35

meditation, 95–98

meetings, for networking, 81

Melbourne
for HMOs, 263
for rent-to-rent, 222
for student/low-income properties, 283

mental attitude, positive, 85–88

Microsoft Project, 175

Mindful Work (Gelles), 97

mindfulness, 335–337

mindset
about, 77
continuing education, 78–80
law of attraction, 91–95
meditation, 95–98
networking, 80–82
positive mental attitude, 85–88
setting goals, 82–85
tips for getting into the right, 333–341
visualization, 88–91

The Miracle Morning (Elrod), 90

money for improvements
for rent-to-rent, 214
as a startup cost for rent-to-rent, 210

monthly rent, negotiating for lease options,
236–237

mortgage broker, 43

mortgages, as a financing option, 27

multi-skilled freelancers, 45

multi-tenant strategies, 10

N

negative equity, 232–233

net income, 131

networking, 46, 80–82

neuro-linguistic programming (NLP), 88

New York, for rent-to-rent, 222

Nice, France, for vacation rentals, 329

niche, finding your, 184–185

Nicklaus, Jack (golfer), 88

NLP (neuro-linguistic programming), 88

nontraditional finance, 74–75

O

off-market deals, facilitating, 185–186

OneDrive (website), 334

ongoing costs

  for lease options, 231

  for rent-to-rent, 211–213

online advertising

  for HMO tenants, 258

  to students, 273

  vacation rentals, 324

online reviews, 48

option to buy, for lease options, 224

other people's money (OTM), 14, 136–137

outcome of project, 142

outsourcing, 44–46

P

Panama, for property development, 177

Pareto principle, 42

Paris

  for rent-to-rent, 222

  for serviced accommodations, 307

passion, as a reason for investing abroad, 24–25

passive income, 12, 38–41

peer-to-peer lending, 75

personal guarantee (PG), 115

personal loans

  as a financing option, 27

  for property development, 167

personal savings, for property development, 167

PG (personal guarantee), 115

photos, on websites, 325

physical benefits, of meditation, 96

planning consultant

  defined, 43

  for property development, 169–170

planning requirements, for HMOs, 251–252

planning restrictions, for serviced accommodations, 301–302

portfolios

  diversifying with multiple revenue streams, 62–65

  running as a business, 12–13, 37–59

positive affirmations, 85–87, 339

positive mental attitude, 85–88

price

  comparing to value, 120

  dynamic pricing, 304, 328

  relying on rising, 67

  for serviced accommodations, 304

private lending, 146–148, 167

processes

  putting in place, 50

  for serviced accommodations, 302–305

productivity apps/tools, 334–335

professional operator, for rent-to-rent, 217

project manager, for property development, 170

promoting your business, 53–55

property

  assessing for development, 161–162

  comparing to other asset classes, 8–9

  controlling, 18, 149–150

  evaluating of rent-to-rent, 213–215

  preparing for serviced accommodations, 299–301

  preparing for use as vacation rentals, 320–324

  subletting, 205–206

property advertisements, 50

property development

  about, 155–157

  assessing property, 161–162

  as a boom strategy, 66

  financing, 165–169

  locations for, 176–177

managing, 169–176

as a shorter-term strategy, 16–17

sourcing opportunities for, 161–164

strategies for, 157–161

Property Forum (website), 46, 54, 79, 191, 340

property information

about, 179–180

as a boom strategy, 67

leads, 180–192

locations for, 196–197

retained buyer's agent, 192–196

property management

about, 31–32

HMOs, 250–251, 255–262

of property development, 169–176

for rent-to-rent, 221–222

student/low-income properties, 281–283

vacation rentals, 327–328

property manager, 43, 347–348

property owner, benefits for with lease options, 232–233

property valuation

about, 119

appraisal research, 133–134

appraisals, 121

comparing price to value, 120

cost approach, 132

effect on financing of, 125–126

evaluating methods for, 132–133

factors influencing, 121–122

importance of, 123–128

income/investment approach, 130–132

market comparison approach, 129–130

maximizing investments, 124

methods of, 128–132

process of, 122–123, 127–128

risk averse nature of appraisers, 126–127

special considerations, 134

yield *vs.* return, 124–125

"The Property Cycle: How to Identify the Best Time to Invest," 334

purchase price, negotiating for lease options, 238

Q

quality of property, for serviced accommodations, 297

QuickBooks (website), 52

R

real estate agents

about, 43

becoming a, 347–348

as a real estate valuer, 123

sourcing properties for development through, 163

real estate appraisal, 120. *See also* property valuation

real estate broker, as a real estate valuer, 123

Real Estate Investing For Dummies, 3rd Edition (Tyson and Griswold), 37, 344

real estate investment trusts (REITs), 348–349

real estate lawyer, 43

RealtyShares (website), 148

recommendations

asking contacts for, 47

for HMO tenants, 258

referrals, for HMO tenants, 258

regulations, for serviced accommodations, 293

regulatory restrictions, for serviced accommodations, 301–302

Remember icon, 3

rent, preparing properties for, 175–176

rent in advance, as a startup cost for rent-to-rent, 210

Rent Manager (website), 53

rental agent, becoming a, 347–348

rental agreement

about, 218

length of lease, 218–219

tenancy agreement, 219

rental contract templates, 50

rental income, earning, 229

Renting Out Your Property For Dummies (Bien and Griswold), 344

renting to students/low-income housing tenants
  about, 265
  as a crunch strategy, 69–70
  drafting tenancy agreements, 275–278
  finding property for, 272–275
  locations for, 283
  managing property for, 281–283
  marketing property for, 272–275
  physically preparing property for, 278–281
  pros and cons of, 268–270
  sourcing property for, 270–272
  what's involved in, 266–267
rent-to-buy. *See* lease options
rent-to-rent
  about, 18, 40, 201–203
  change of use, 208–209
  choosing an approach for, 206–207
  as a crunch strategy, 69
  earning income with, 211–213
  ethical, 204
  financial model, 209–213
  finding tenants, 220–221
  image problem of, 203–204
  locations for, 222
  ongoing costs, 211–213
  property management for, 221–222
  property suitable for, 205
  rental agreement, 218–219
  shoestring budget, 210–211
  sourcing property for, 213–217
  startup costs, 209–210
  subletting property, 205–206
repayment loans, 109–110
reservations, managing, 303–304
retained buyer's agent, 192–196
return, yield *vs.*, 124–125
return on investment (ROI), 124
revenue streams, diversifying with multiple, 62–65
review, for vacation rentals, 327
Rightmove (website), 185
risk, managing with meditation, 95–98

risk profile, assessing your, 28–31
Roddick, Anita (founder of The Body Shop), 26
ROI (return on investment), 124
Roomi (website), 250

S

safeguards, negotiating for lease options, 239–240
safety
  of tenants, 280–281
  of vacation rentals, 323–324
sale, preparing properties for, 175–176
sales-based strategy, 66
Salesforce (website), 52
San Antonio, for lease options, 241
San Diego, for serviced accommodations, 307
San Francisco, for HMOs, 263
schedule, for property development, 174–175
Scotland, for student/low-income properties, 283
seasonality, 316–318
second-charge loans, 115
The Secret Daily Teachings (website), 91, 341
security deposit
  as a startup cost for rent-to-rent, 209
  for student/low-income properties, 277–278
sellers
  open to lease options, 234–235
  pitching to potential, 186–187
  as a real estate valuer, 122
seller's market, 65–68
selling yourself, 144–145
serviced accommodations
  about, 64, 285–286
  locations for, 307
  managing on an ongoing basis, 306
  planning restrictions, 301–302
  preparing properties for, 299–301
  processes and systems for, 302–305
  pros and cons of, 289–294
  regulatory restrictions, 301–302
  service levels for, 294–296

services provided, 287–288

sourcing properties for, 296–298

target audience for, 289

types of, 286–287

vacation rentals *vs.*, 310–311

shoestring budget, for rent-to-rent, 210–211

shorter-term strategies, 16–17, 62–63

Signable (website), 52

size of property

as a factor influencing value, 121

for serviced accommodations, 297

Sleepio (website), 341

slumlords, 203–204

social media marketing software, 52

software, 51–53

sources, for continuing education, 78–79

space available, for rent-to-rent, 214

Spain

for lease options, 240–241

for property development, 177

for property information, 197

for vacation rentals, 329

SpareRoom (website), 54, 250, 258

special considerations, for valuing property, 134

Sprout Social (website), 52

Squarespace (website), 52

Stamp Duty land Tax, 238

standard residential investment mortgage, 112–113

startup costs, for rent-to-rent, 209–210

strategies

about, 7–8

blending, 14–20

choosing, 20–21

comparing property to other asset classes, 8–9

finances, 13–14

high-earning, 10–11

International, 11–12

longer-term, 17–20, 62–63

market fluctuations, 65–71

matching for lease options, 227

multi-tenant, 10

for property development, 157–161

running portfolio as a business, 12–13

sales-based, 66

shorter-term, 16–17, 62–63

tips for, 343–351

stress management, 95–98

structural surveys, fees for, 110

Student (website), 273

Student Accommodation (website), 273

students/low-income housing tenants, renting to

about, 265

as a crunch strategy, 69–70

drafting tenancy agreements, 275–278

finding property for, 272–275

locations for, 283

managing property for, 281–283

marketing property for, 272–275

physically preparing property for, 278–281

pros and cons of, 268–270

sourcing property for, 270–272

what's involved in, 266–267

subletting property, 205–206

supply of property, as a factor influencing value, 122

surveyors, 123

Sydney, for serviced accommodations, 307

systems

investing in for your business, 49–53

for serviced accommodations, 302–305

T

target audience

for HMOs, 249

preparing properties for, 278–279

property development and, 159–160

for rent-to-rent, 214

for serviced accommodations, 289, 296

tax advisor, 43

taxes, vacation rentals and, 311

Technical stuff icon, 4

technology, investing in for your business, 49–53

tenancy agreements
  about, 219
  drafting, 275–278
  for HMOs, 256–257
tenant onboarding process, 50
tenants
  finding, 220–221
  finding and vetting for HMOs, 258–260
  managing for HMOs, 260–261
  vetting, 275
term, of loans, 104
term loans, 115–117
Think and Grow Rich (Hill), 88
ThinkUp, 339
third-party assessments, fees for, 110
Thomas, Stefan (author)
  Business Networking For Dummies, 81
thoughts, focusing on, 93–94
Tip icon, 3
Tokyo
  for serviced accommodations, 307
  for student/low-income properties, 283
Toronto, for student/low-income properties, 283
tradespeople, 43
tradespeople, for property development, 171
traditional finance
  about, 72–74, 101
  assessing options for, 112–117
  bridge loans, 113–115
  choosing a product, 117–118
  commercial mortgages, 113
  considerations for, 104–110
  credit report, 111
  fee considerations, 110
  fixed-rate *vs.* adjustable-rate loans, 105–107
  International *vs.* domestic, 118
  land development loans, 115–117
  link between leverage and growth, 102–103
  loan guarantees, 116
  loan length, 107
  loan-to-value balance, 108–109

options for, 103–104
  repayment *vs.* interest-only loans, 109–110
  second-charge loans, 115
  standard residential investment mortgage, 112–113
translator, 43
Trustpilot (website), 48
TweetDeck (website), 52
Twitter (website), 341
Tyson, Eric (author)
  Real Estate Investing For Dummies, 3rd Edition, 37, 344

U

Uber, 304
Udemy (website), 79, 334
United Kingdom
  for lease options, 241
  for property development, 177
  for property information, 197
  for rent-to-rent, 222
  for student/low-income properties, 283
  for vacation rentals, 329
United States
  for HMOs, 263
  for lease options, 241
  for property development, 177
  for property information, 197
  for rent-to-rent, 222
  for serviced accommodations, 307
  for student/low-income properties, 283
  for vacation rentals, 329
The Universe Has Your Back (Bernstein), 90
Upwork (website), 47, 334
utility bills, for HMO tenants, 259

V

vacation rentals
  about, 309–310
  cash flow planning for, 314–316

cost planning for, 314–316

locations for, 312–314, 329

managing, 327–328

marketing, 324–327

preparing property for, 320–324

seasonality, 316–318

serviced accommodation *vs.*, 310–311

sourcing properties for, 318–319

tax advantages of, 311

valuation

about, 13–14, 119

appraisal research, 133–134

appraisals, 121

comparing price to value, 120

cost approach, 132

effect on financing of, 125–126

evaluating methods for, 132–133

factors influencing, 121–122

importance of, 123–128

income/investment approach, 130–132

market comparison approach, 129–130

maximizing investments, 124

methods of, 128–132

process of, 122–123, 127–128

risk averse nature of appraisers, 126–127

special considerations, 134

yield *vs.* return, 124–125

valuation fee, 110

value

adding, 19–20, 61, 66, 156, 208

comparing price to, 120

factors that influence, 121–122

valuers, 123

Vancouver, for serviced accommodations, 307

variable mortgage, 72

virtual assistant, 44

vision board, 337–338

visualization, 88–91, 338

void periods, 11, 245, 292, 315, 350

VRBO (website), 324

W

Warning icon, 4

wear and tear, preparing for, 279–280

websites

Adobe Sign, 52

Airbnb, 285, 324

Association of Serviced Apartment Providers (ASAP), 293

Booking.com, 286, 303, 324

census data, 250

Cheat Sheet, 4

Coursera, 79

craigslist, 54, 273

CrowdProperty, 148

DocuSign, 52

Dropbox, 334

Evernote, 334

Eviivo's, 303

Experian, 259

Facebook, 55, 341

Fiverr, 47, 334

FlipKey, 324

FreshBooks, 52

Fundrise, 148

Gmail, 335

Google Calendar, 334

Google Drive, 334

having your own, 144, 325

Headspace, 336

HomeAway, 324

Hotpads, 54

iCloud, 334

importance of having for your business, 144

Infusionsoft, 52, 335

Instagram, 341

LinkedIn, 55

OneDrive, 334

Property Forum, 46, 54, 79, 191, 340

QuickBooks, 52

real estate education, 4

websites *(continued)*
  RealtyShares, 148
  Rent Manager, 53
  Rightmove, 185
  Roomi, 250
  Salesforce, 52
  The Secret Daily Teachings, 341
  Signable, 52
  Sleepio, 341
  SpareRoom, 54, 250, 258
  Sprout Social, 52
  Squarespace, 52
  Student, 273
  Student Accommodation, 273
  ThinkUp, 339
  Trustpilot, 48
  TweetDeck, 52
  Twitter, 341
  Udemy, 79, 334
  Upwork, 47, 334
  VRBO, 324
  Wimdu, 304–305
  WordPress, 52
  world property prices, 27
  Wunderflats, 304–305
  Xero, 52
  Yelp, 48
  Zillow, 54, 185
  Zoopla, 250
Wimdu (website), 304–305
word-of-mouth marketing, to students, 273–274
WordPress (website), 52
Wunderflats (website), 304–305

X

Xero (website), 52

Y

Yelp (website), 48
yield
  about, 38, 131
  potential, 250
  return *vs.*, 124–125
yourself
  selling, 144–145
  sourcing properties for development, 163–164

Z

Zillow (website), 54, 185
Zoopla (website), 250

About the Author

Nicholas Wallwork is a leading international real estate market commentator, entrepreneur, investor, and developer. Nicholas heads up several real estate and investment companies and has produced and presented a number of real estate TV shows on Sky TV in the UK. As an author, he writes a multitude of educational content dedicated to supporting landlords, real estate professionals, and investors across the industry through www.propertyforum.com (a real estate chat forum, educational hub, and news portal) and www.bullmarketboard.com (a stock market investing chat forum, hub, and news portal).

Nicholas has a demonstrated track record of working on successful developments and investments in the real estate industry. He has a wide breadth of real estate experience with specific expertise in developing houses in multiple occupation, micro studio and co-living apartment blocks, and private rented-sector developments. He also has experience developing healthcare and assisted living properties.

Nicholas can be contacted at me@nicholaswallwork.com for any business enquiries. He is also on LinkedIn, Facebook, and Instagram (@nicholas_wallwork).

Dedication

This book is dedicated to my soul mate and amazing wife, Britta Wallwork, and to my amazing, always positive family Siènna, Skyla, and Silàs. Thank you, Britta, for believing in me always and without question, right from the outset. We will always dream big and continue to enjoy every moment as though it's our last.

Author's Acknowledgments

It has been a major dream of mine to one day write a book, and I'm extremely grateful to have been given this opportunity, one that I'm hopeful will lead to many more projects with Wiley. It's a huge team effort writing a book, and I'm specifically grateful to Annie Knight for taking the time to listen to my initial proposal and then for introducing me to my acquisitions editor, Tracy Boggier. Thank you so much for taking me seriously over all those other proposals and making that introduction when you did. I'm forever grateful to you for that.

Tracy has been amazing. She's so generous with her limited time. Tracy is approachable and has helped point me in the right direction a number of times while championing me and my pitch throughout. Without her, there might not have been a book at all, so thank you again, Tracy. I'm truly grateful for your continued support.

A big thank you to Elizabeth Kuball, my project editor. You've been most helpful helping keep me on track, giving general advice, and writing tips, and you've done a brilliant job understanding and assisting with the UK/US nuances while writing the book.

Thanks also go out to my wife and best friend, Britta, and all my family (hi, Mum, Dad, Andy, and my brother Simon!) and extended crazy Dutch family (John, Yvonne, Joyce, Maurice, and Daphne) and friends both here and in Holland (sorry, I can't name you all!) who hear nonstop about my latest projects and big ideas.

A massive thank you to my best friend and business partner, Chris Sturmer; there's nothing better than working with your friend and I wouldn't be where I am today without our awesome partnership, for which I'm truly grateful. We've certainly defied mixing business with pleasure.

A huge thank you to Claire for your help and support throughout. You're fantastic!

Thanks to Robert for your trust and ongoing partnership. Thanks also to some of my insanely talented, loyal, and supportive team: Kelly, Michelle, Lee, Stephanie, and Kath. We couldn't do it without you guys. A massive and heart felt *thank you!*

A shout-out to Michael Hammond for working with us so closely. It's been a pleasure working on both our businesses together with such synergy. Thanks to "mate" (you know who you are — that's Ben Collins for the rest of the world) for believing in me when I came up with the idea of my first real estate company all those years ago and supporting the vision — it worked right!

Thank you to all our JV investors who have trusted and believed in us over the years. I'm proud we've been able to create win/win investments for us all.

Finally, thank you to all my mentors, successful people I've followed over the years, and to the law of attraction for always delivering. I'm looking forward to the next step already. Always be growing, onward and upward!

Publisher's Acknowledgments

Senior Acquisitions Editor: Tracy Boggier
Project Editor: Elizabeth Kuball
Copy Editor: Elizabeth Kuball
Technical Editor: Joana Meding

Production Editor: Magesh Elangovan
Cover Photos: © jamesteohart/iStockphoto

PERSONAL ENRICHMENT

Staying Sharp	**Facebook**	**Guitar**	**Investing**	**Beekeeping**	**Digital Photography**
9781119187790	9781119179030	9781119293354	9781119293347	9781119310068	9781119235606
USA $26.00	USA $21.99	USA $24.99	USA $22.99	USA $22.99	USA $24.99
CAN $31.99	CAN $25.99	CAN $29.99	CAN $27.99	CAN $27.99	CAN $29.99
UK £19.99	UK £16.99	UK £17.99	UK £16.99	UK £16.99	UK £17.99

 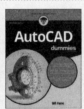  

Meditation	**Pregnancy**	**Samsung Galaxy S7**	**iPhone**	**Crocheting**	**Nutrition**
9781119251163	9781119235491	9781119279952	9781119283133	9781119287117	9781119130246
USA $24.99	USA $26.99	USA $24.99	USA $24.99	USA $24.99	USA $22.99
CAN $29.99	CAN $31.99	CAN $29.99	CAN $29.99	CAN $29.99	CAN $27.99
UK £17.99	UK £19.99	UK £17.99	UK £17.99	UK £16.99	UK £16.99

PROFESSIONAL DEVELOPMENT

Windows 10	**AutoCAD**	**Excel 2016**	**QuickBooks 2017**	**macOS Sierra**	**LinkedIn**	**Windows 10 ALL-IN-ONE**
9781119311041	9781119255796	9781119293439	9781119281467	9781119280651	9781119251132	9781119310563
USA $24.99	USA $39.99	USA $26.99	USA $26.99	USA $29.99	USA $24.99	USA $34.00
CAN $29.99	CAN $47.99	CAN $31.99	CAN $31.99	CAN $35.99	CAN $29.99	CAN $41.99
UK £17.99	UK £27.99	UK £19.99	UK £19.99	UK £21.99	UK £17.99	UK £24.99

SharePoint 2016	**Fundamental Analysis**	**Networking**	**Office 2016**	**Office 365**	**Salesforce.com**	**Coding**
9781119181705	9781119263593	9781119257769	9781119293477	9781119265313	9781119239314	9781119293323
USA $29.99	USA $26.99	USA $29.99	USA $26.99	USA $24.99	USA $29.99	USA $29.99
CAN $35.99	CAN $31.99	CAN $35.99	CAN $31.99	CAN $29.99	CAN $35.99	CAN $35.99
UK £21.99	UK £19.99	UK £21.99	UK £19.99	UK £17.99	UK £21.99	UK £21.99